W9-BUU-066

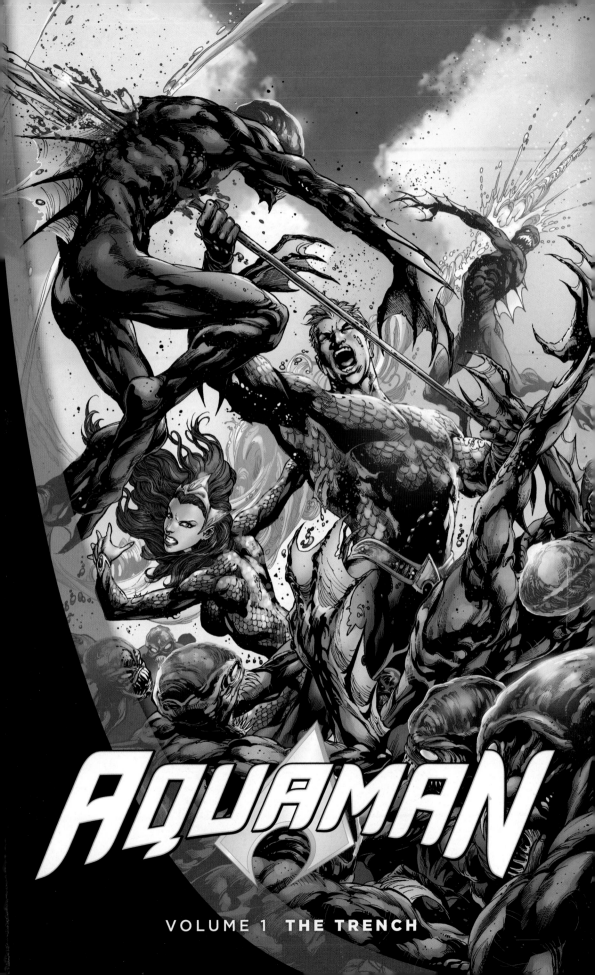

AQUAMAN

VOLUME 1 THE TRENCH

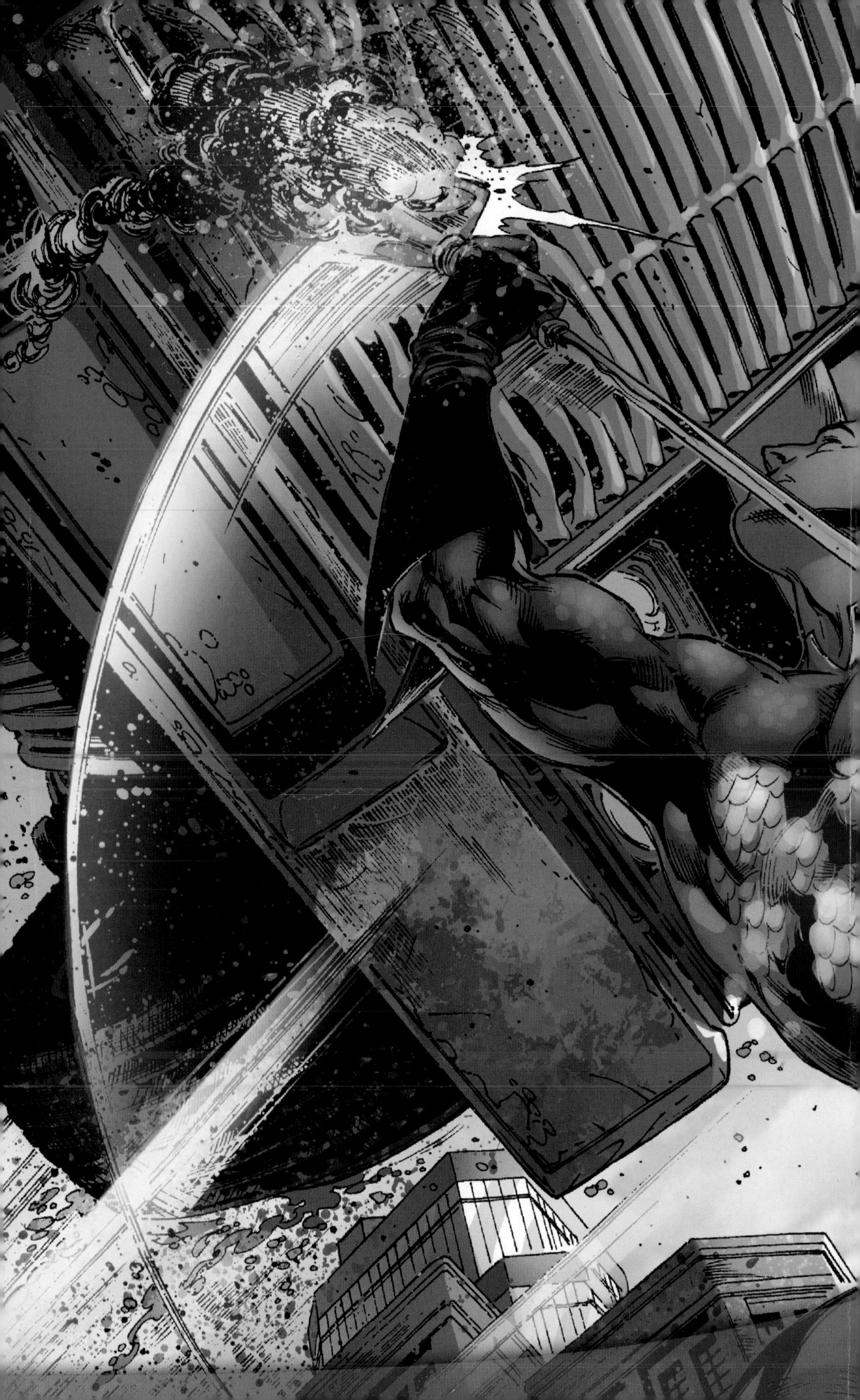

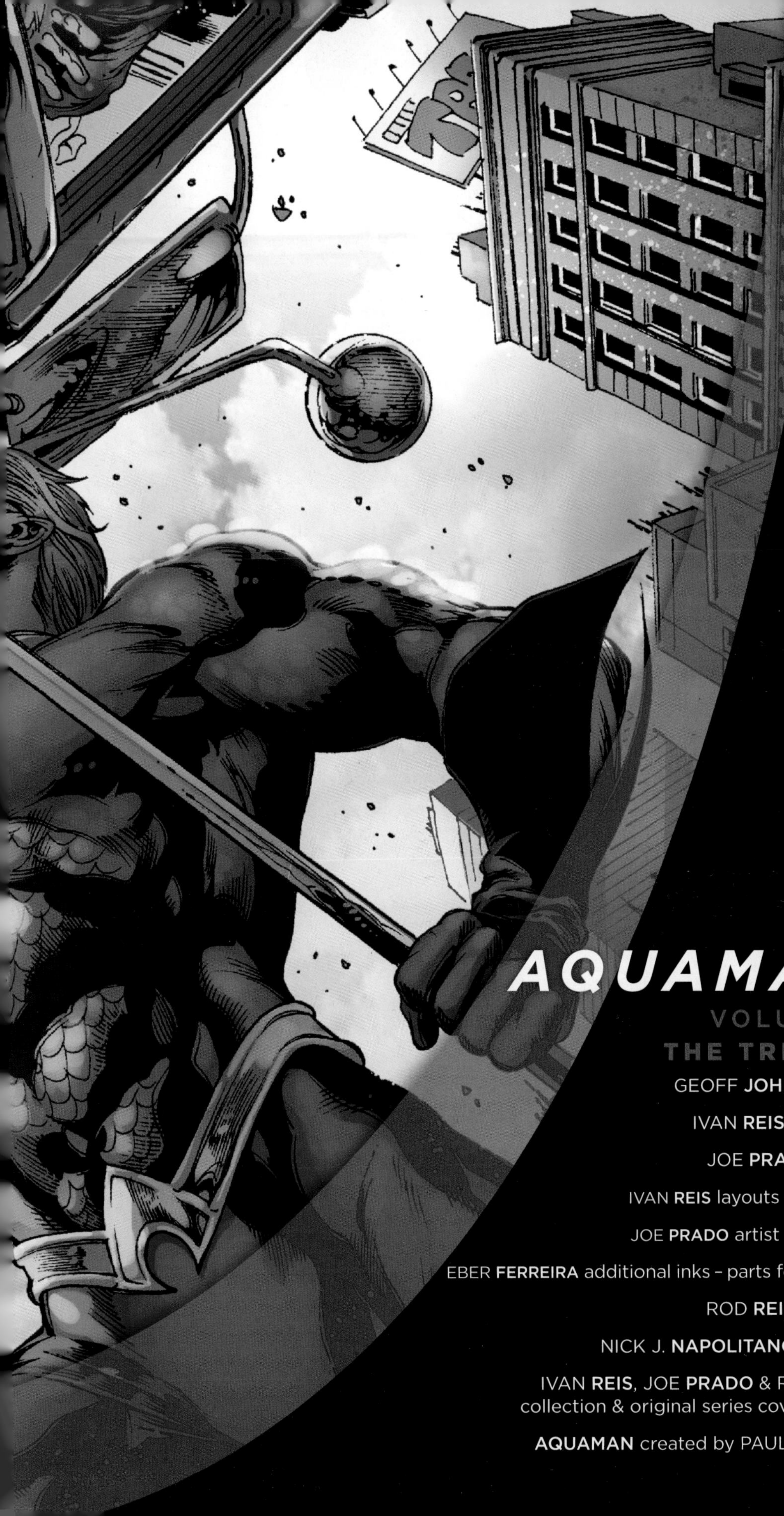

AQUAMAN

VOLUME 1

THE TRENCH

GEOFF **JOHNS** writer

IVAN **REIS** penciller

JOE **PRADO** inker

IVAN **REIS** layouts – part six

JOE **PRADO** artist – part six

EBER **FERREIRA** additional inks – parts four & five

ROD **REIS** colorist

NICK J. **NAPOLITANO** letterer

IVAN **REIS**, JOE **PRADO** & ROD **REIS**
collection & original series cover artists

AQUAMAN created by PAUL **NORRIS**

PAT McCALLUM Editor – Original Series SEAN MACKIEWICZ Assistant Editor – Original Series
PETER HAMBOUSSI Editor ROBBIN BROSTERMAN Design Director – Books
ROBBIE BIEDERMAN Publication Design

BOB HARRAS VP – Editor-in-Chief

DIANE NELSON President DAN DIDIO and JIM LEE Co-Publishers
GEOFF JOHNS Chief Creative Officer
JOHN ROOD Executive VP – Sales, Marketing and Business Development
AMY GENKINS Senior VP – Business and Legal Affairs NAIRI GARDINER Senior VP – Finance
JEFF BOISON VP – Publishing Operations MARK CHIARELLO VP – Art Direction and Design
JOHN CUNNINGHAM VP – Marketing TERRI CUNNINGHAM VP – Talent Relations and Services
ALISON GILL Senior VP – Manufacturing and Operations HANK KANALZ Senior VP – Digital
JAY KOGAN VP – Business and Legal Affairs, Publishing JACK MAHAN VP – Business Affairs, Talent
NICK NAPOLITANO VP – Manufacturing Administration SUE POHJA VP – Book Sales
COURTNEY SIMMONS Senior VP – Publicity BOB WAYNE Senior VP – Sales

AQUAMAN VOLUME 1: THE TRENCH
Published by DC Comics. Cover and compilation Copyright © 2012 DC Comics.
All Rights Reserved.

Originally published in single magazine form in AQUAMAN 1-6 Copyright © 2011, 2012 DC Comics.
All Rights Reserved. All characters, their distinctive likenesses and related elements featured in this publication
are trademarks of DC Comics. The stories, characters and incidents featured in this publication are entirely fictional.
DC Comics does not read or accept unsolicited ideas, stories or artwork.

DC Comics, 1700 Broadway, New York, NY 10019
A Warner Bros. Entertainment Company.
Printed by RR Donnelley, Salem, VA, USA. 8/3/12. First Printing.

HC ISBN: 978-1-4012-3551-2
SC ISBN: 978-1-4012-3710-3

Library of Congress Cataloging-in-Publication Data

Johns, Geoff, 1973-
Aquaman. Volume 1, The trench / Geoff Johns, Ivan Reis, Joe Prado.
p. cm.
"Originally published in single magazine form in AQUAMAN 1-6."
ISBN 978-1-4012-3551-2
1. Graphic novels. I. Reis, Ivan. II. Prado, Joe. III. Title. IV. Title: Trench.
PN6728.A68J64 2012
741.5'973—dc23
2012018771

SUSTAINABLE
FORESTRY
INITIATIVE

Certified Chain of Custody
At Least 25% Certified Forest Content
www.sfiprogram.org
SFI-01042
APPLIES TO TEXT STOCK ONLY

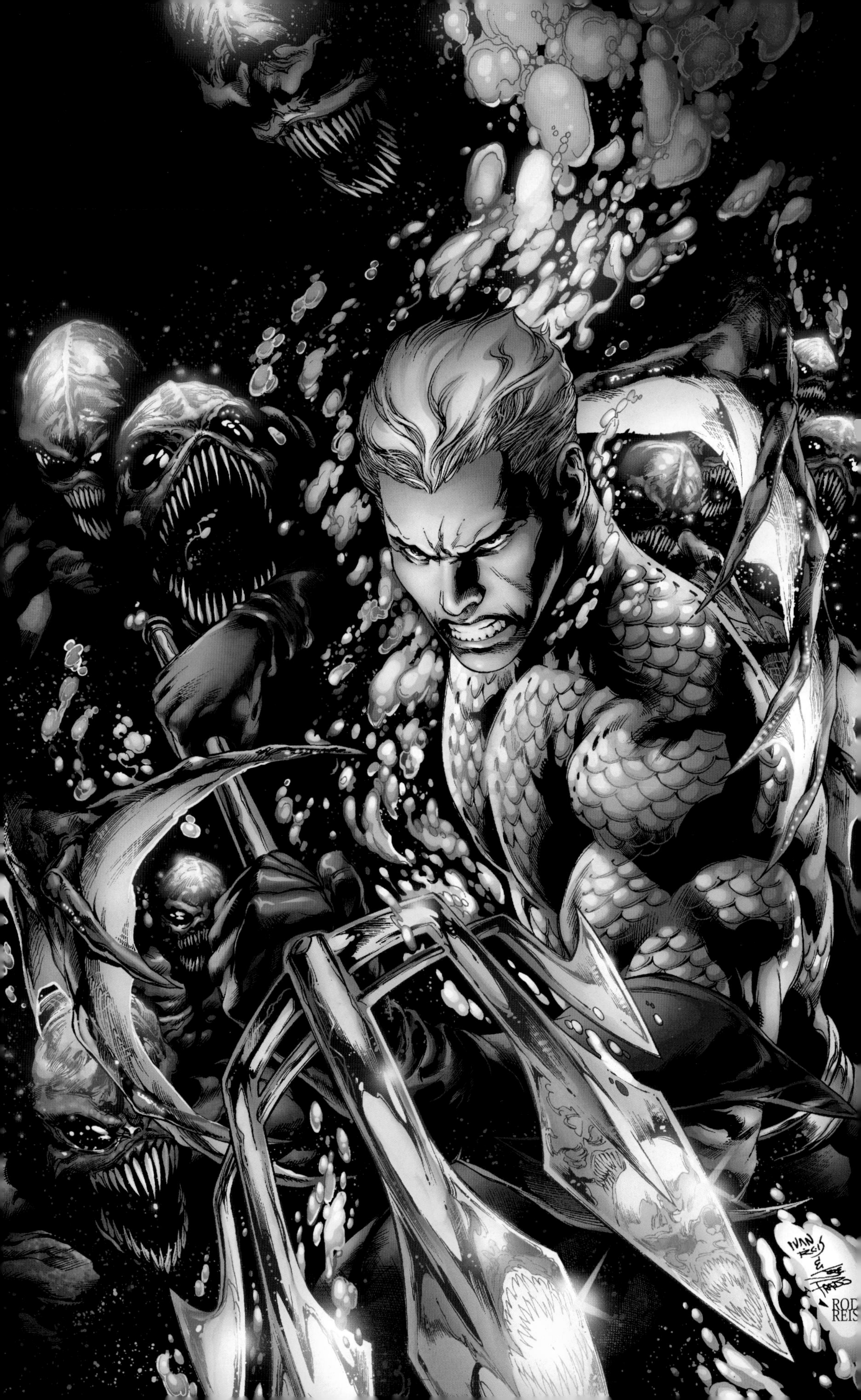

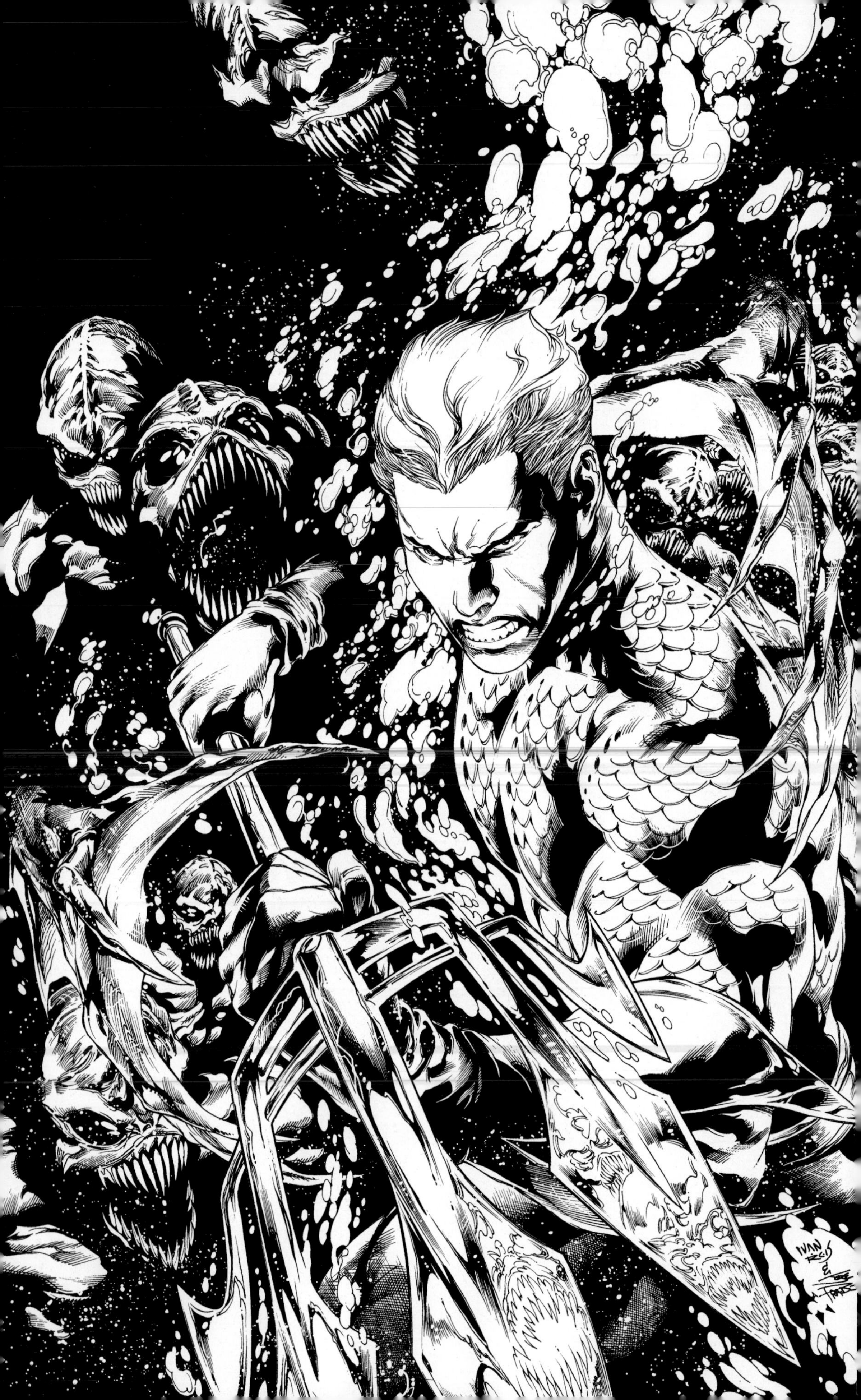

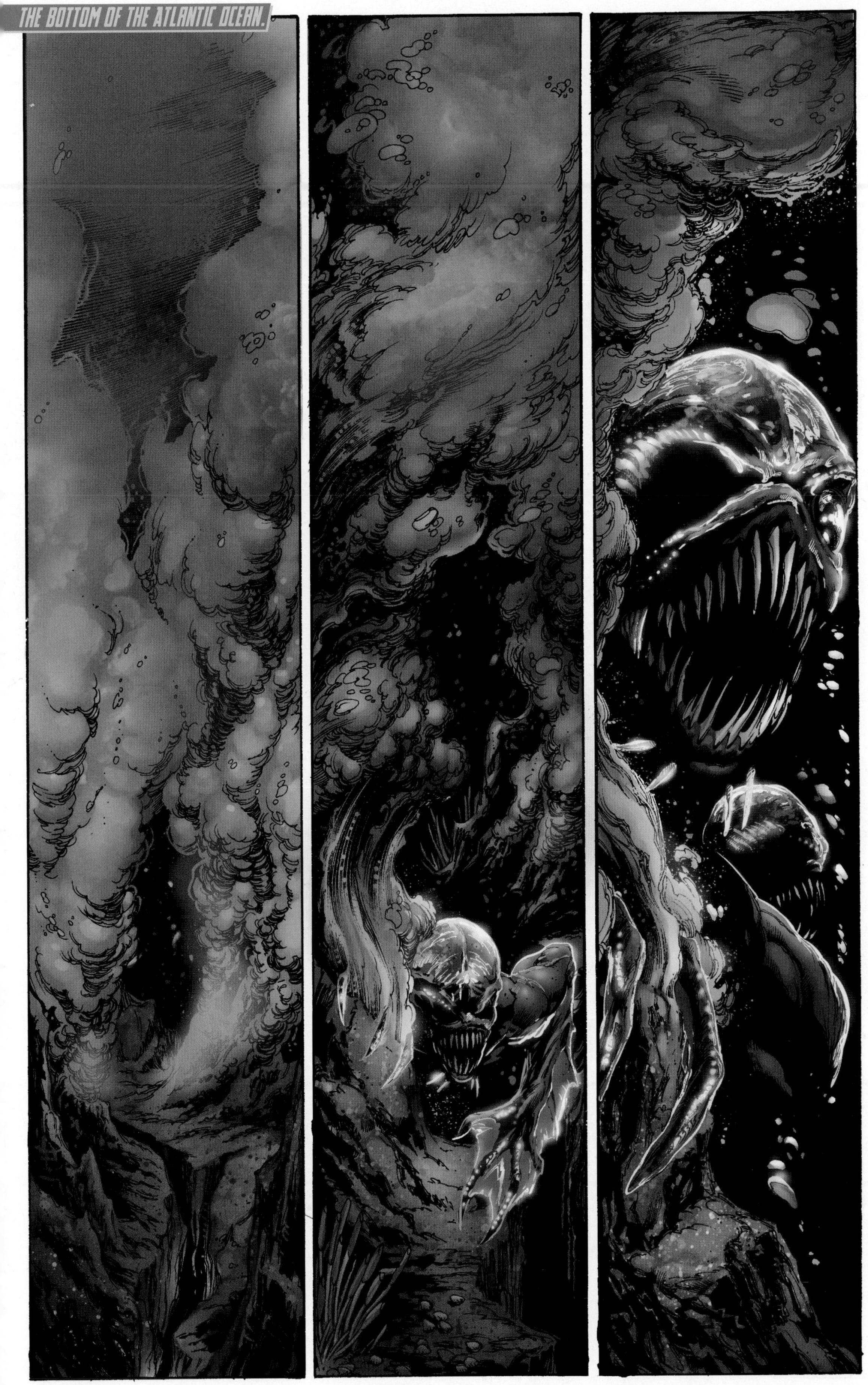
THE BOTTOM OF THE ATLANTIC OCEAN.

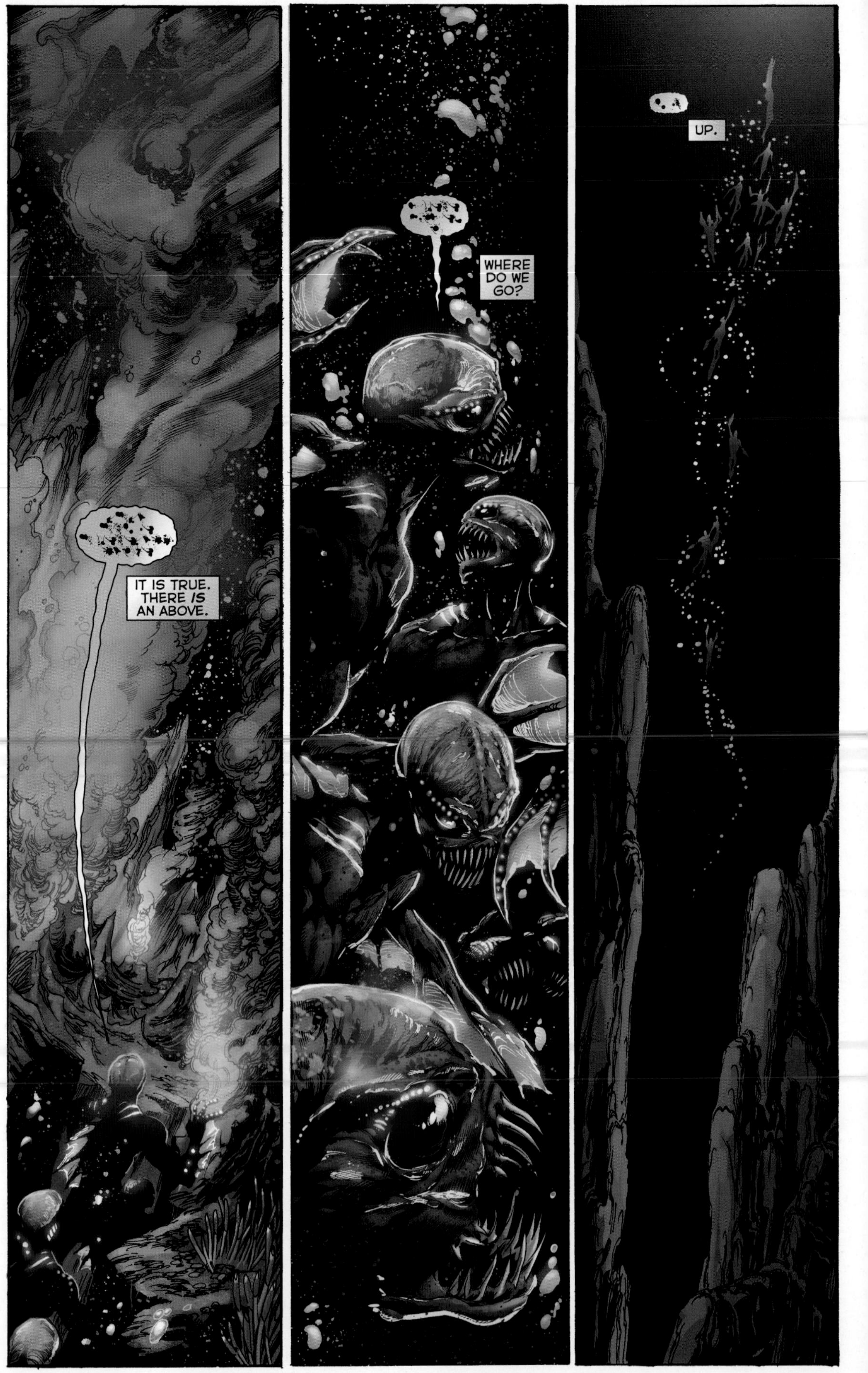
IT IS TRUE. THERE IS AN ABOVE.
WHERE DO WE GO?
UP.

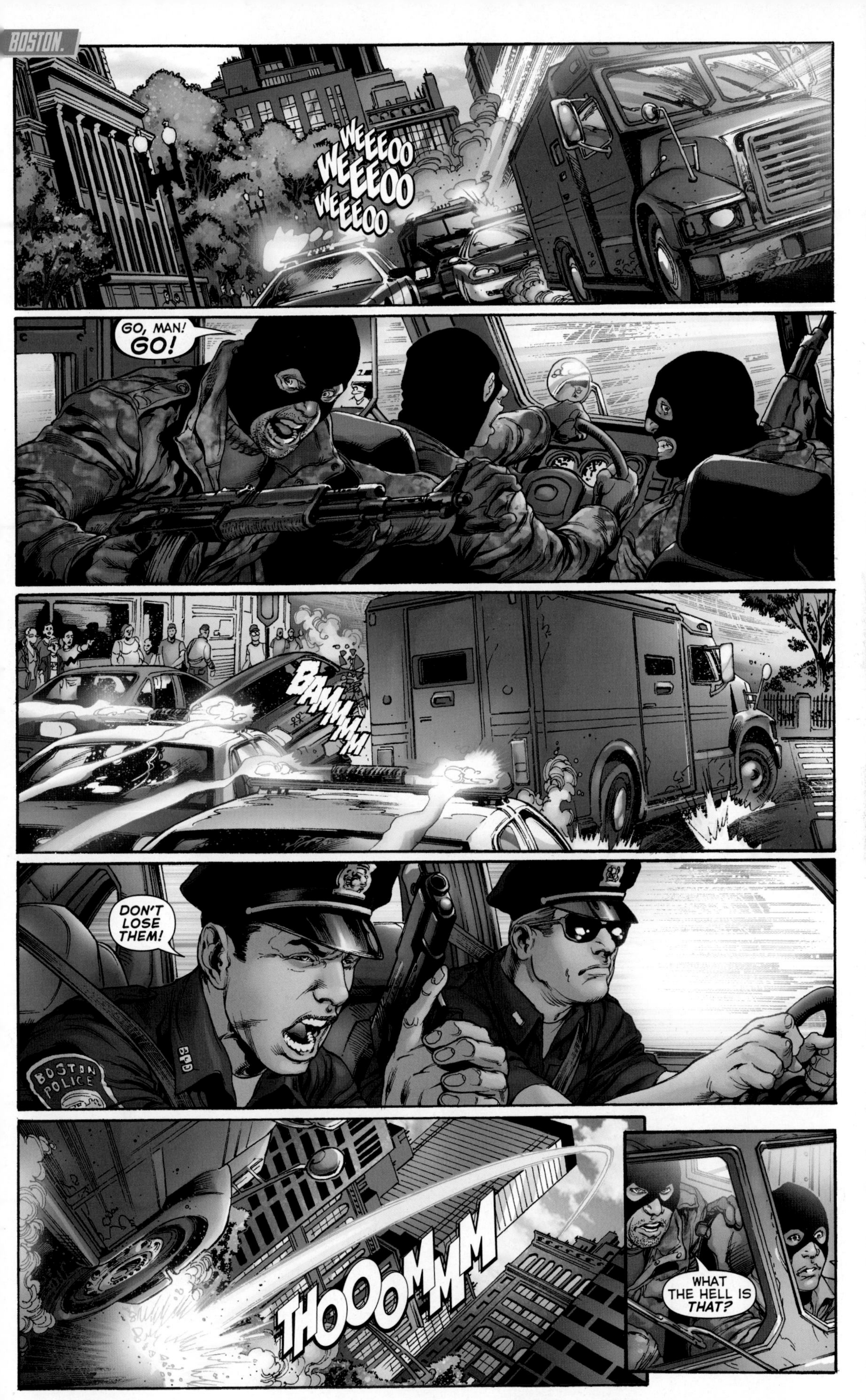
BOSTON.
WEEEOO
WEEEOO
WEEEOO
GO, MAN! GO!
BAMMMM
DON'T LOSE THEM!
THOOOMMM
WHAT THE HELL IS THAT?

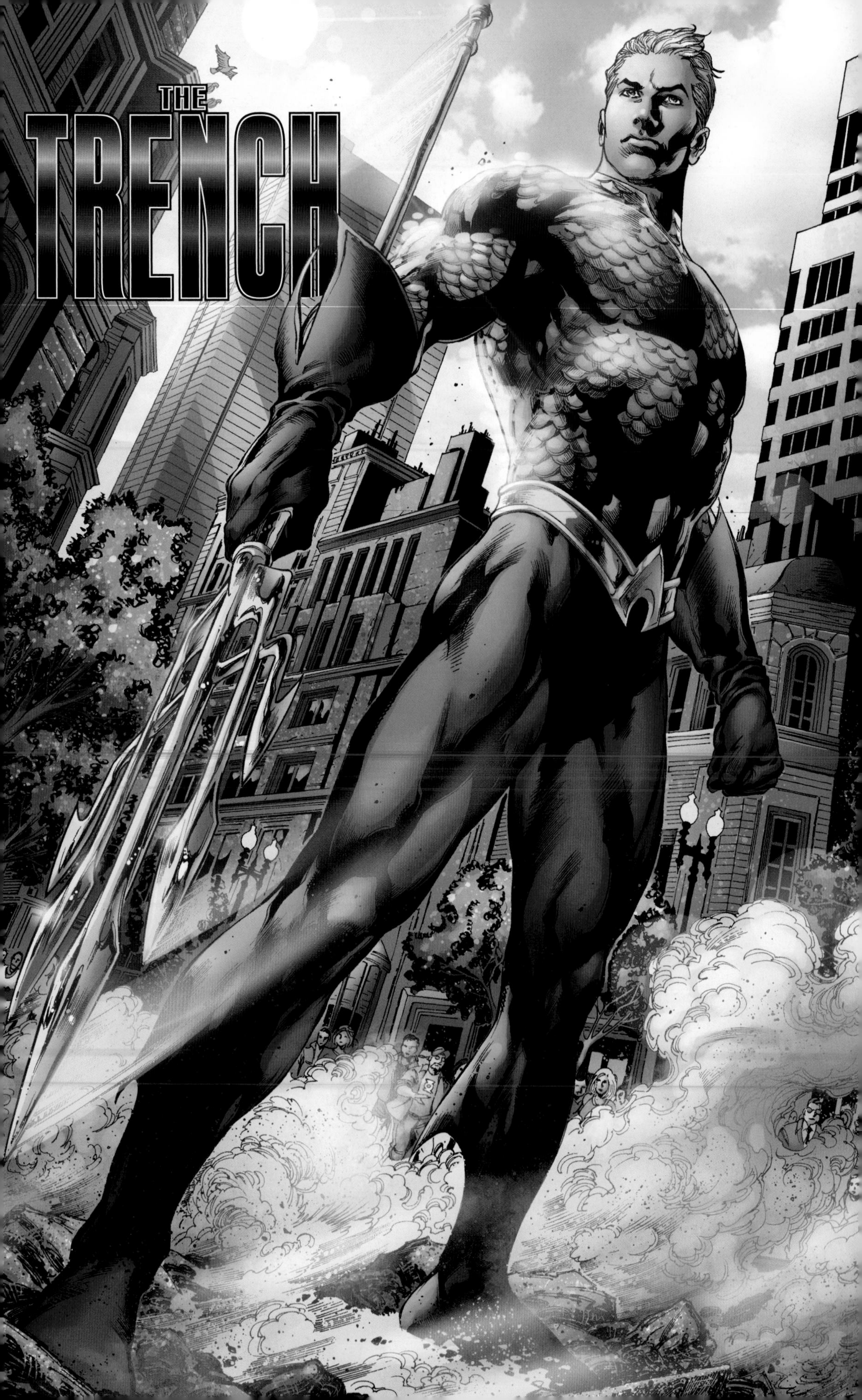
THE
TRENCH

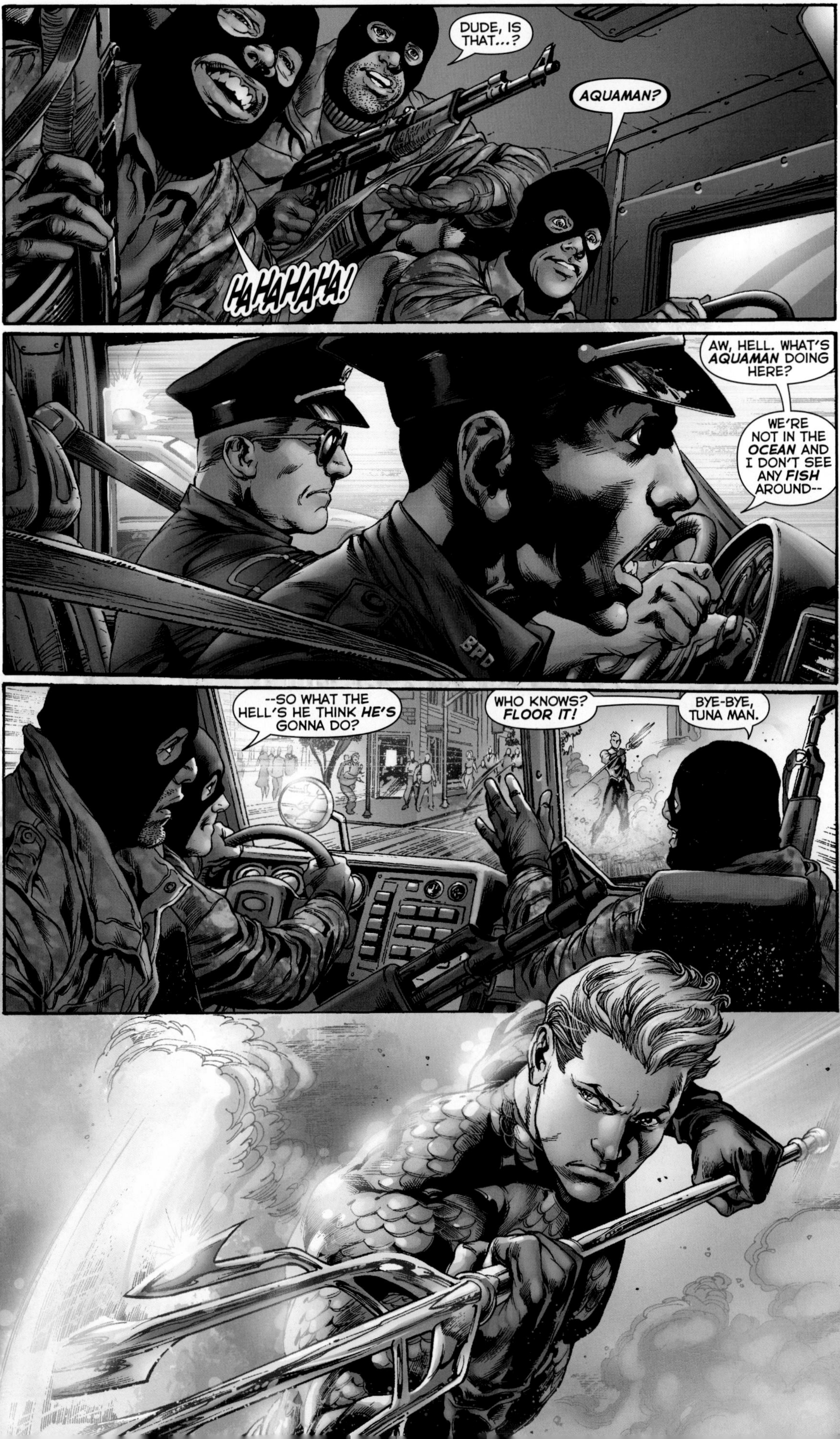
DUDE, IS THAT...?
AQUAMAN?
HAHAHAHA!
AW, HELL. WHAT'S *AQUAMAN* DOING HERE?
WE'RE NOT IN THE *OCEAN* AND I DON'T SEE ANY *FISH* AROUND--
--SO WHAT THE HELL'S HE THINK *HE'S* GONNA DO?
WHO KNOWS? *FLOOR IT!*
BYE-BYE, TUNA MAN.

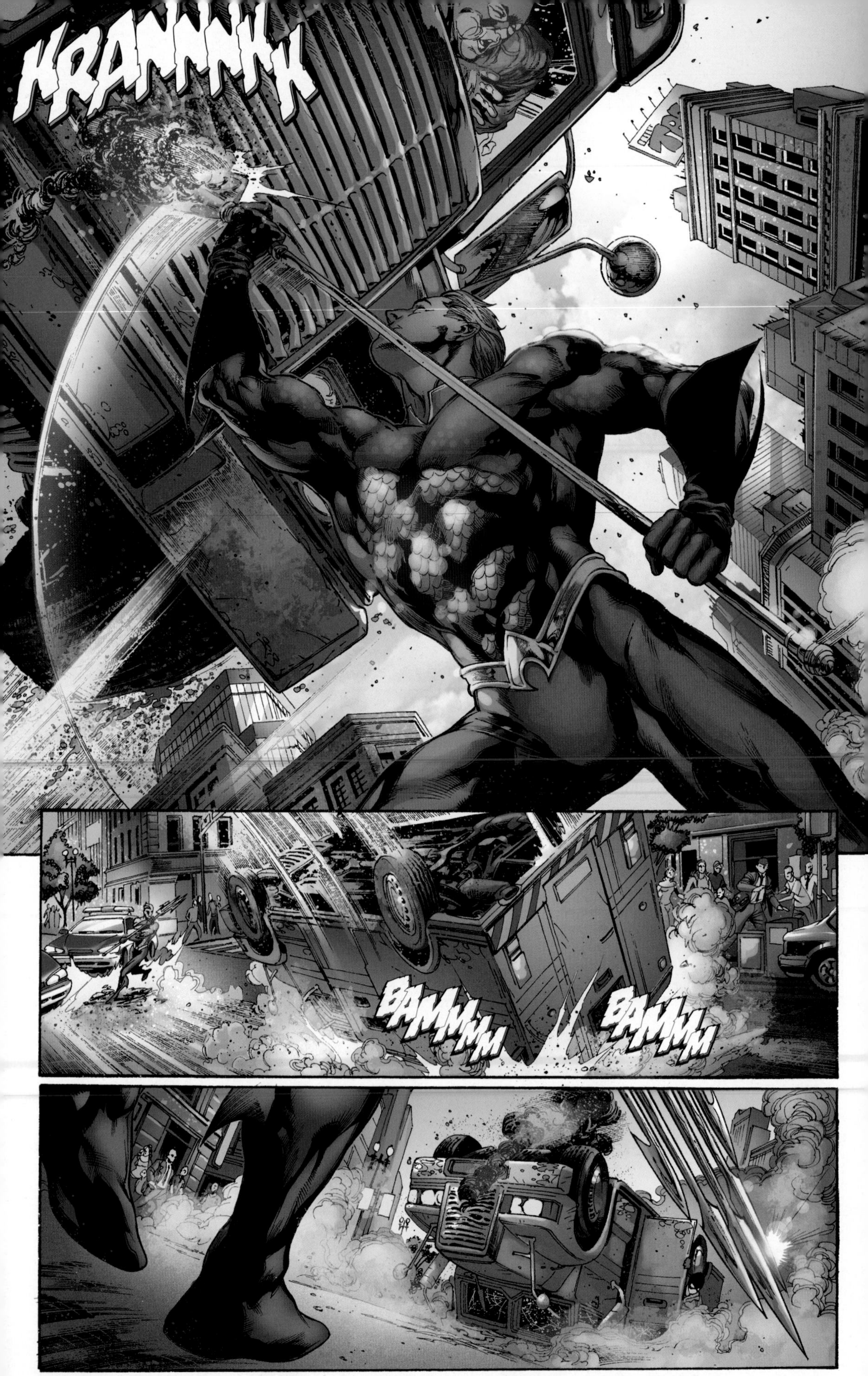
KRANNNKK
BAMMMM
BAMMMM

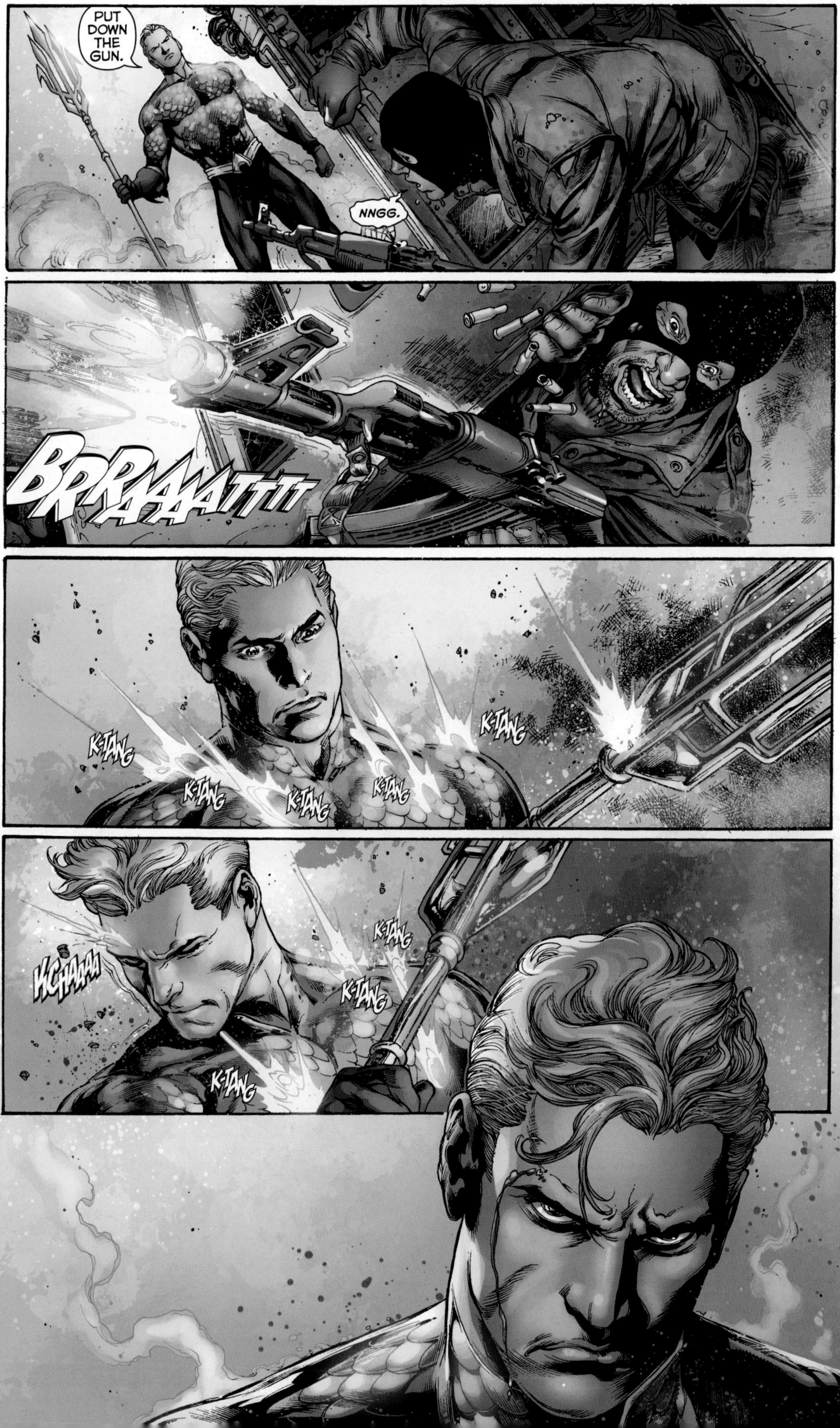

PUT DOWN THE GUN.
NNGG.
BRRAAAATTTT
K-TANG
K-TANG
K-TANG
K-TANG
K-TANG
KCHAAAA
K-TANG
K-TANG
K-TANG

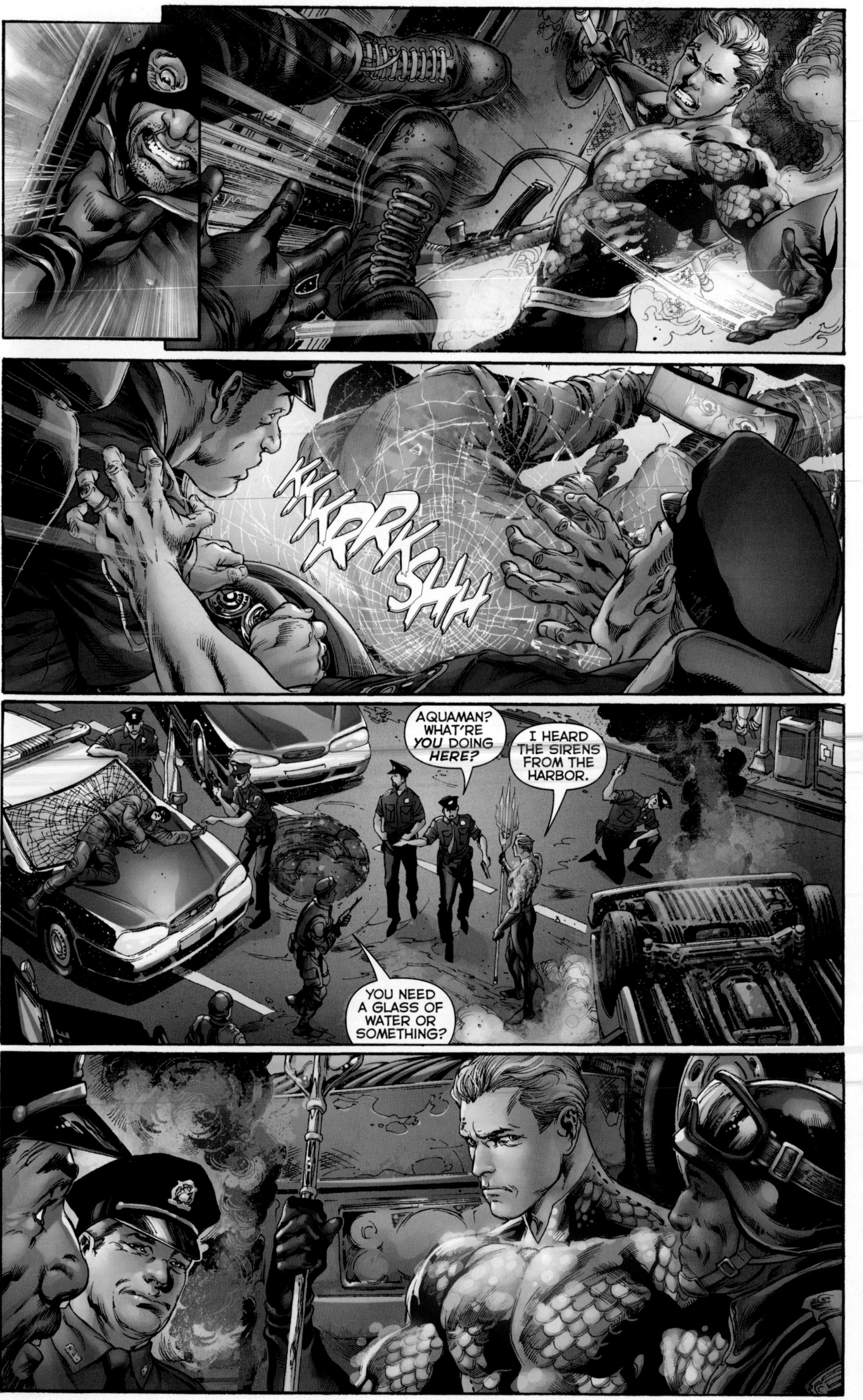
KKKRRKSHH
AQUAMAN? WHAT'RE *YOU* DOING *HERE?*
I HEARD THE SIRENS FROM THE HARBOR.
YOU NEED A GLASS OF WATER OR SOMETHING?

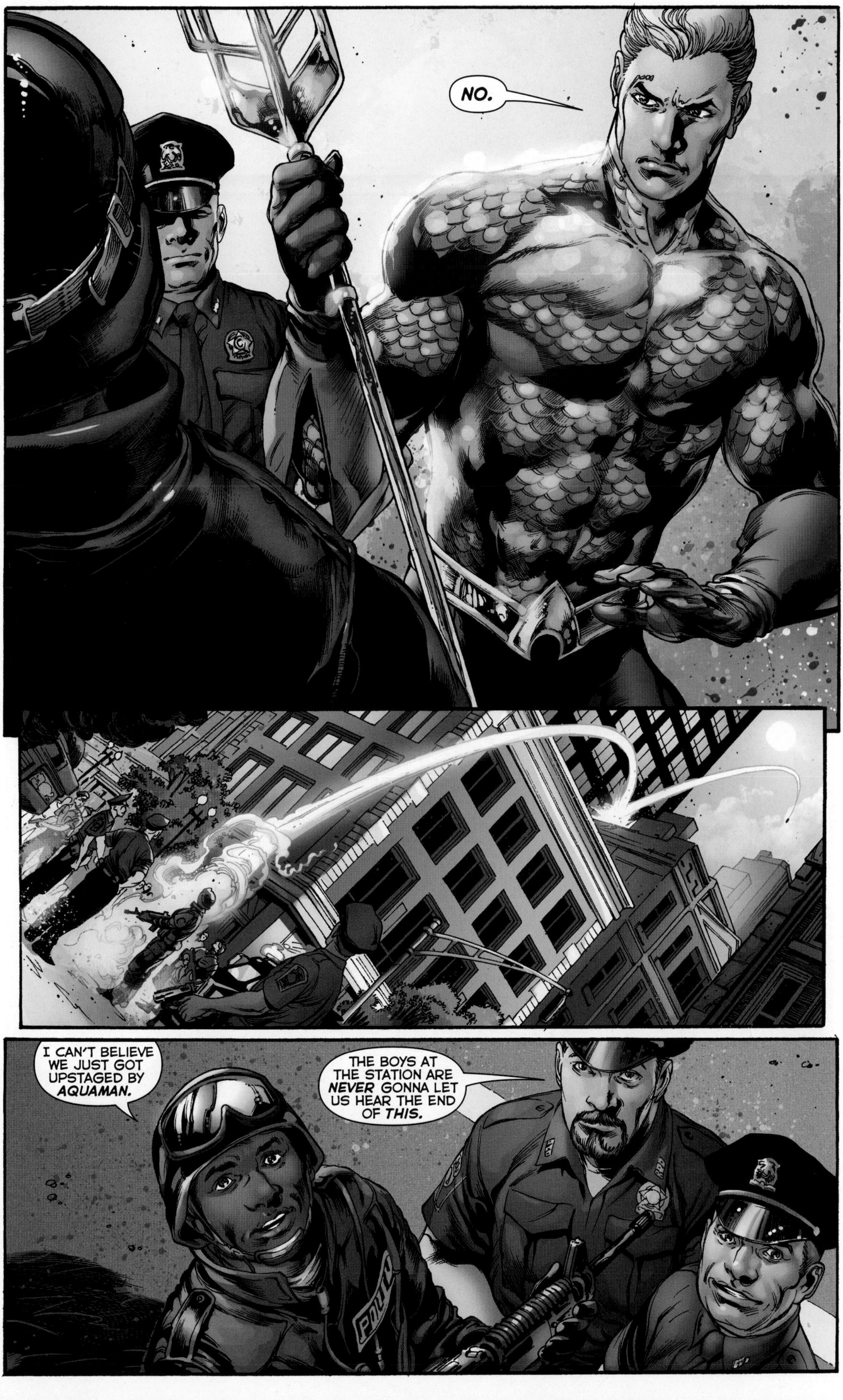
NO.
I CAN'T BELIEVE WE JUST GOT UPSTAGED BY AQUAMAN.
THE BOYS AT THE STATION ARE NEVER GONNA LET US HEAR THE END OF THIS.

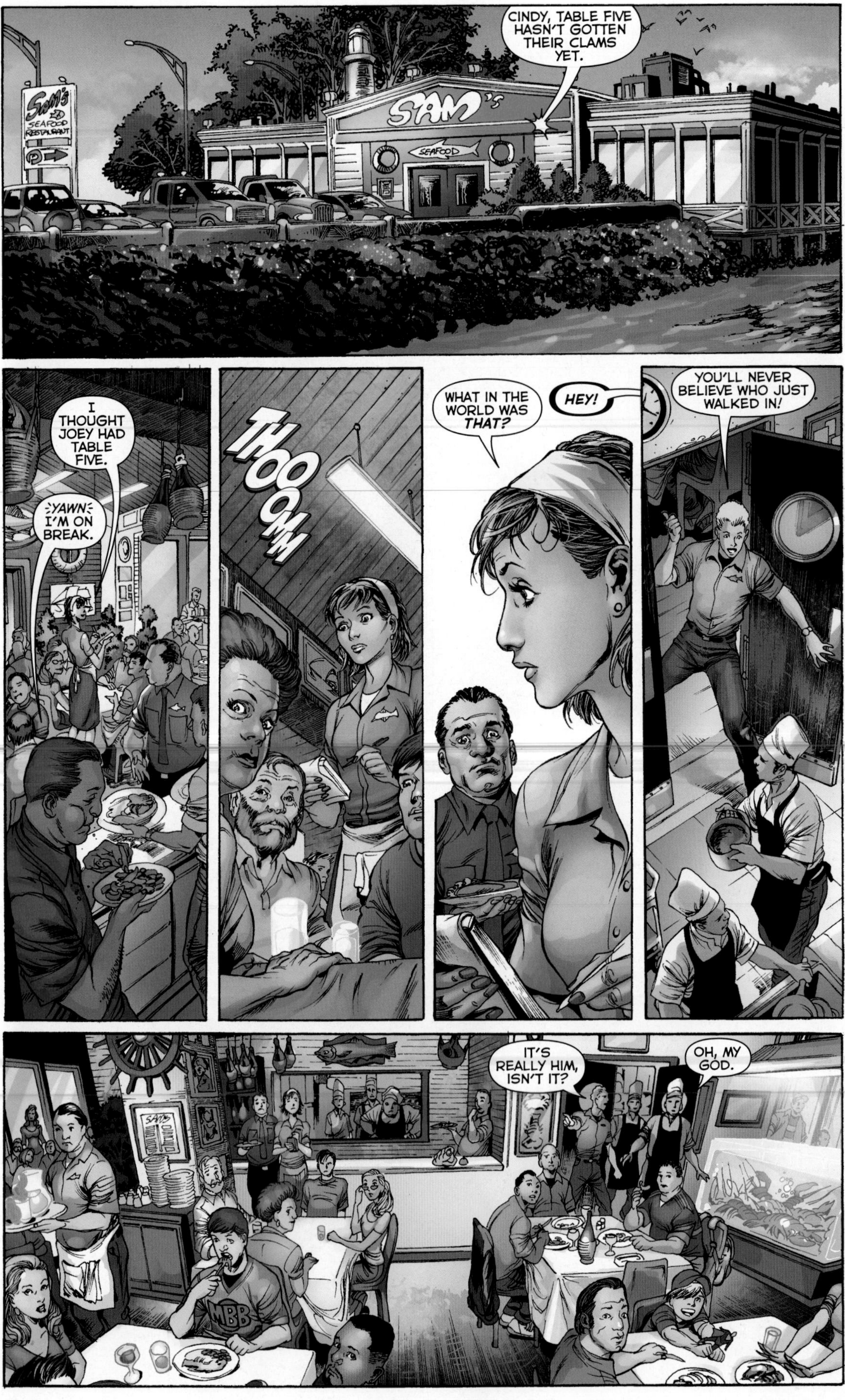
SAM'S SEAFOOD RESTAURANT
SAM'S
SEAFOOD
CINDY, TABLE FIVE HASN'T GOTTEN THEIR CLAMS YET.
I THOUGHT JOEY HAD TABLE FIVE.
YAWN I'M ON BREAK.
THOOOMM
WHAT IN THE WORLD WAS THAT?
HEY!
YOU'LL NEVER BELIEVE WHO JUST WALKED IN!
IT'S REALLY HIM, ISN'T IT?
OH, MY GOD.
MBB

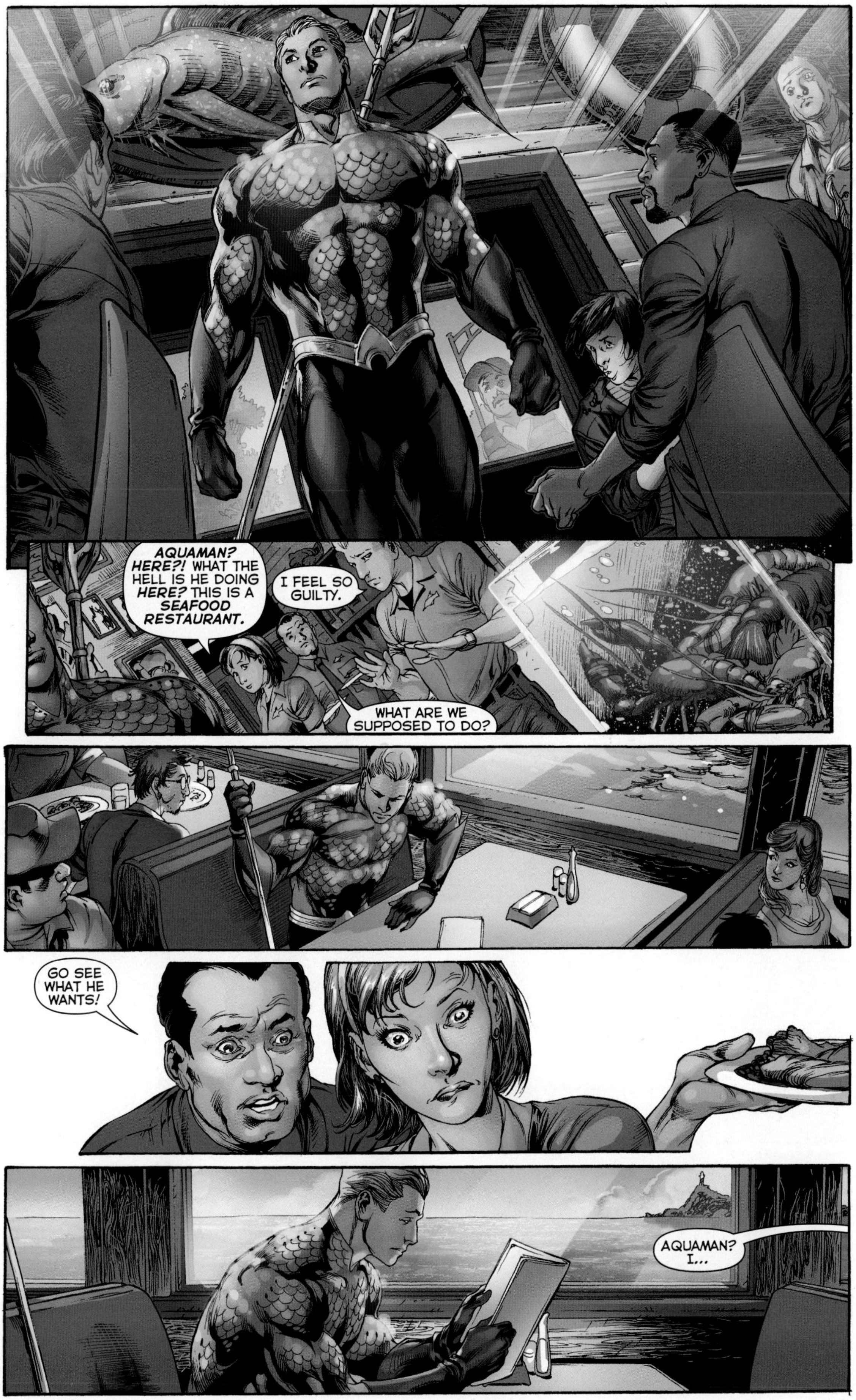
AQUAMAN? HERE?! WHAT THE HELL IS HE DOING HERE? THIS IS A SEAFOOD RESTAURANT.
I FEEL SO GUILTY.
WHAT ARE WE SUPPOSED TO DO?
GO SEE WHAT HE WANTS!
AQUAMAN? I...

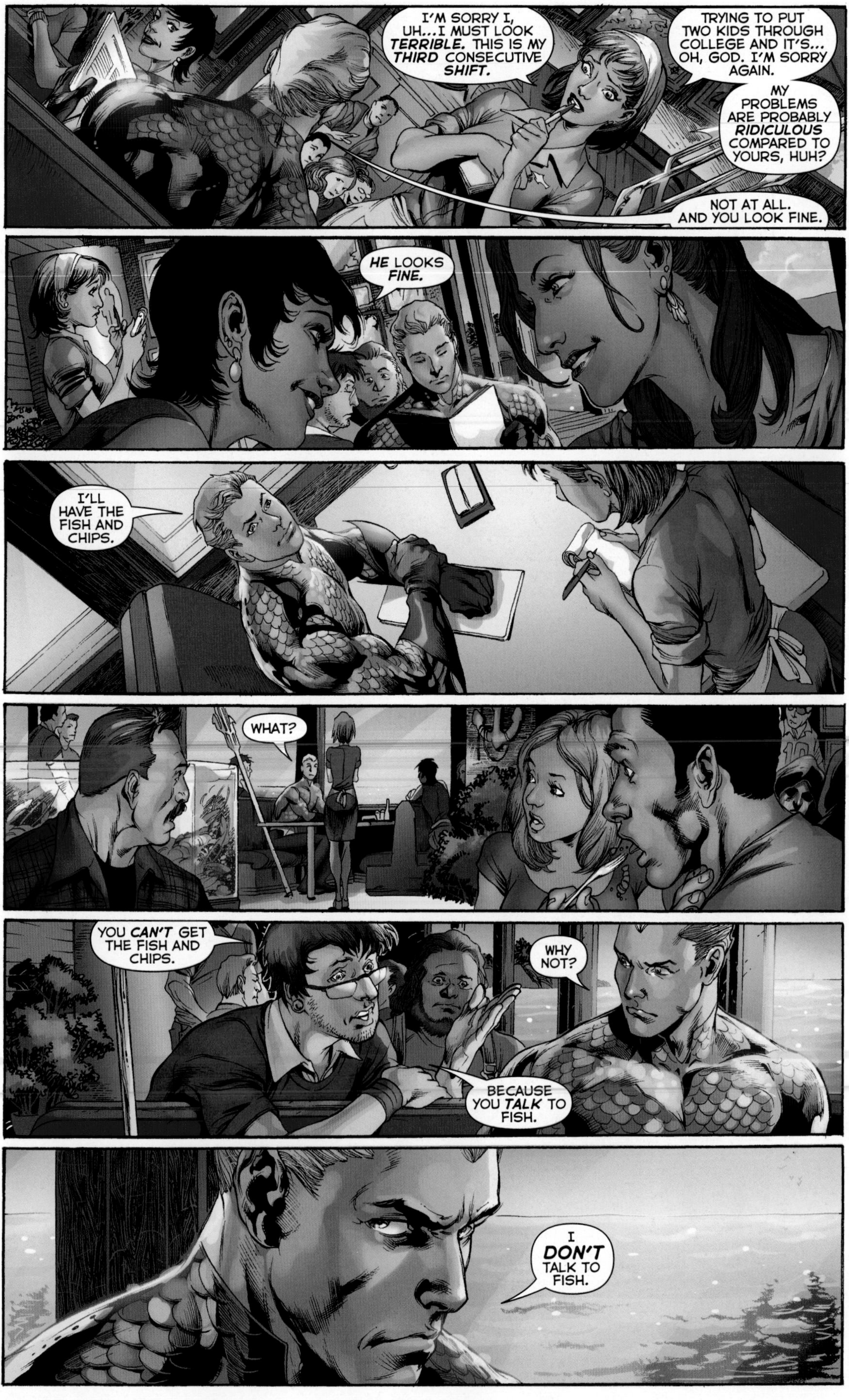
I'M SORRY I, UH...I MUST LOOK TERRIBLE. THIS IS MY THIRD CONSECUTIVE SHIFT.
TRYING TO PUT TWO KIDS THROUGH COLLEGE AND IT'S... OH, GOD. I'M SORRY AGAIN.
MY PROBLEMS ARE PROBABLY RIDICULOUS COMPARED TO YOURS, HUH?
NOT AT ALL. AND YOU LOOK FINE.
HE LOOKS FINE.
I'LL HAVE THE FISH AND CHIPS.
WHAT?
YOU CAN'T GET THE FISH AND CHIPS.
WHY NOT?
BECAUSE YOU TALK TO FISH.
I DON'T TALK TO FISH.

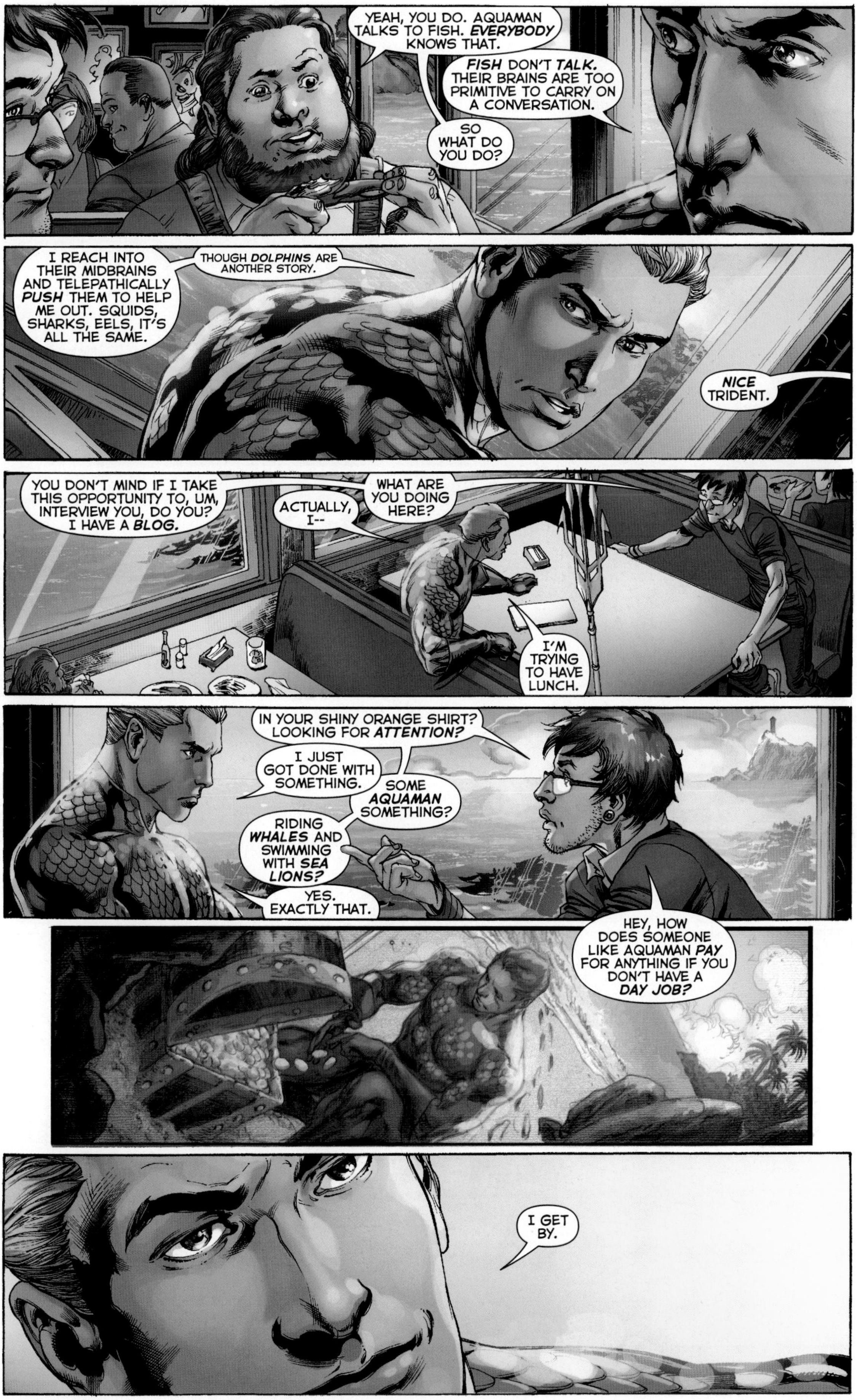
YEAH, YOU DO. AQUAMAN TALKS TO FISH. EVERYBODY KNOWS THAT.
FISH DON'T TALK. THEIR BRAINS ARE TOO PRIMITIVE TO CARRY ON A CONVERSATION.
SO WHAT DO YOU DO?
I REACH INTO THEIR MIDBRAINS AND TELEPATHICALLY PUSH THEM TO HELP ME OUT. SQUIDS, SHARKS, EELS, IT'S ALL THE SAME.
THOUGH DOLPHINS ARE ANOTHER STORY.
NICE TRIDENT.
YOU DON'T MIND IF I TAKE THIS OPPORTUNITY TO, UM, INTERVIEW YOU, DO YOU? I HAVE A BLOG.
ACTUALLY, I--
WHAT ARE YOU DOING HERE?
I'M TRYING TO HAVE LUNCH.
IN YOUR SHINY ORANGE SHIRT? LOOKING FOR ATTENTION?
I JUST GOT DONE WITH SOMETHING.
SOME AQUAMAN SOMETHING?
RIDING WHALES AND SWIMMING WITH SEA LIONS?
YES. EXACTLY THAT.
HEY, HOW DOES SOMEONE LIKE AQUAMAN PAY FOR ANYTHING IF YOU DON'T HAVE A DAY JOB?
I GET BY.

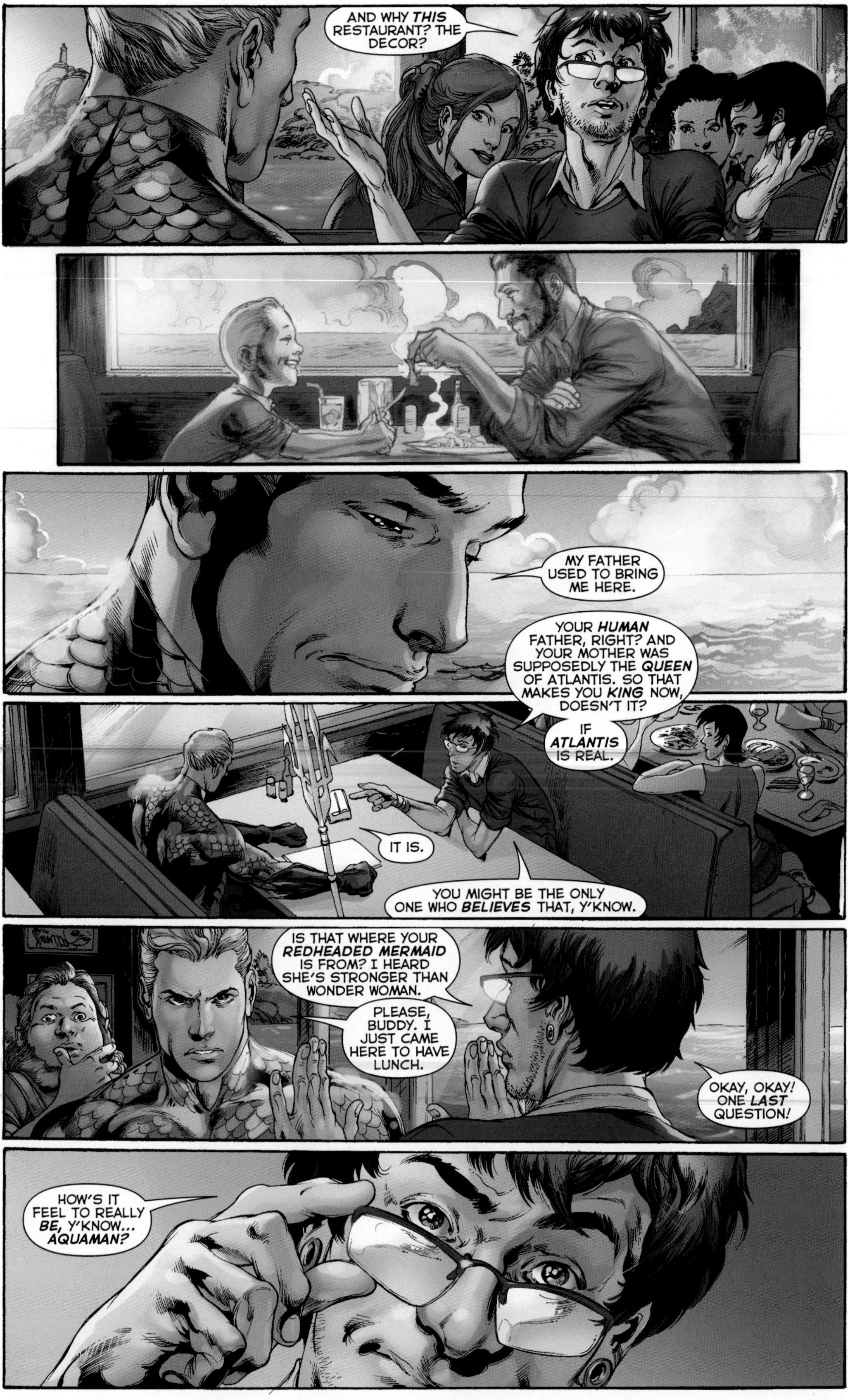
AND WHY THIS RESTAURANT? THE DECOR?
MY FATHER USED TO BRING ME HERE.
YOUR HUMAN FATHER, RIGHT? AND YOUR MOTHER WAS SUPPOSEDLY THE QUEEN OF ATLANTIS. SO THAT MAKES YOU KING NOW, DOESN'T IT?
IF ATLANTIS IS REAL.
IT IS.
YOU MIGHT BE THE ONLY ONE WHO BELIEVES THAT, Y'KNOW.
IS THAT WHERE YOUR REDHEADED MERMAID IS FROM? I HEARD SHE'S STRONGER THAN WONDER WOMAN.
PLEASE, BUDDY. I JUST CAME HERE TO HAVE LUNCH.
OKAY, OKAY! ONE LAST QUESTION!
HOW'S IT FEEL TO REALLY BE, Y'KNOW... AQUAMAN?

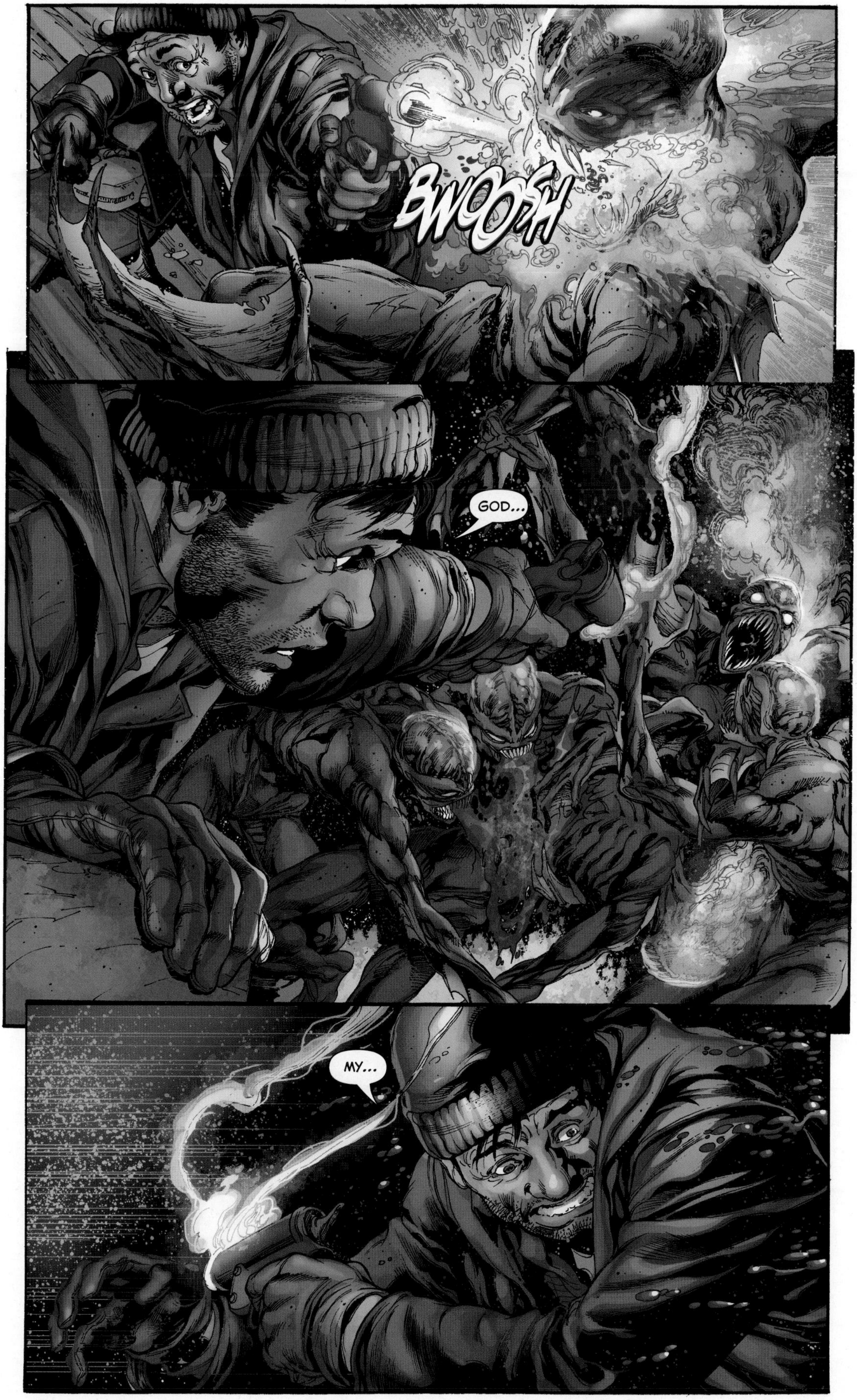
BWOOSH
GOD...
MY...

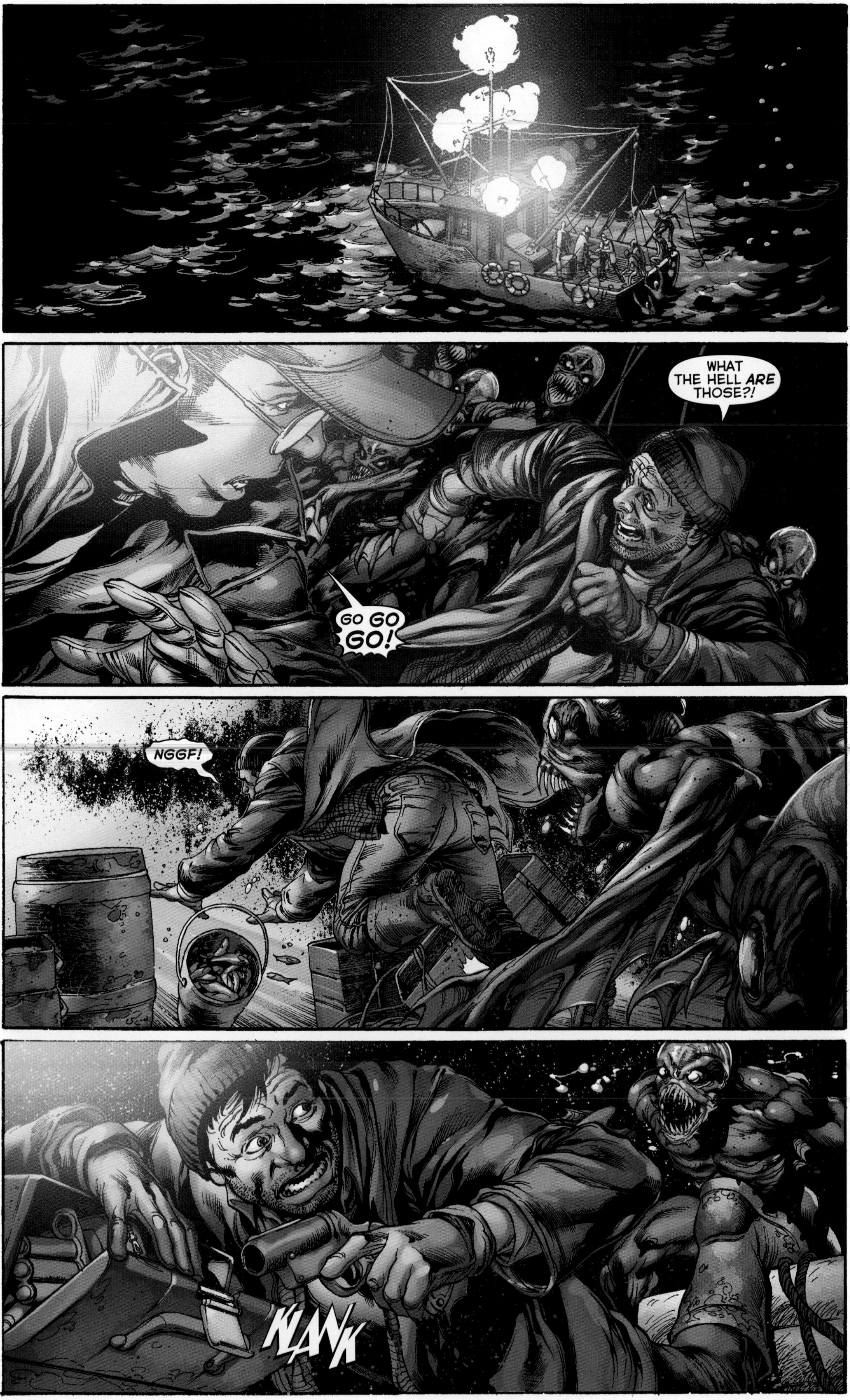
WHAT THE HELL ARE THOSE?!
GO GO GO!
NGGF!
KLANK

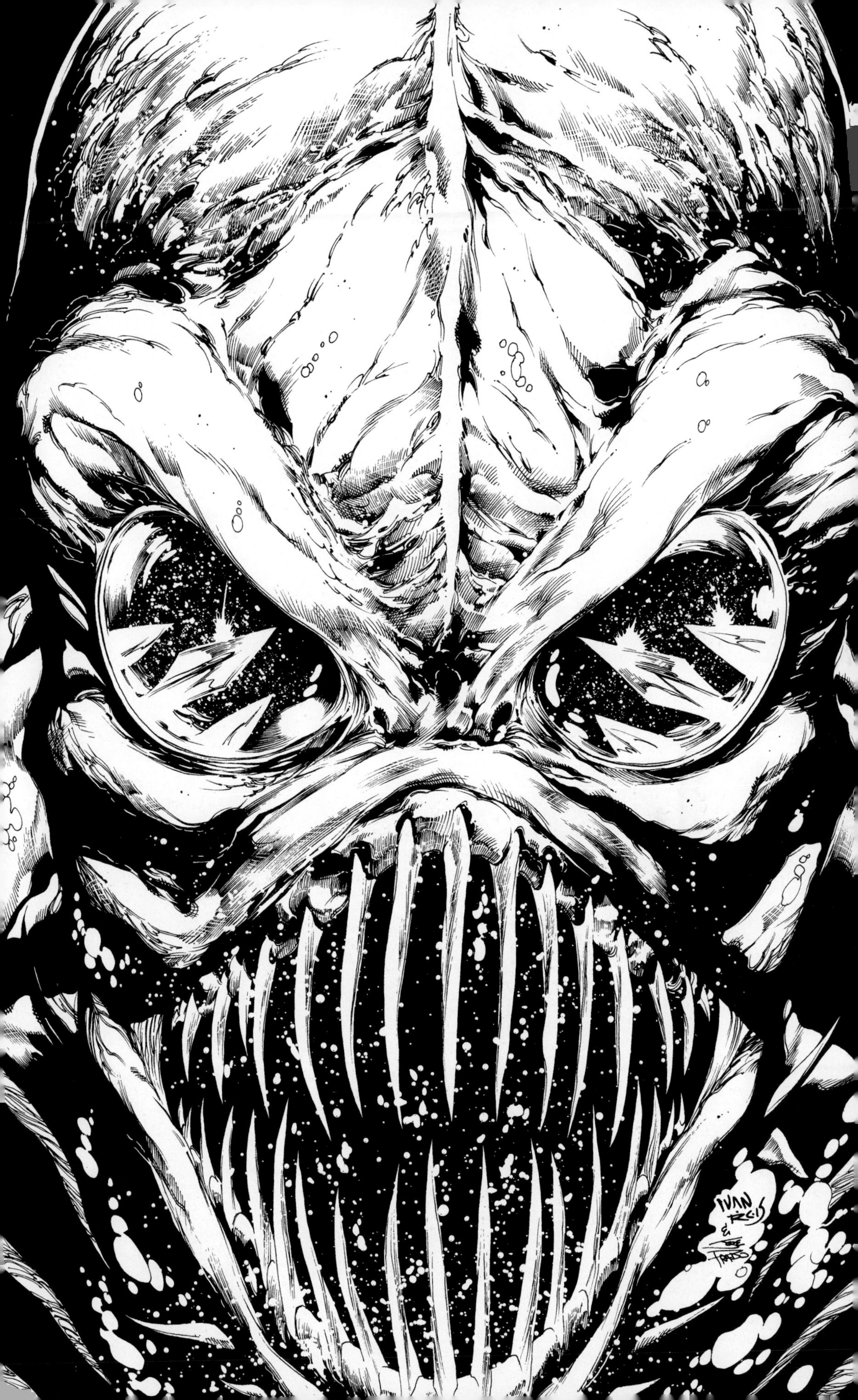

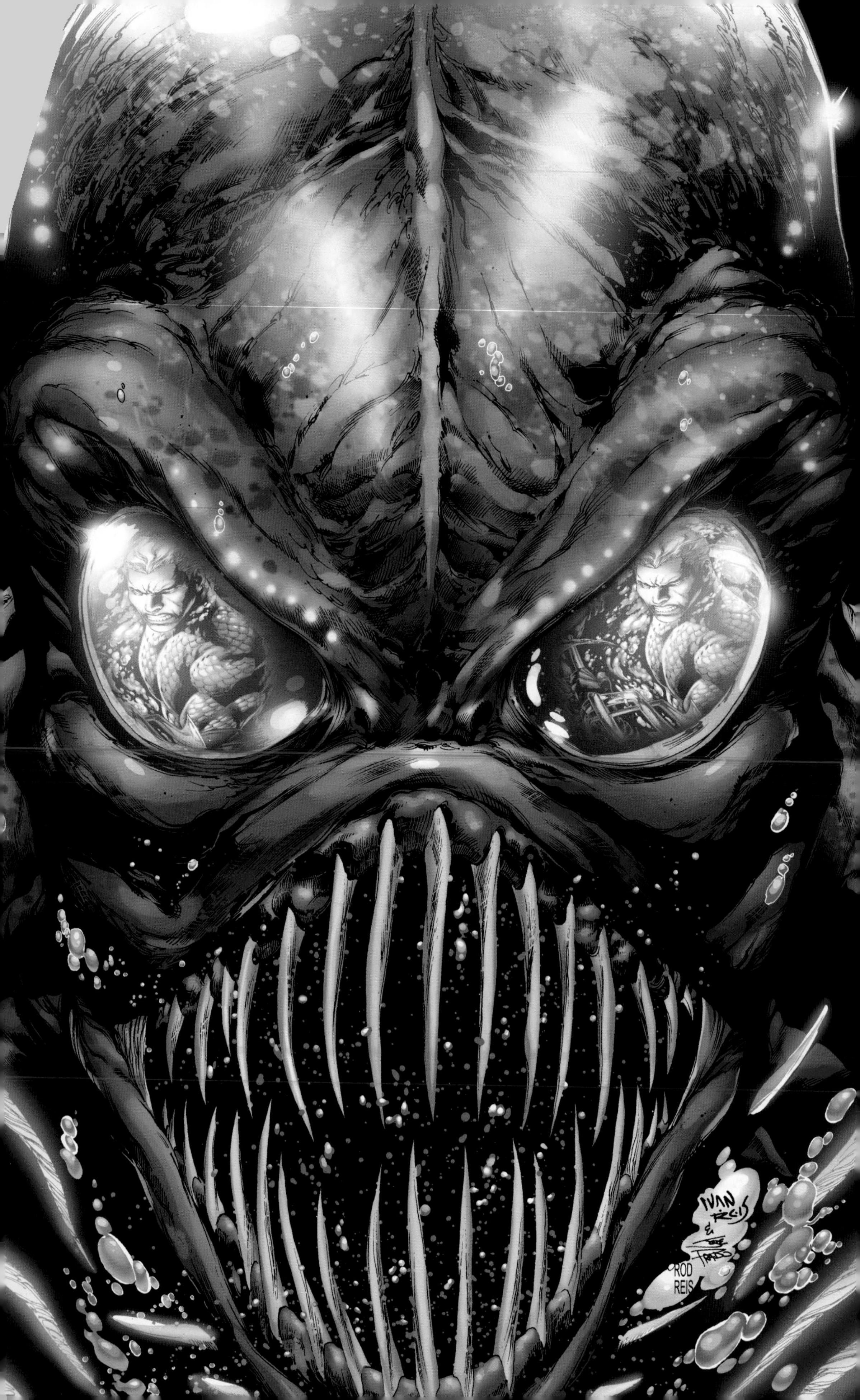
ROD
REIS

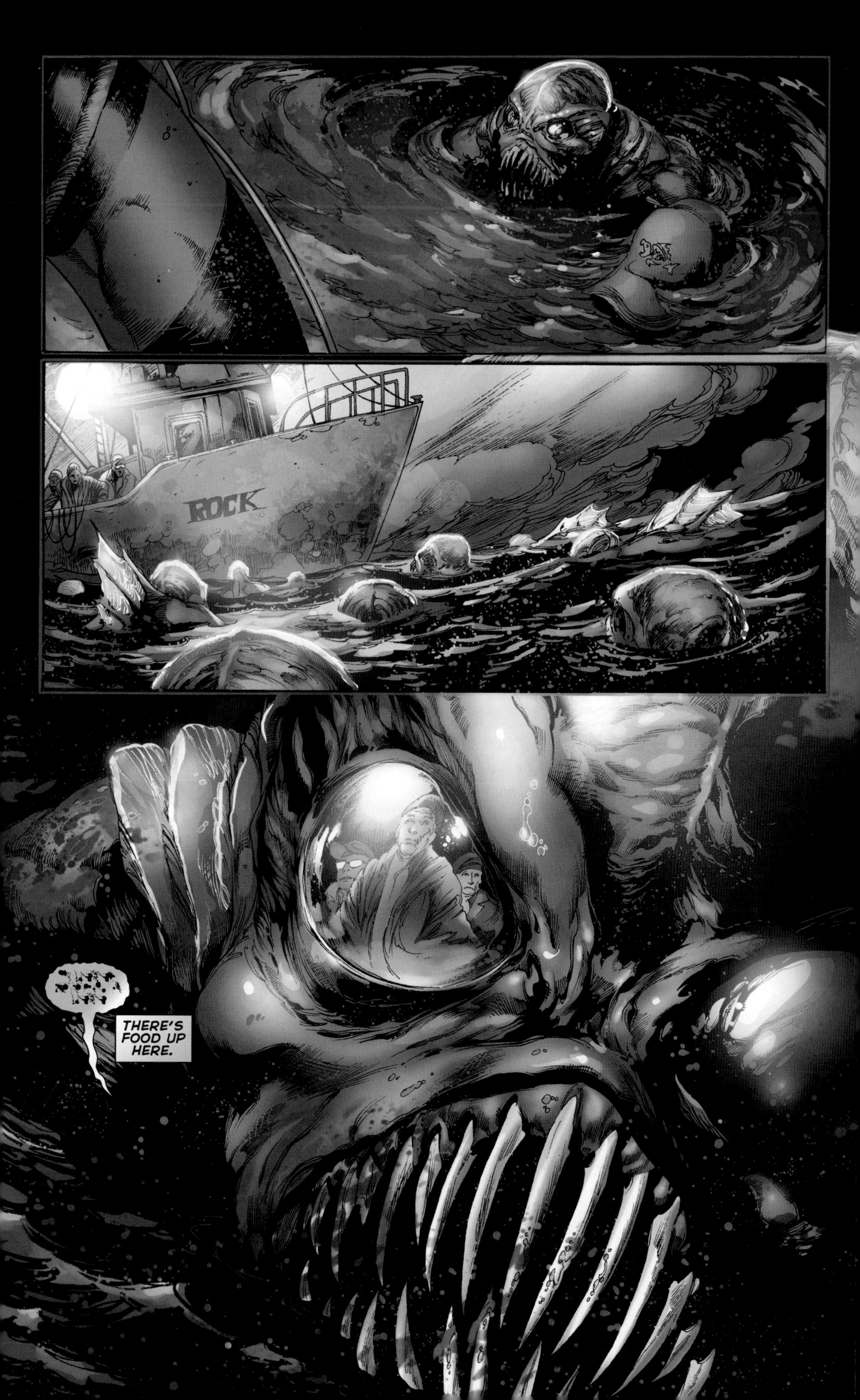
ROCK
THERE'S FOOD UP HERE.

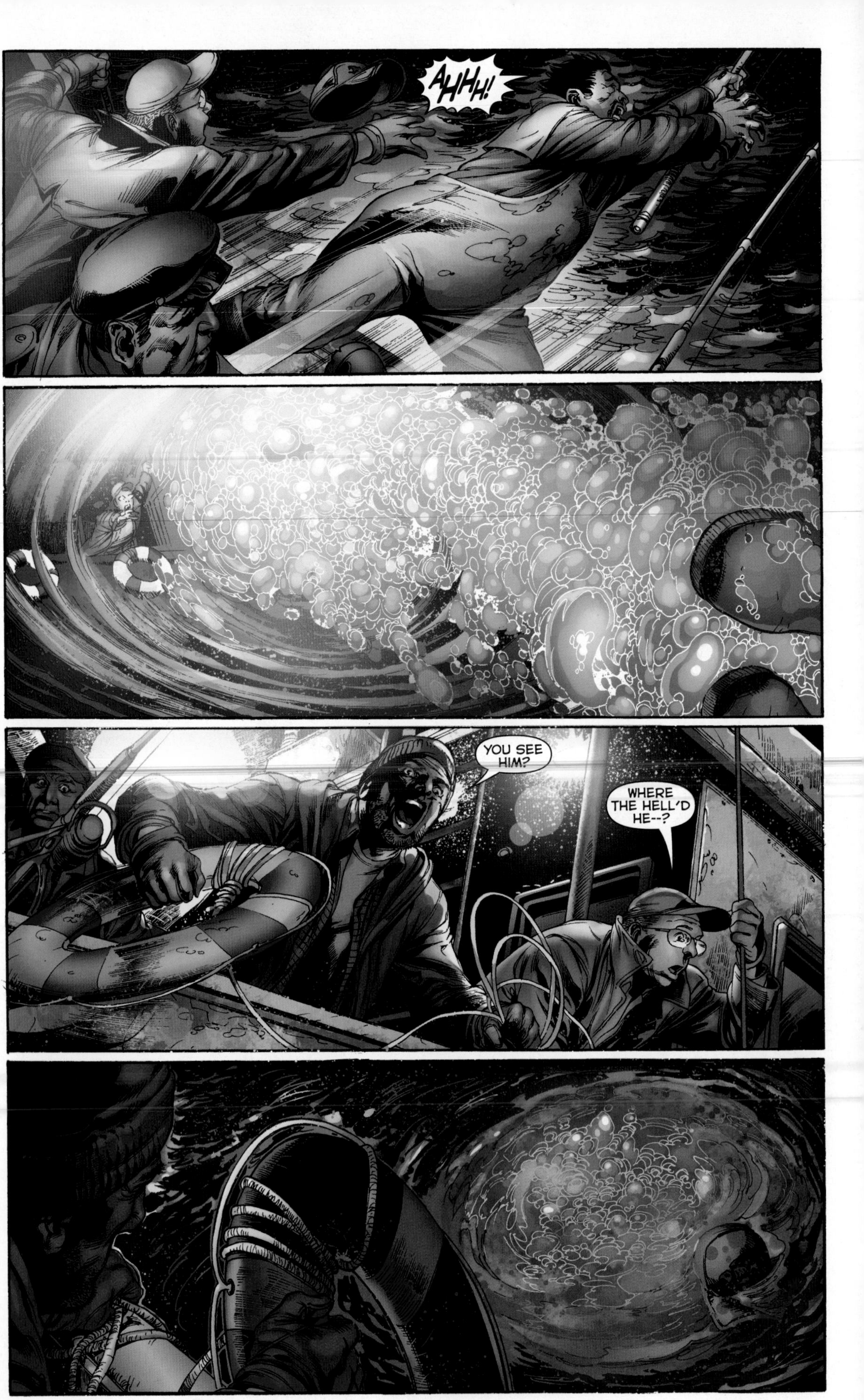
AHHH!
YOU SEE HIM?
WHERE THE HELL'D HE--?

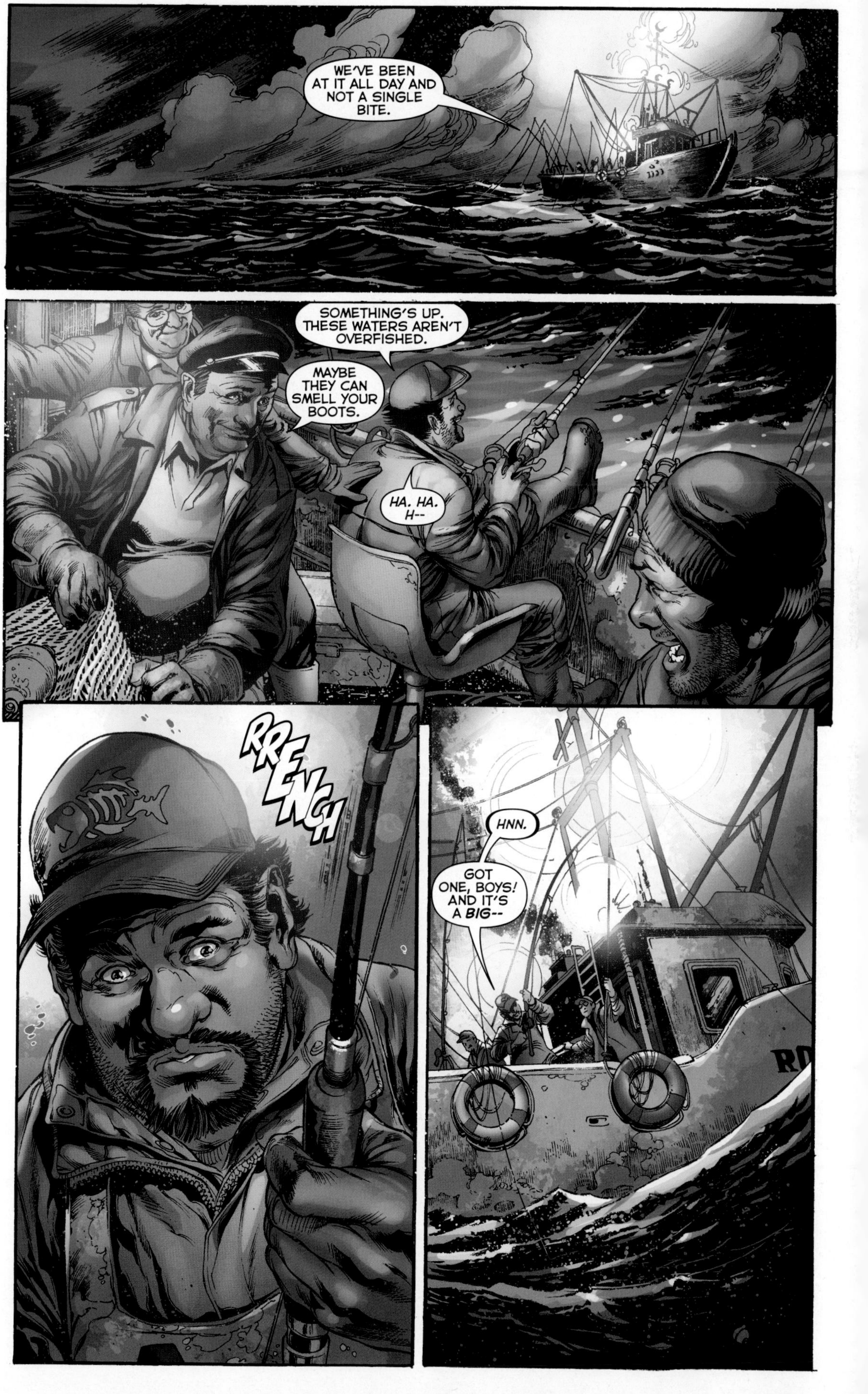
WE'VE BEEN AT IT ALL DAY AND NOT A SINGLE BITE.
SOMETHING'S UP. THESE WATERS AREN'T OVERFISHED.
MAYBE THEY CAN SMELL YOUR BOOTS.
HA. HA. H--
RRENCH
HNN.
GOT ONE, BOYS! AND IT'S A BIG--

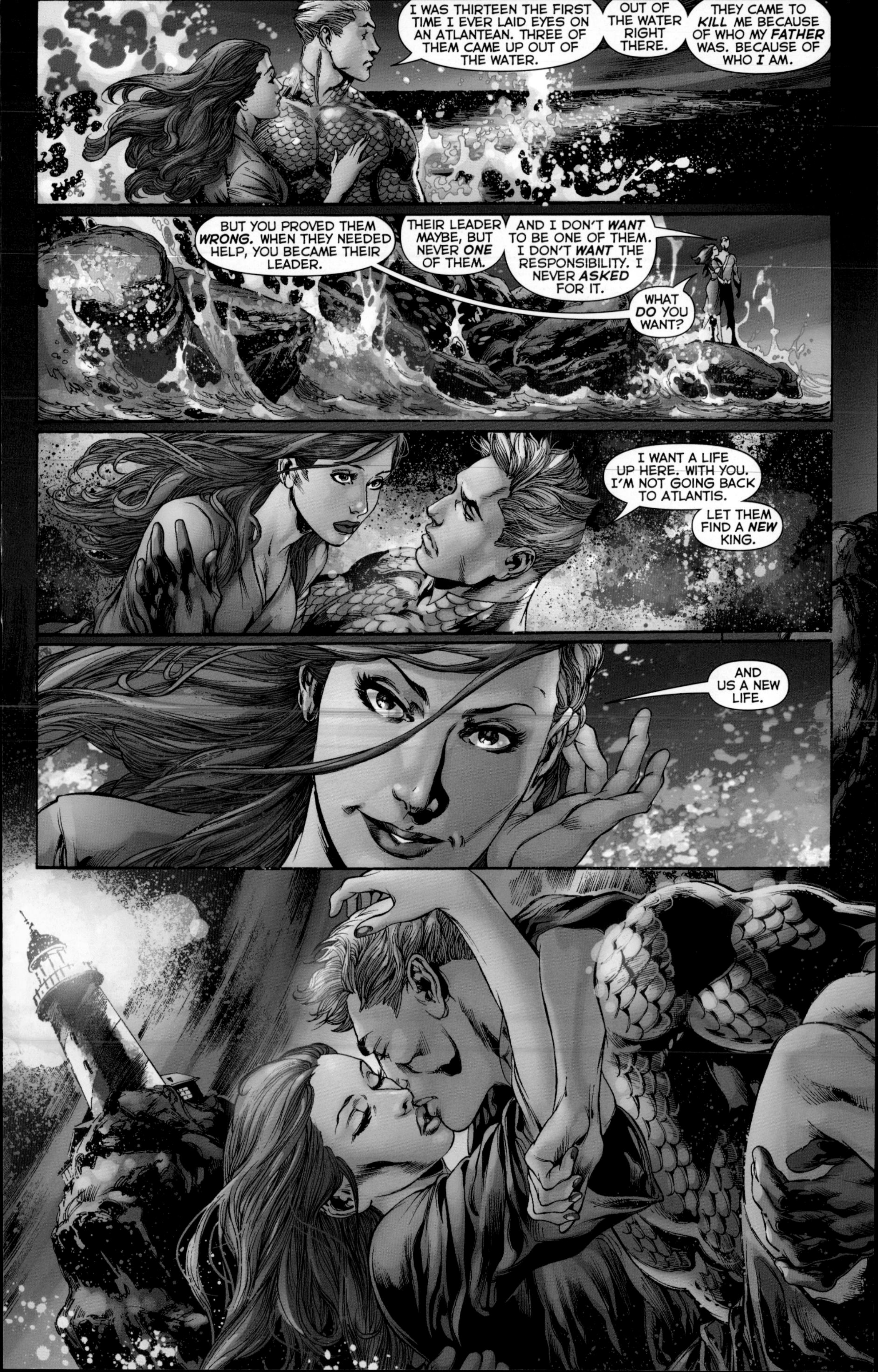

I WAS THIRTEEN THE FIRST TIME I EVER LAID EYES ON AN ATLANTEAN. THREE OF THEM CAME UP OUT OF THE WATER.
OUT OF THE WATER RIGHT THERE.
THEY CAME TO KILL ME BECAUSE OF WHO MY FATHER WAS. BECAUSE OF WHO I AM.
BUT YOU PROVED THEM WRONG. WHEN THEY NEEDED HELP, YOU BECAME THEIR LEADER.
THEIR LEADER MAYBE, BUT NEVER ONE OF THEM.
AND I DON'T WANT TO BE ONE OF THEM. I DON'T WANT THE RESPONSIBILITY. I NEVER ASKED FOR IT.
WHAT DO YOU WANT?
I WANT A LIFE UP HERE. WITH YOU. I'M NOT GOING BACK TO ATLANTIS.
LET THEM FIND A NEW KING.
AND US A NEW LIFE.

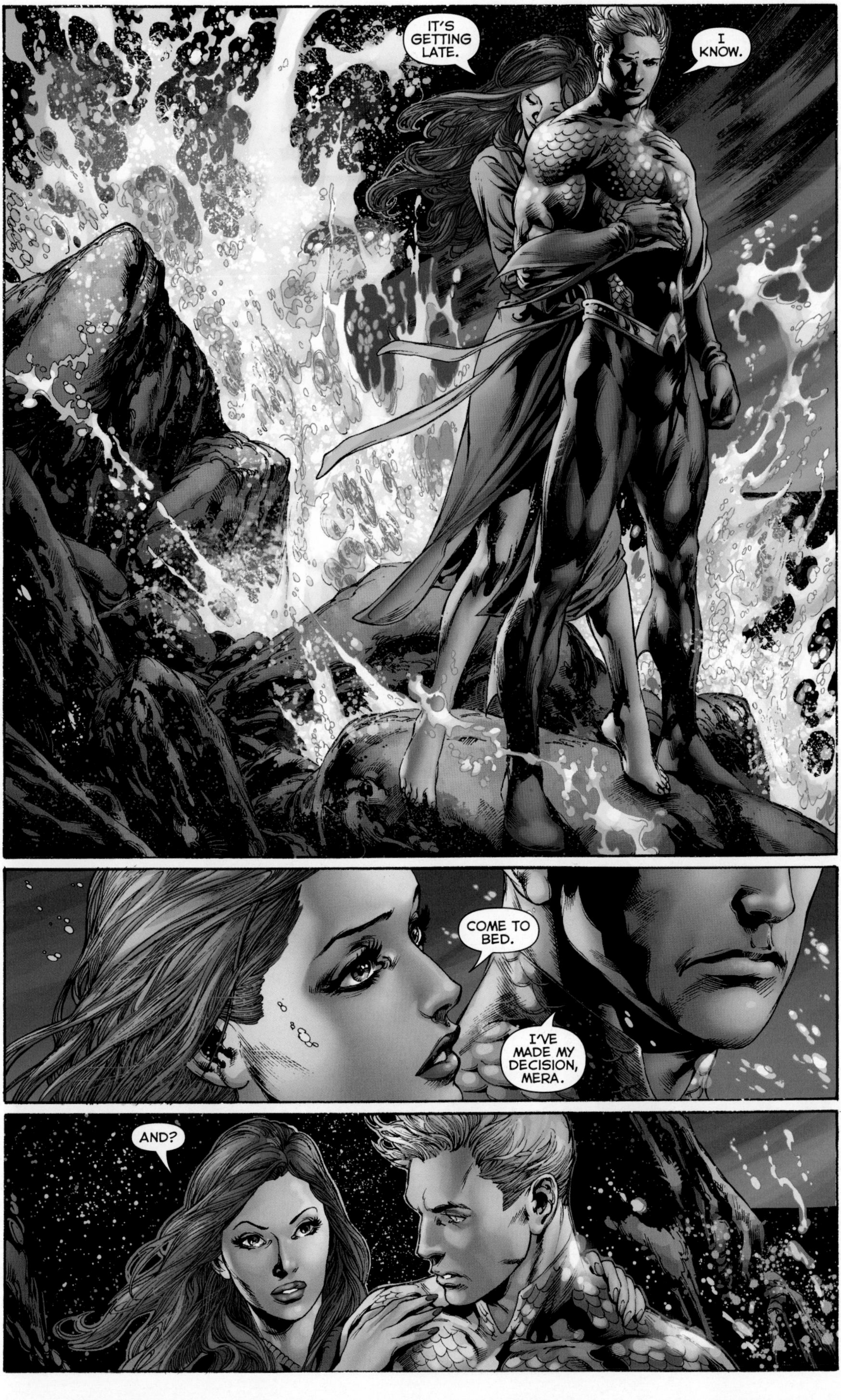
IT'S GETTING LATE.
I KNOW.
COME TO BED.
I'VE MADE MY DECISION, MERA.
AND?

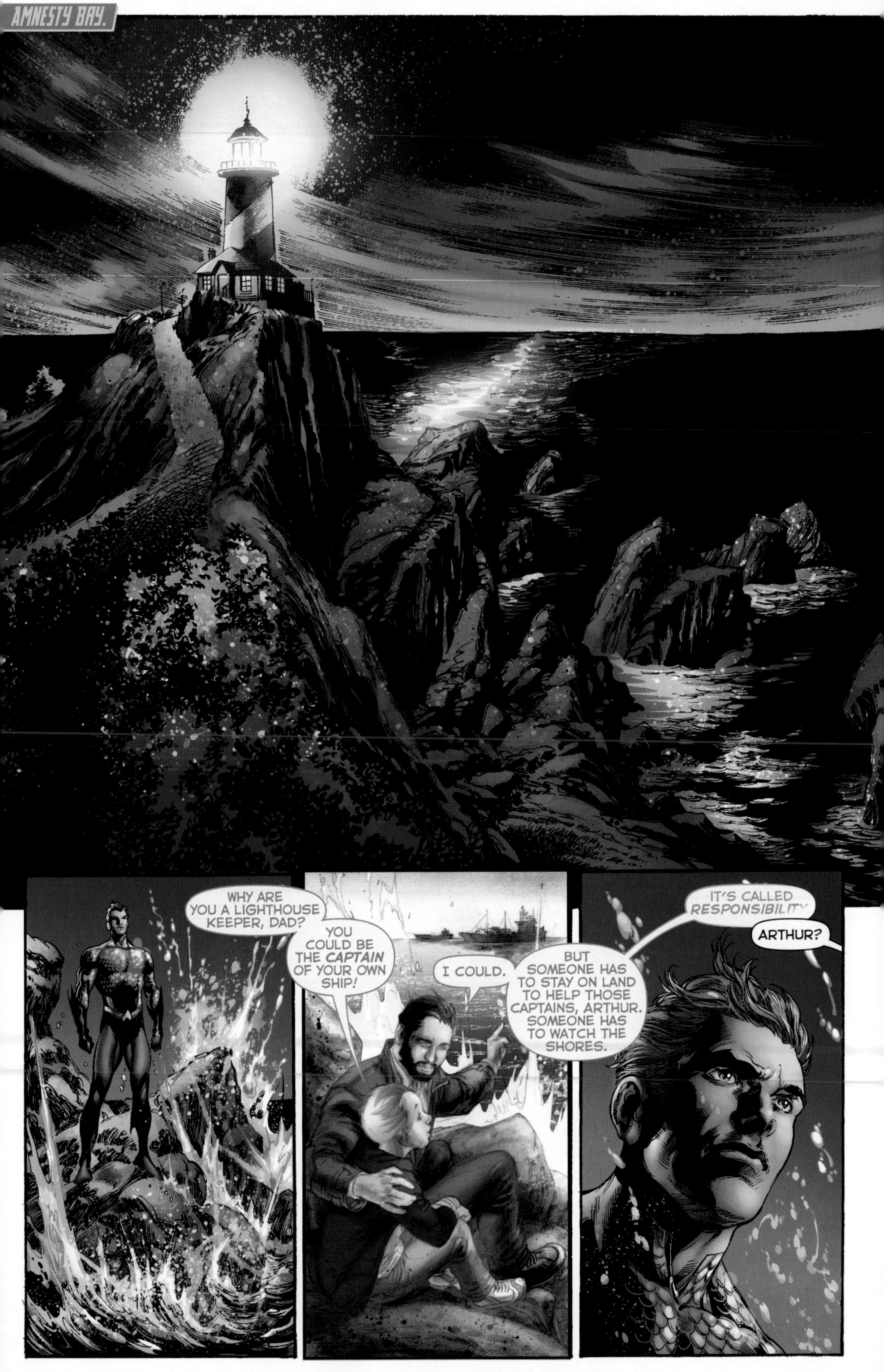
AMNESTY BAY.
WHY ARE YOU A LIGHTHOUSE KEEPER, DAD?
YOU COULD BE THE CAPTAIN OF YOUR OWN SHIP!
I COULD.
BUT SOMEONE HAS TO STAY ON LAND TO HELP THOSE CAPTAINS, ARTHUR. SOMEONE HAS TO WATCH THE SHORES.
IT'S CALLED RESPONSIBILITY.
ARTHUR?

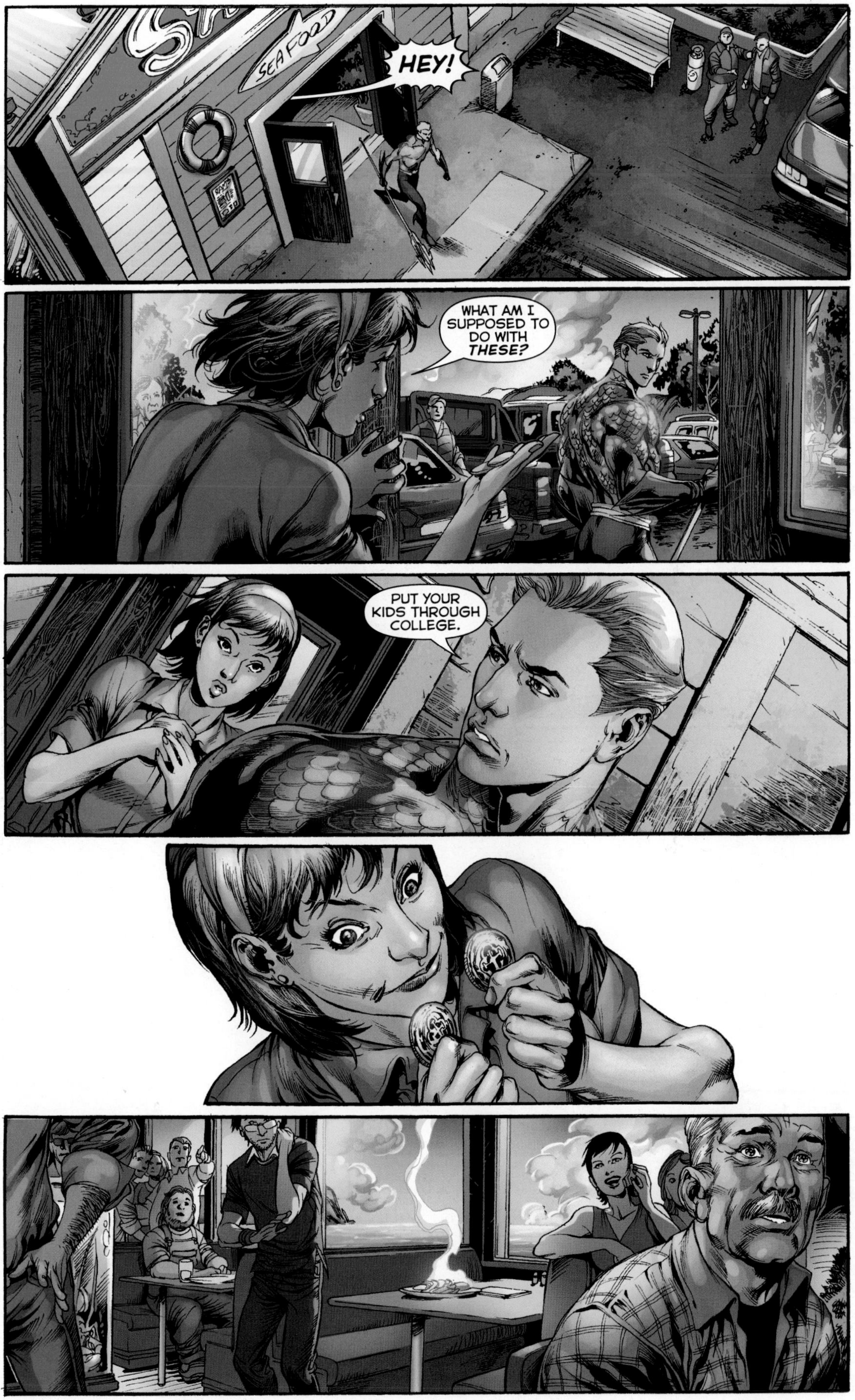
SEAFOOD
HEY!
WHAT AM I SUPPOSED TO DO WITH *THESE?*
PUT YOUR KIDS THROUGH COLLEGE.

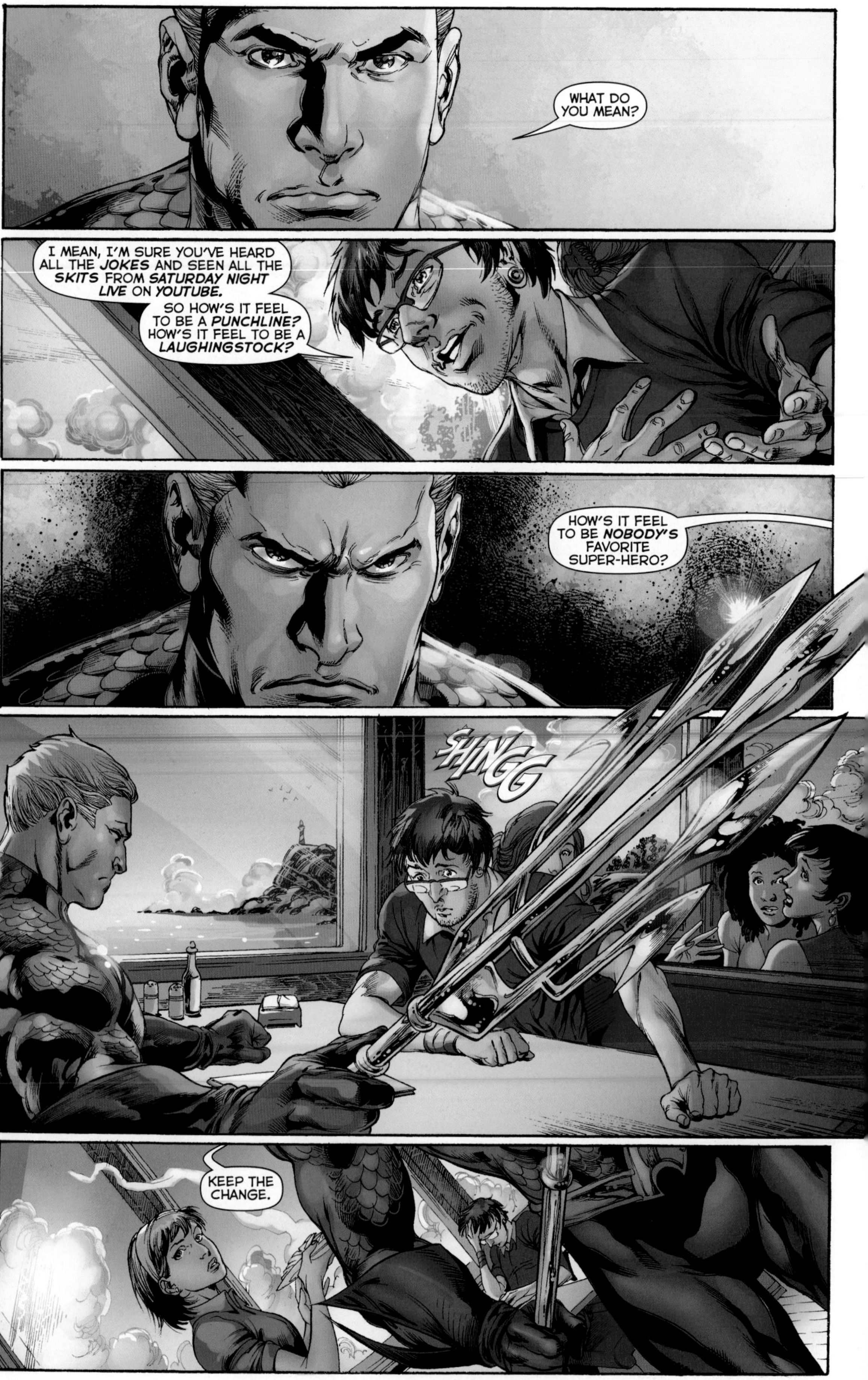
WHAT DO YOU MEAN?
I MEAN, I'M SURE YOU'VE HEARD ALL THE JOKES AND SEEN ALL THE SKITS FROM SATURDAY NIGHT LIVE ON YOUTUBE.
SO HOW'S IT FEEL TO BE A PUNCHLINE? HOW'S IT FEEL TO BE A LAUGHINGSTOCK?
HOW'S IT FEEL TO BE NOBODY'S FAVORITE SUPER-HERO?
SHINGG
KEEP THE CHANGE.

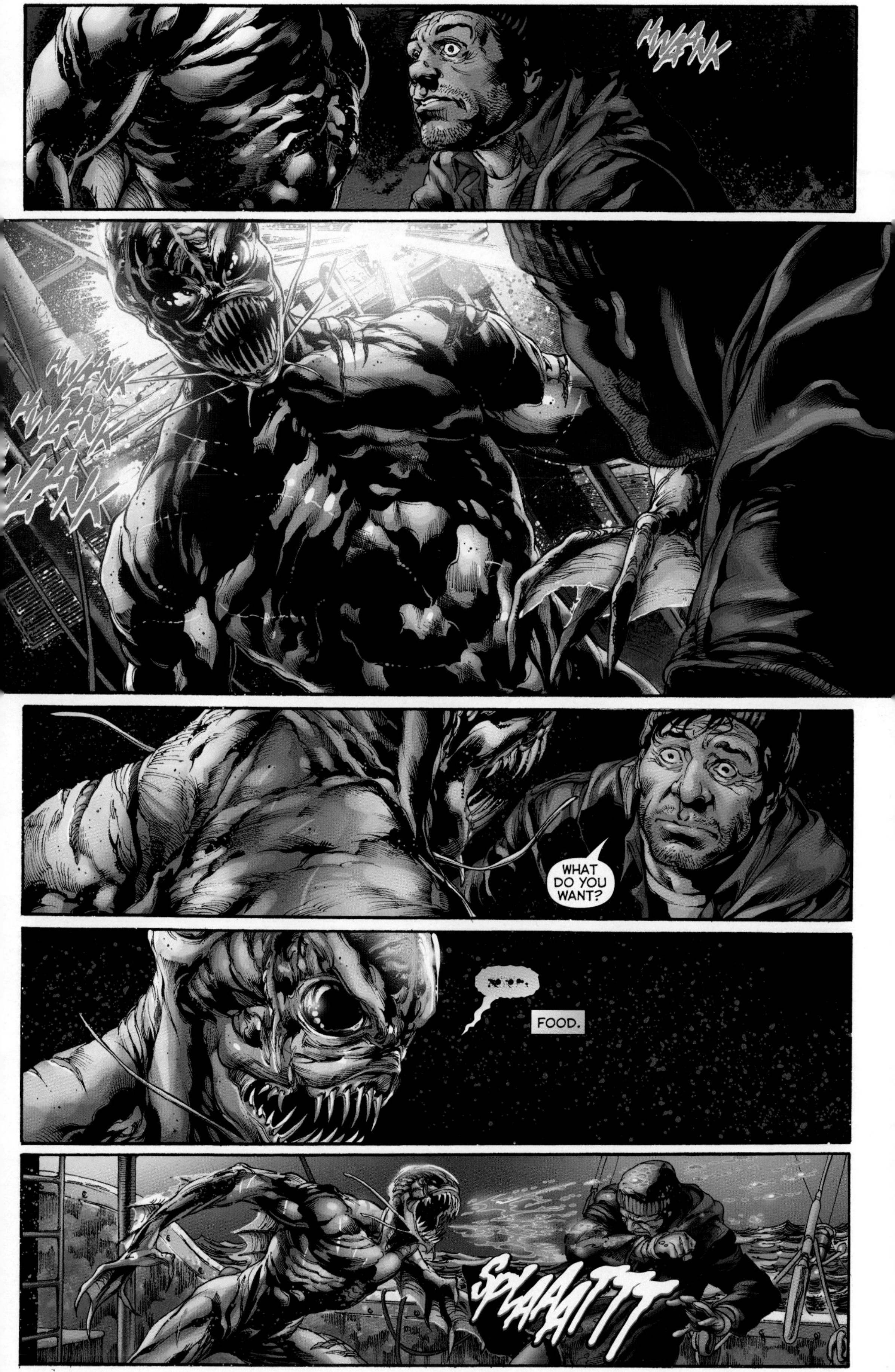
HWANK
HWANK
HWANK
WANK
WHAT DO YOU WANT?
FOOD.
SPLAAATTT

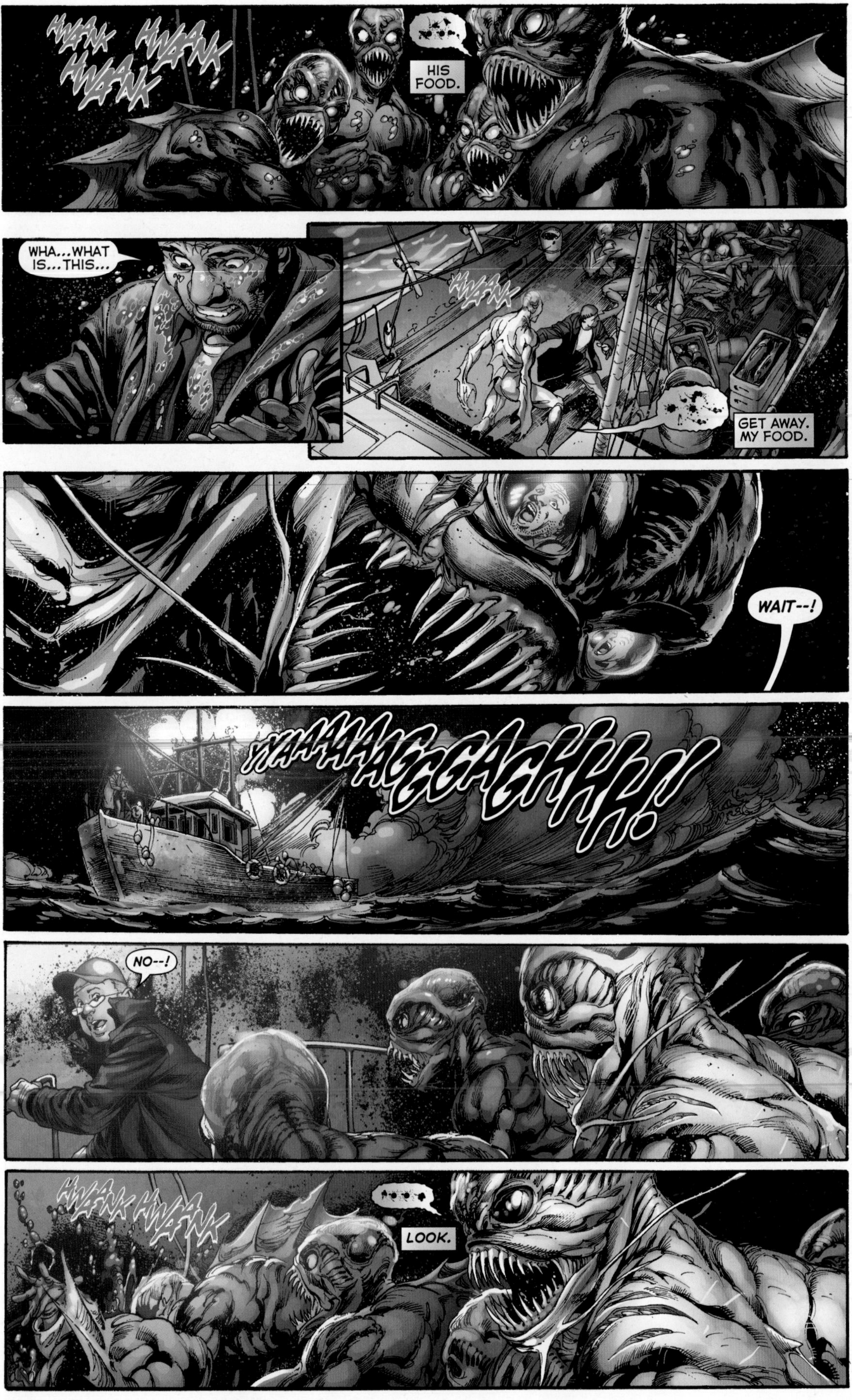

HWANK HWANK HWANK HWANK
HIS FOOD.
WHA...WHAT IS...THIS...
HWANK
GET AWAY. MY FOOD.
WAIT--!
YYAAAAAAGGGACHHH!
NO--!
HWANK HWANK
LOOK.

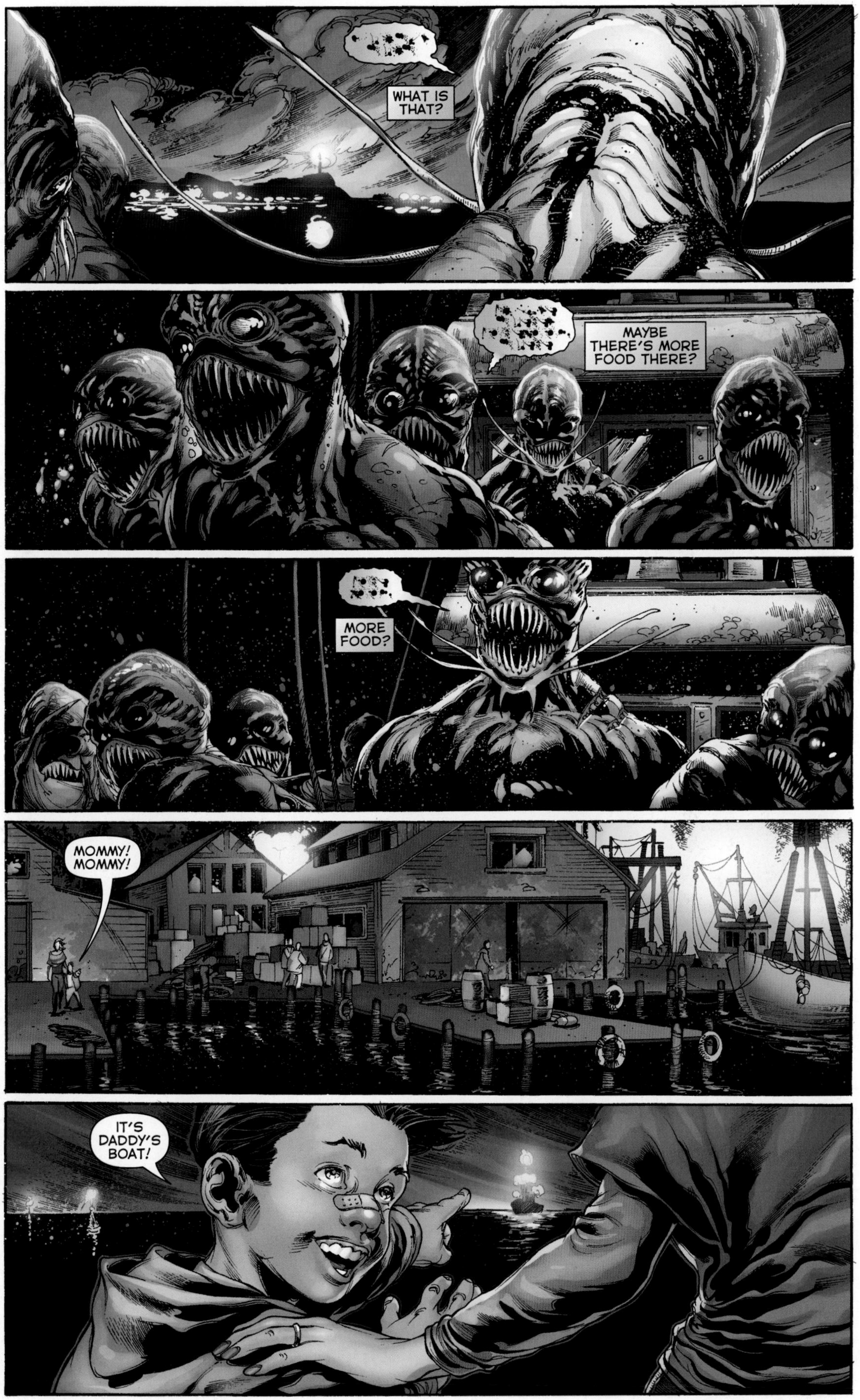
WHAT IS THAT?
MAYBE THERE'S MORE FOOD THERE?
MORE FOOD?
MOMMY! MOMMY!
IT'S DADDY'S BOAT!

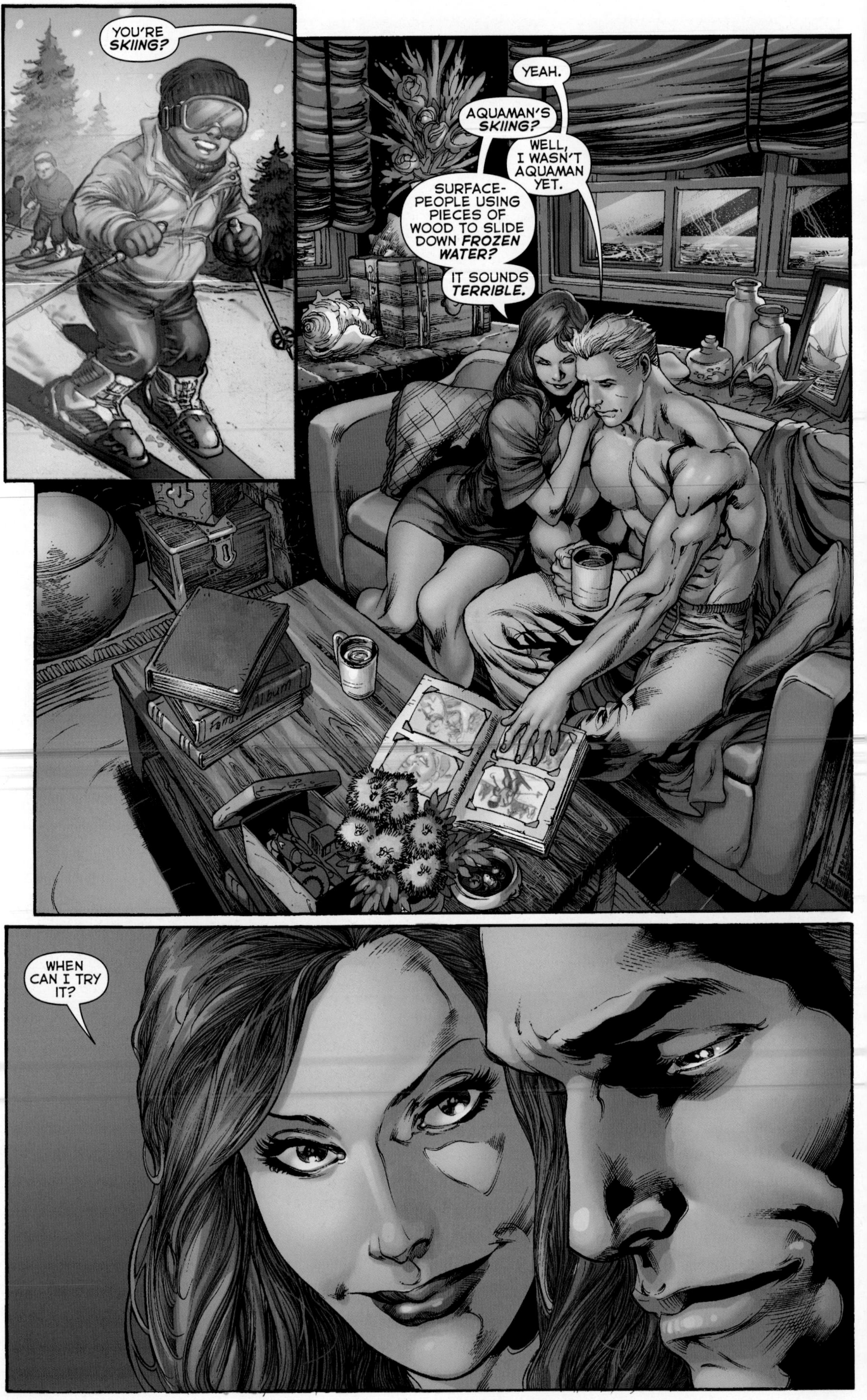
YOU'RE SKIING?
YEAH.
AQUAMAN'S SKIING?
WELL, I WASN'T AQUAMAN YET.
SURFACE-PEOPLE USING PIECES OF WOOD TO SLIDE DOWN FROZEN WATER?
IT SOUNDS TERRIBLE.
WHEN CAN I TRY IT?

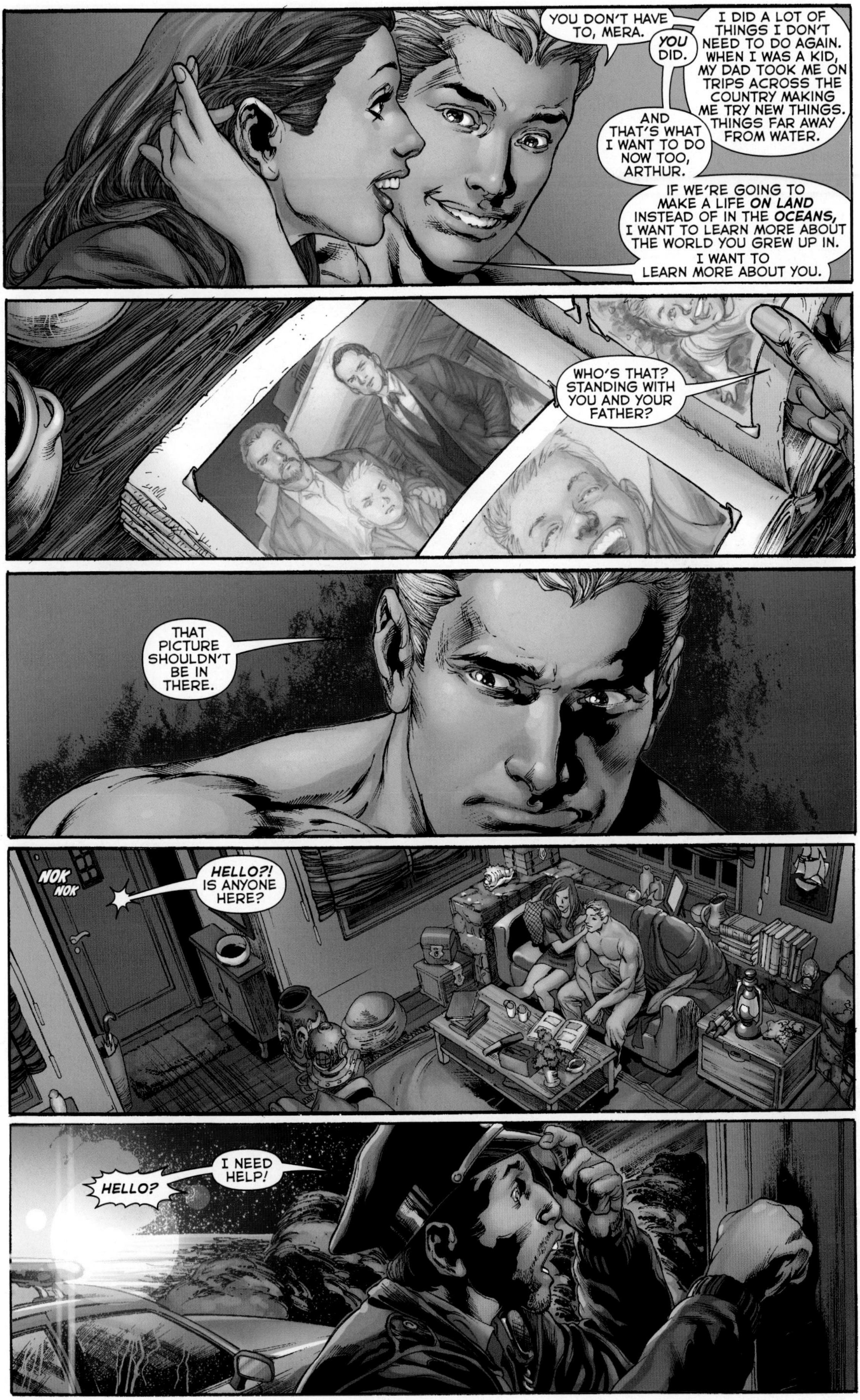
YOU DON'T HAVE TO, MERA.
YOU DID.
I DID A LOT OF THINGS I DON'T NEED TO DO AGAIN. WHEN I WAS A KID, MY DAD TOOK ME ON TRIPS ACROSS THE COUNTRY MAKING ME TRY NEW THINGS. THINGS FAR AWAY FROM WATER.
AND THAT'S WHAT I WANT TO DO NOW TOO, ARTHUR.
IF WE'RE GOING TO MAKE A LIFE ON LAND INSTEAD OF IN THE OCEANS, I WANT TO LEARN MORE ABOUT THE WORLD YOU GREW UP IN.
I WANT TO LEARN MORE ABOUT YOU.
WHO'S THAT? STANDING WITH YOU AND YOUR FATHER?
THAT PICTURE SHOULDN'T BE IN THERE.
NOK NOK
HELLO?! IS ANYONE HERE?
HELLO?
I NEED HELP!

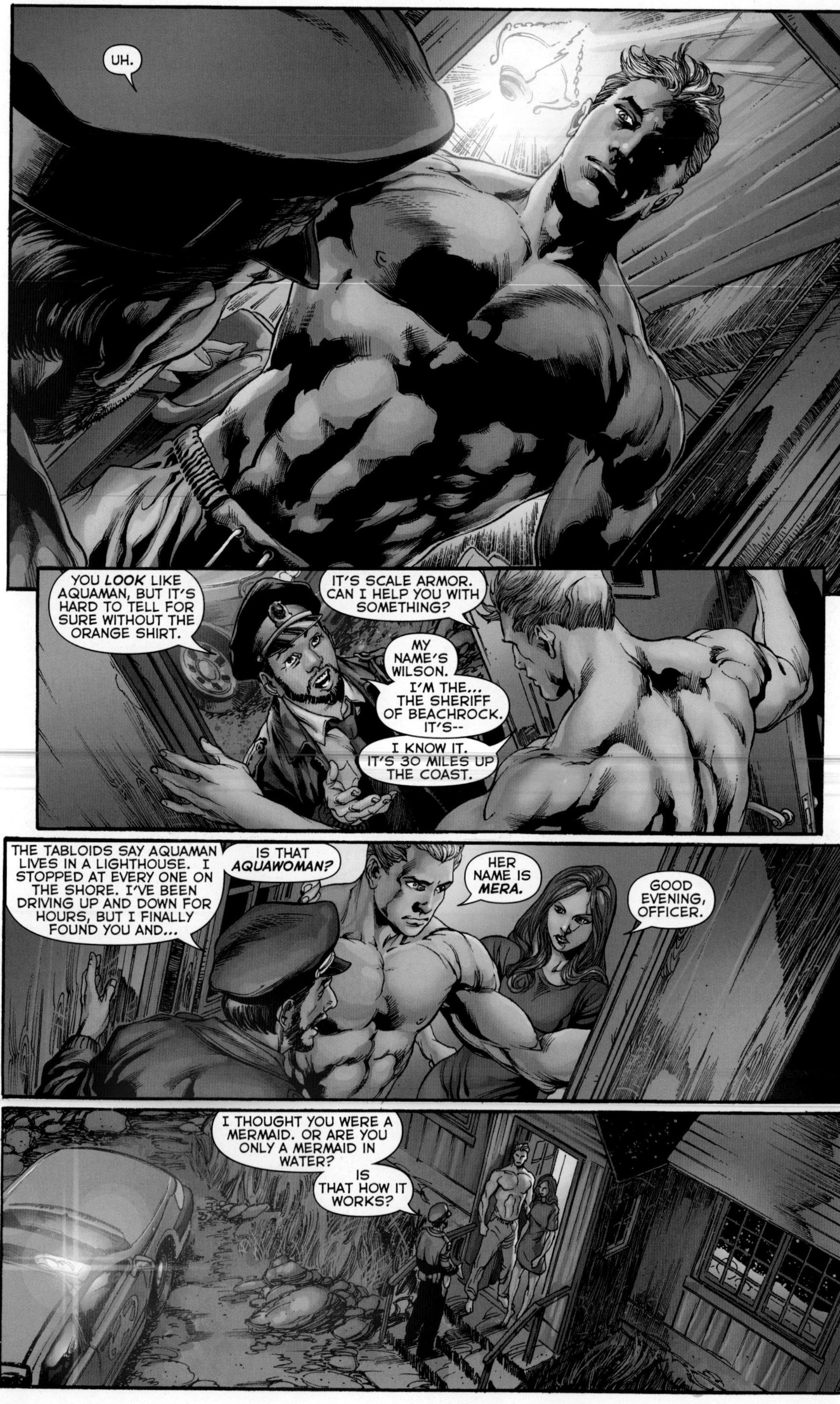
UH.
YOU LOOK LIKE AQUAMAN, BUT IT'S HARD TO TELL FOR SURE WITHOUT THE ORANGE SHIRT.
IT'S SCALE ARMOR. CAN I HELP YOU WITH SOMETHING?
MY NAME'S WILSON.
I'M THE... THE SHERIFF OF BEACHROCK. IT'S--
I KNOW IT. IT'S 30 MILES UP THE COAST.
THE TABLOIDS SAY AQUAMAN LIVES IN A LIGHTHOUSE. I STOPPED AT EVERY ONE ON THE SHORE. I'VE BEEN DRIVING UP AND DOWN FOR HOURS, BUT I FINALLY FOUND YOU AND...
IS THAT AQUAWOMAN?
HER NAME IS MERA.
GOOD EVENING, OFFICER.
I THOUGHT YOU WERE A MERMAID. OR ARE YOU ONLY A MERMAID IN WATER?
IS THAT HOW IT WORKS?

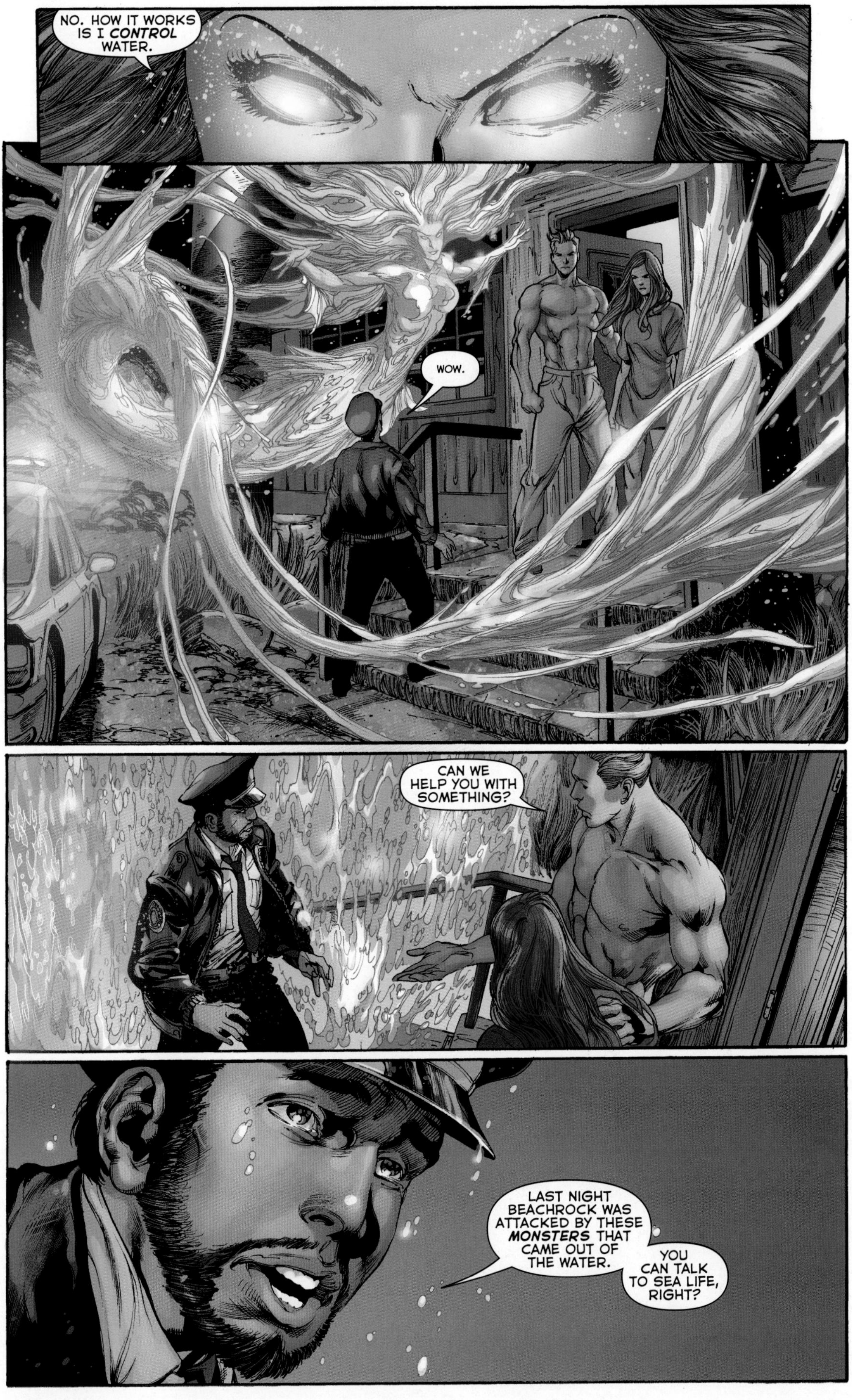
NO. HOW IT WORKS IS I *CONTROL* WATER.
WOW.
CAN WE HELP YOU WITH SOMETHING?
LAST NIGHT BEACHROCK WAS ATTACKED BY THESE *MONSTERS* THAT CAME OUT OF THE WATER.
YOU CAN TALK TO SEA LIFE, RIGHT?

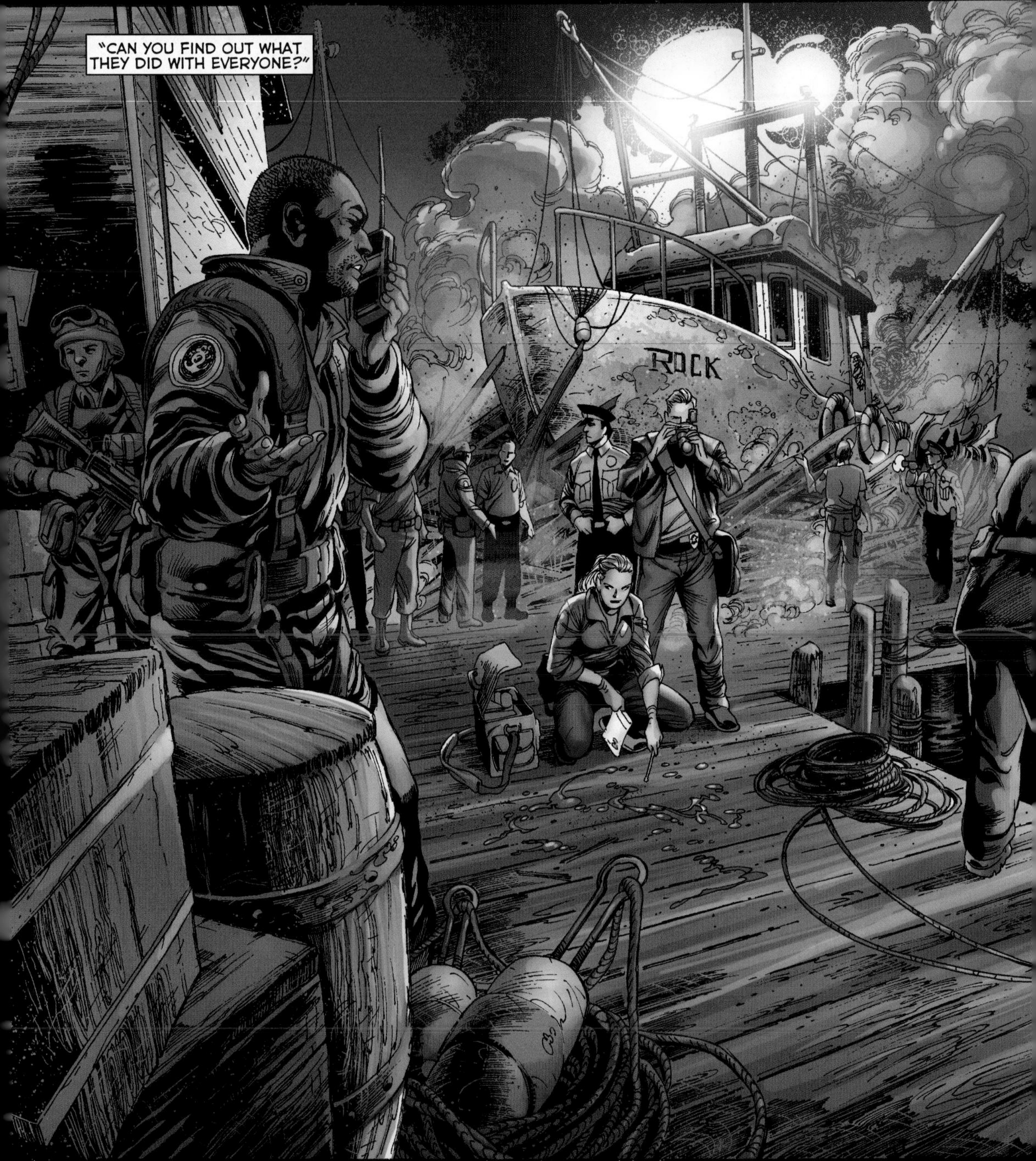
"CAN YOU FIND OUT WHAT THEY DID WITH EVERYONE?"
ROCK

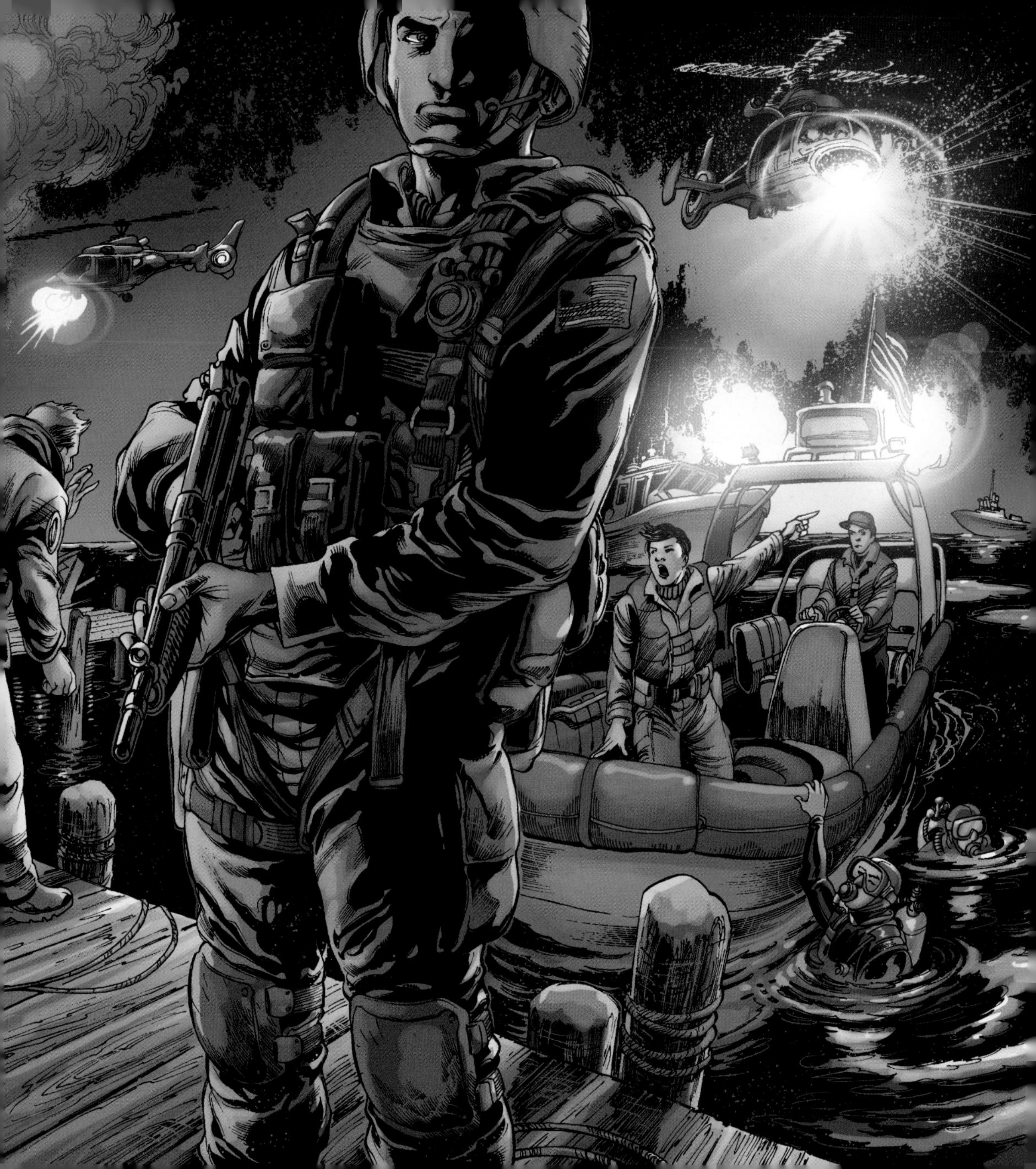

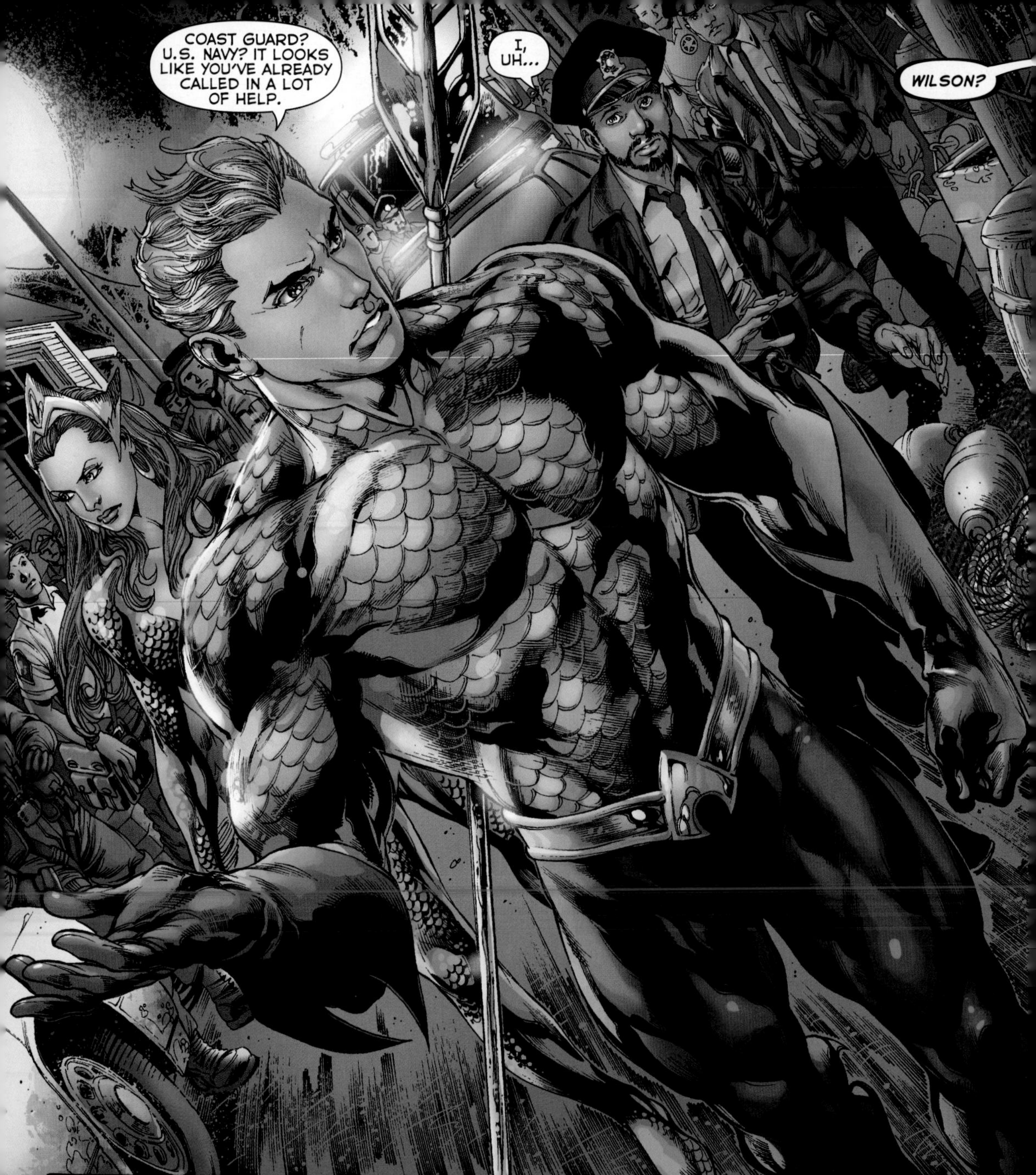
COAST GUARD? U.S. NAVY? IT LOOKS LIKE YOU'VE ALREADY CALLED IN A LOT OF HELP.
I, UH...
WILSON?

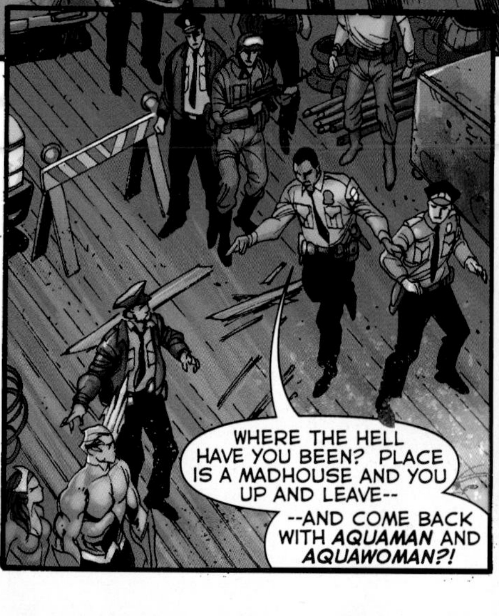
WHERE THE HELL HAVE YOU BEEN? PLACE IS A MADHOUSE AND YOU UP AND LEAVE--
--AND COME BACK WITH *AQUAMAN* AND *AQUAWOMAN?!*

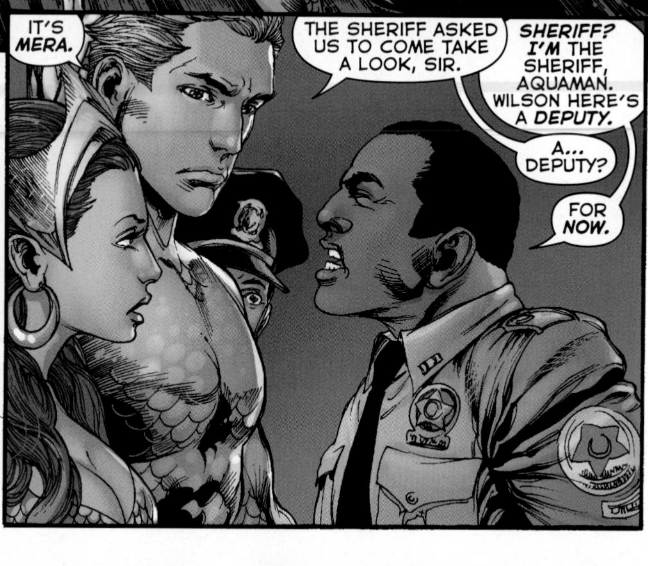
IT'S *MERA.*
THE SHERIFF ASKED US TO COME TAKE A LOOK, SIR.
SHERIFF? I'M THE SHERIFF, AQUAMAN. WILSON HERE'S A *DEPUTY.*
A... DEPUTY?
FOR *NOW.*

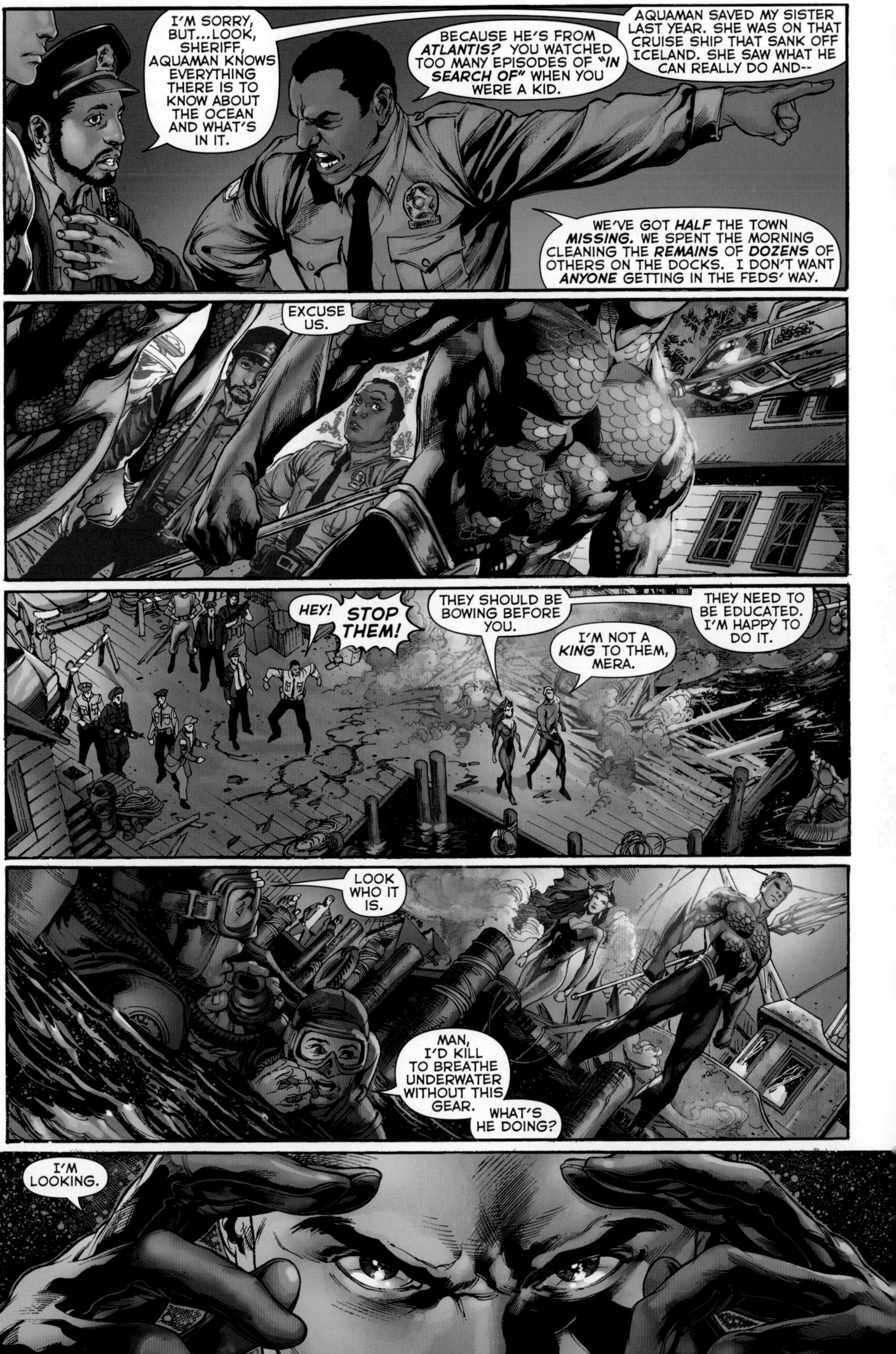
I'M SORRY, BUT...LOOK, SHERIFF, AQUAMAN KNOWS EVERYTHING THERE IS TO KNOW ABOUT THE OCEAN AND WHAT'S IN IT.
BECAUSE HE'S FROM ATLANTIS? YOU WATCHED TOO MANY EPISODES OF "IN SEARCH OF" WHEN YOU WERE A KID.
AQUAMAN SAVED MY SISTER LAST YEAR. SHE WAS ON THAT CRUISE SHIP THAT SANK OFF ICELAND. SHE SAW WHAT HE CAN REALLY DO AND--
WE'VE GOT HALF THE TOWN MISSING. WE SPENT THE MORNING CLEANING THE REMAINS OF DOZENS OF OTHERS ON THE DOCKS. I DON'T WANT ANYONE GETTING IN THE FEDS' WAY.
EXCUSE US.
HEY!
STOP THEM!
THEY SHOULD BE BOWING BEFORE YOU.
I'M NOT A KING TO THEM, MERA.
THEY NEED TO BE EDUCATED. I'M HAPPY TO DO IT.
LOOK WHO IT IS.
MAN, I'D KILL TO BREATHE UNDERWATER WITHOUT THIS GEAR.
WHAT'S HE DOING?
I'M LOOKING.

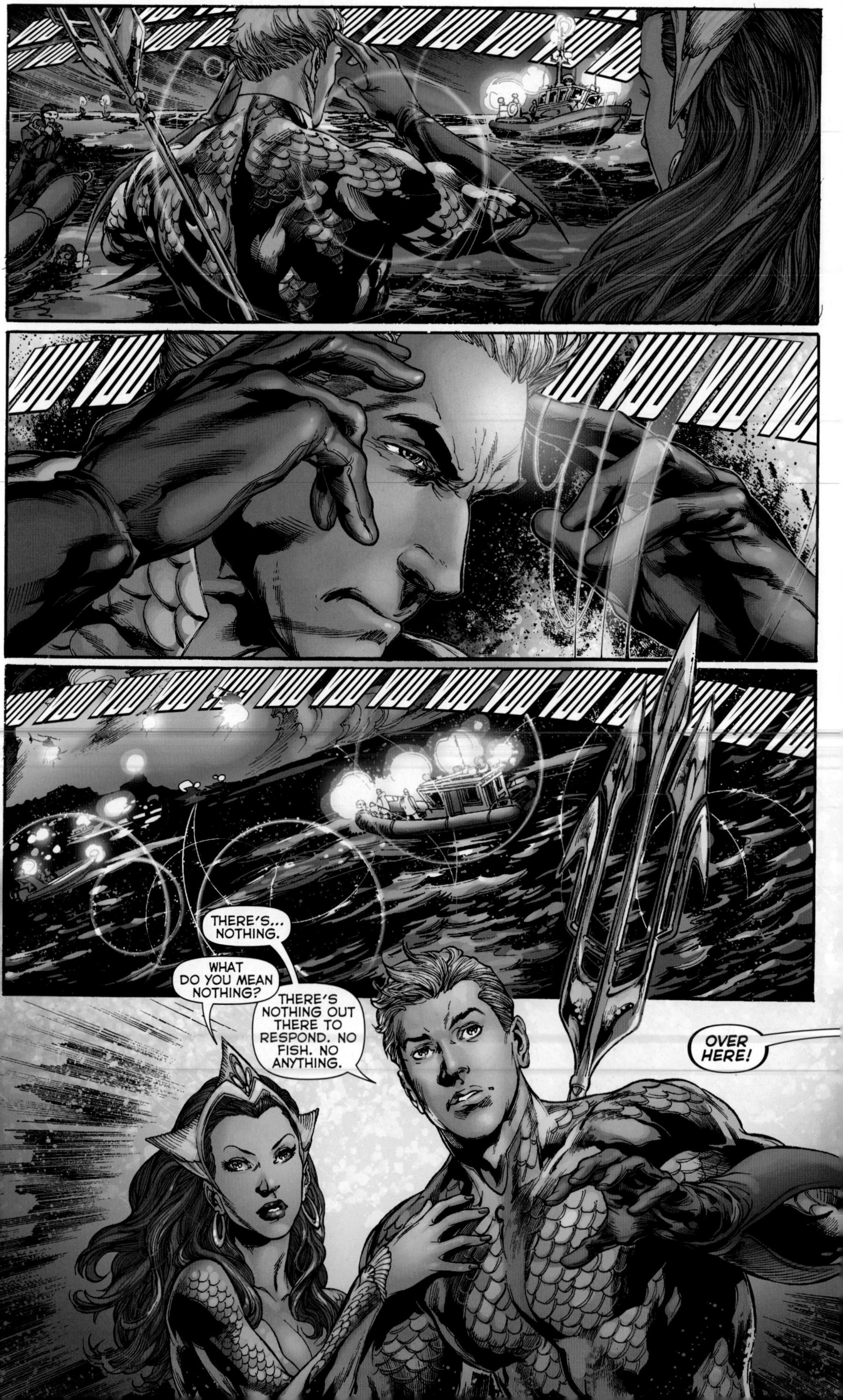
THERE'S... NOTHING.
WHAT DO YOU MEAN NOTHING?
THERE'S NOTHING OUT THERE TO RESPOND. NO FISH. NO ANYTHING.
OVER HERE!

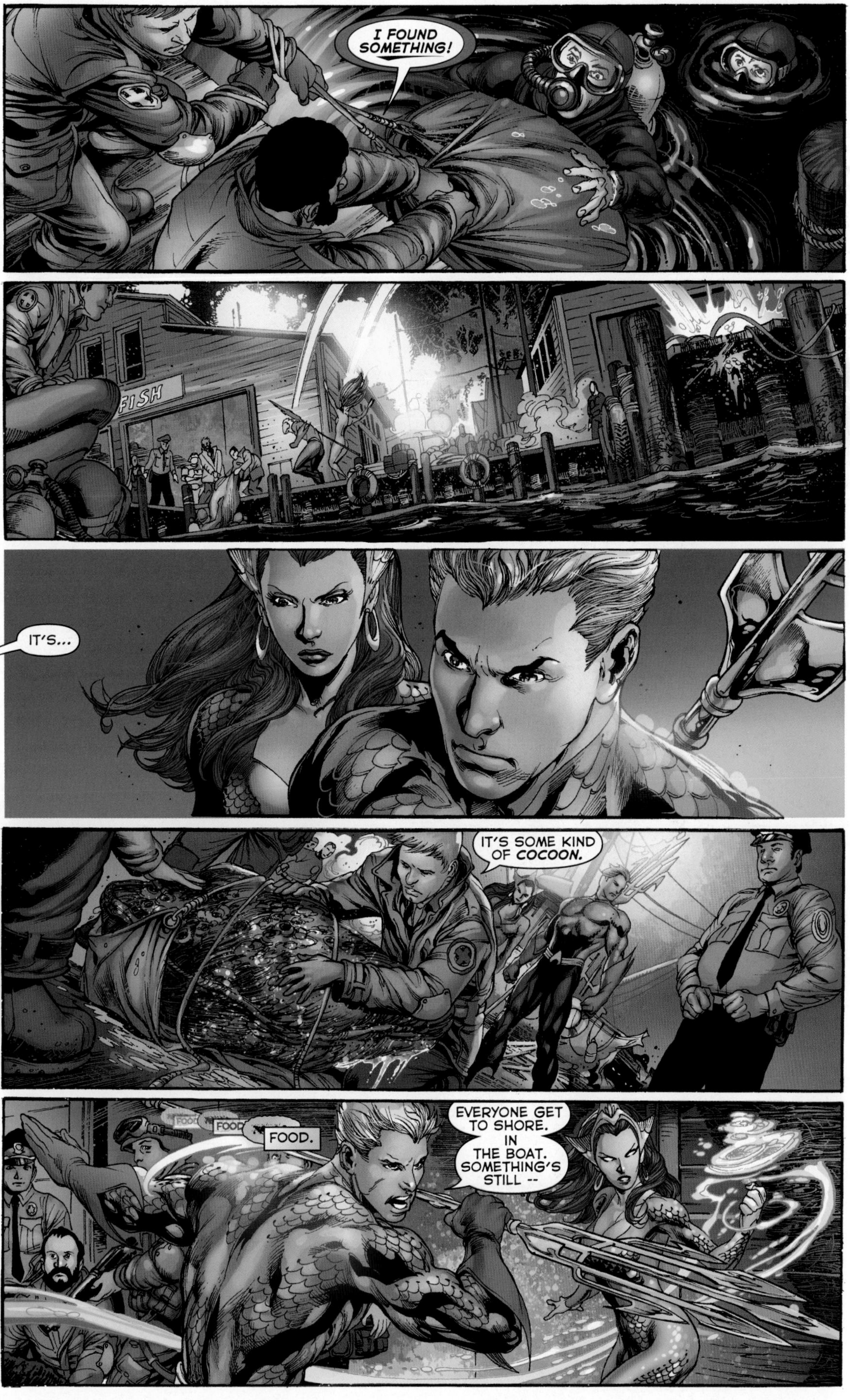
I FOUND SOMETHING!
FISH
IT'S...
IT'S SOME KIND OF COCOON.
FOOD
FOOD
FOOD.
EVERYONE GET TO SHORE. IN THE BOAT. SOMETHING'S STILL --

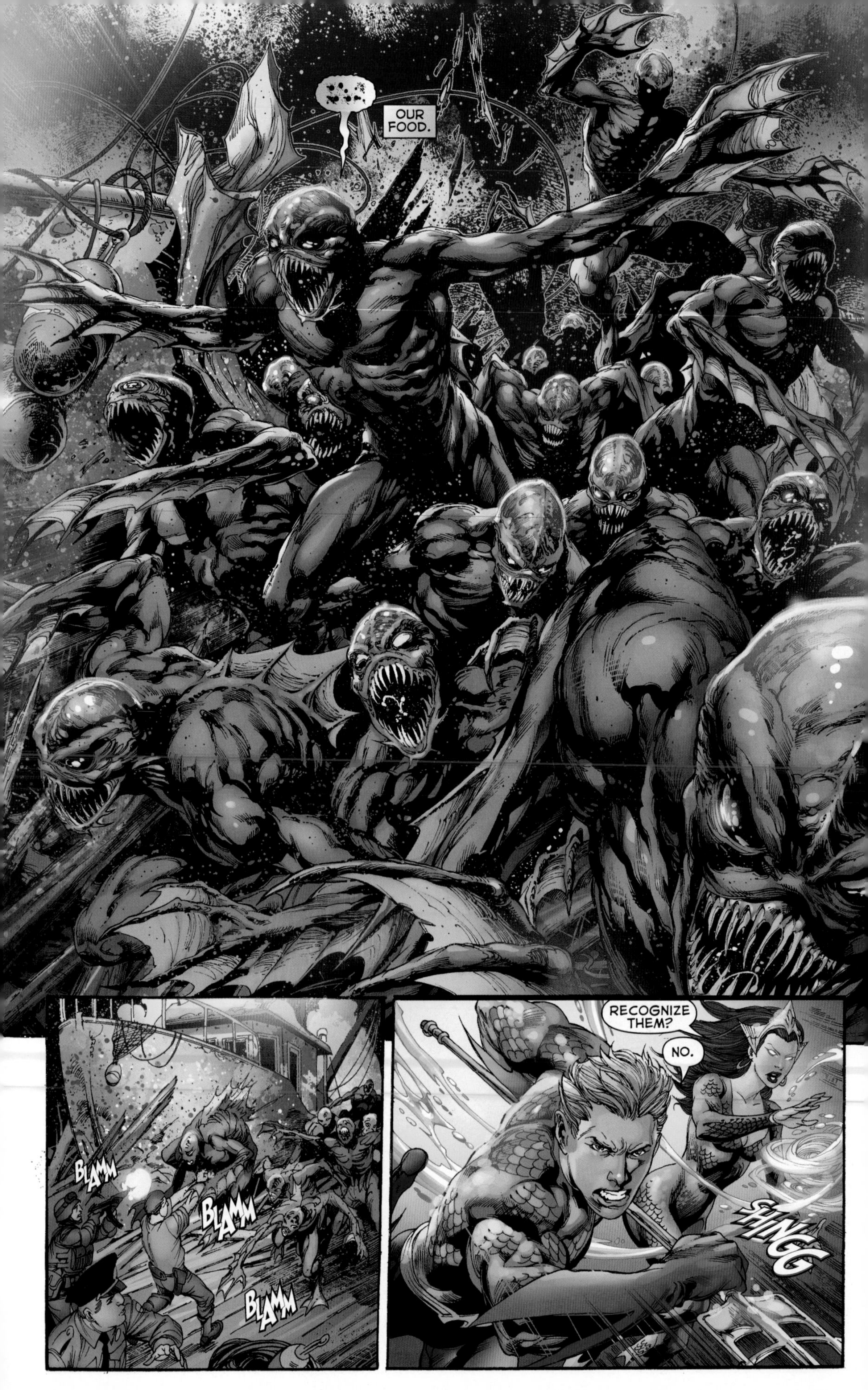
OUR FOOD.
BLAMM
BLAMM
BLAMM
RECOGNIZE THEM?
NO.
SHINGG

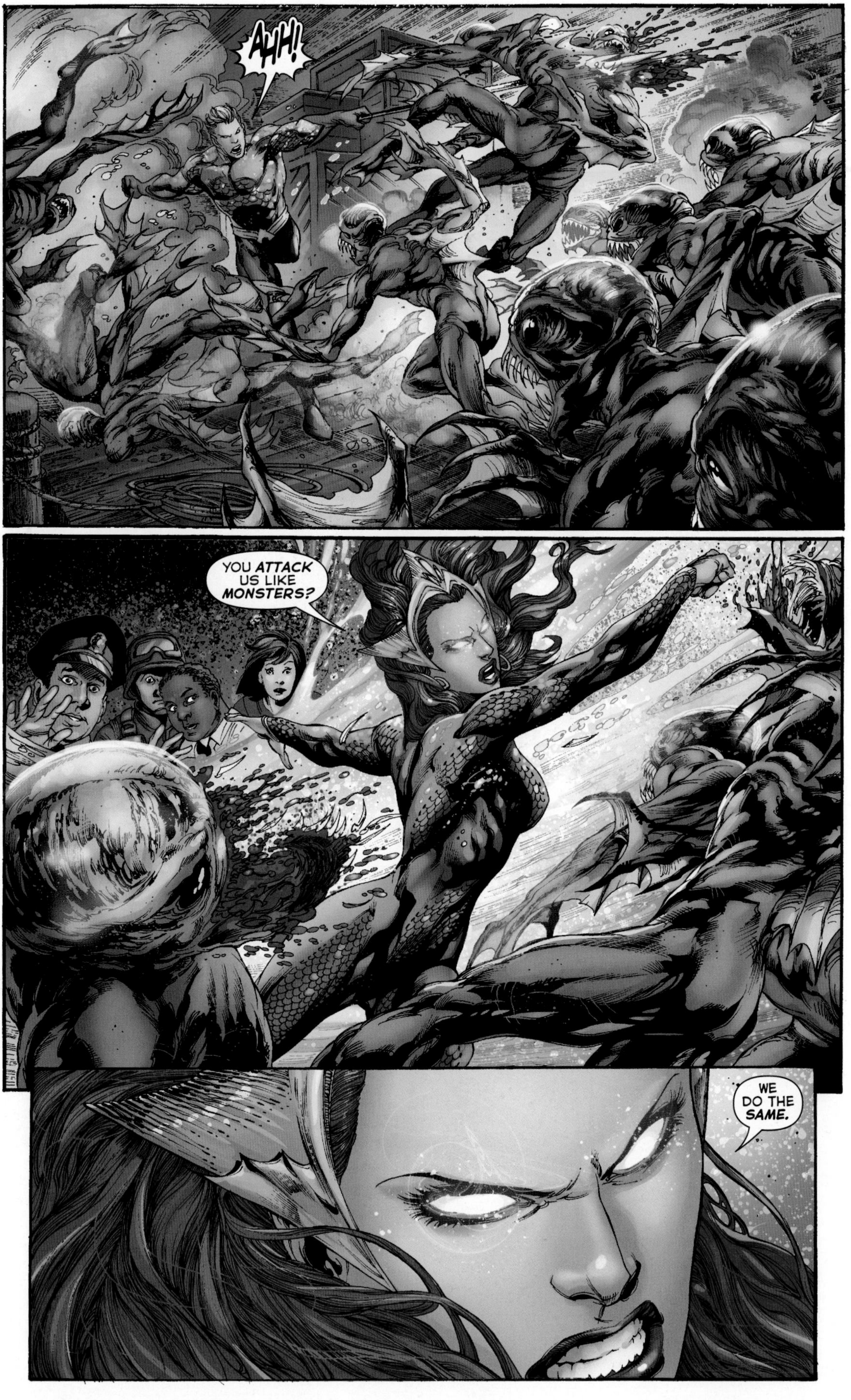
AHH!
YOU ATTACK US LIKE MONSTERS?
WE DO THE SAME.

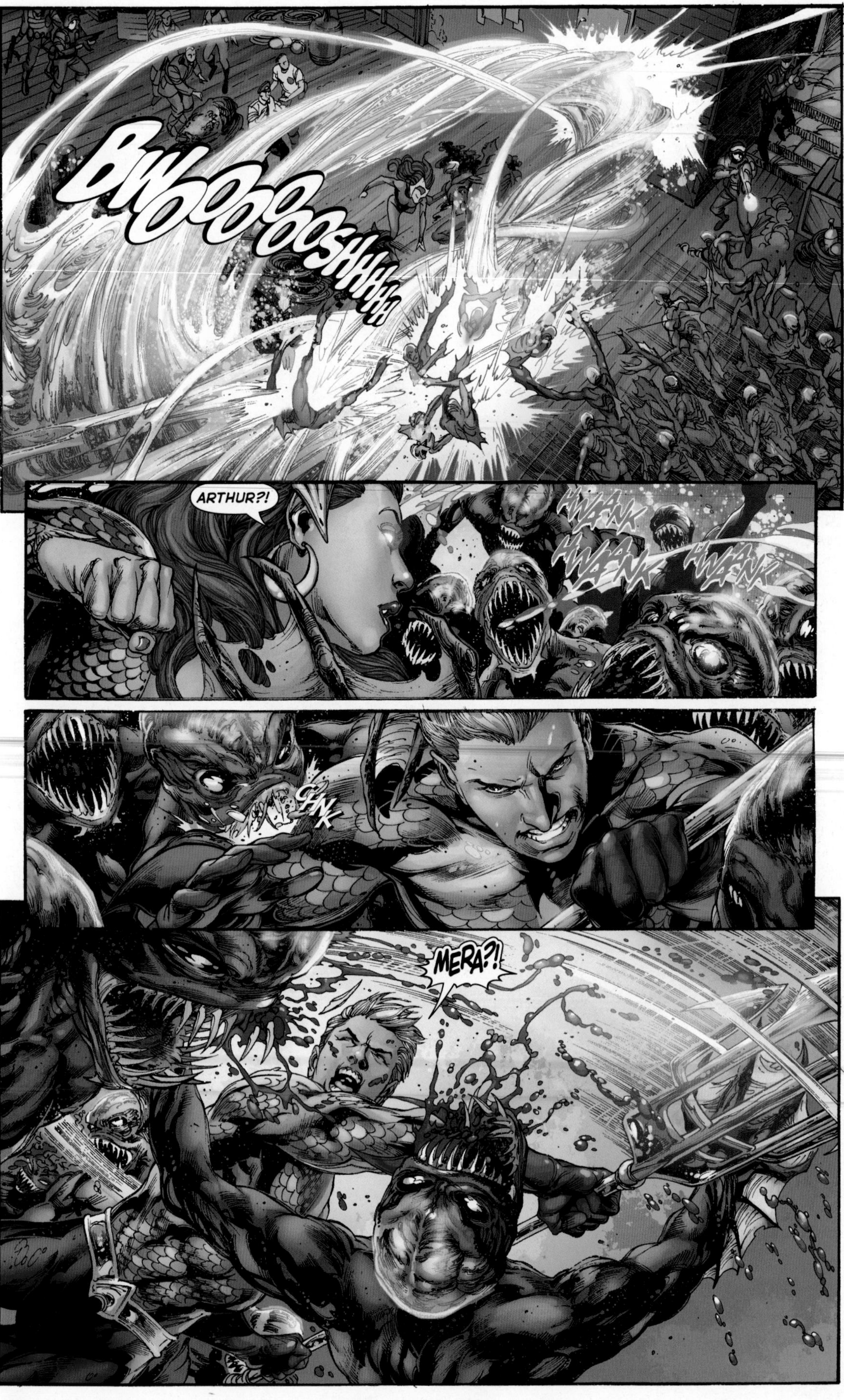
BWOOOOOOSHHHH
ARTHUR?!
HWANK
HWANK
HWANK
HWANK
CHNK
MERA?!

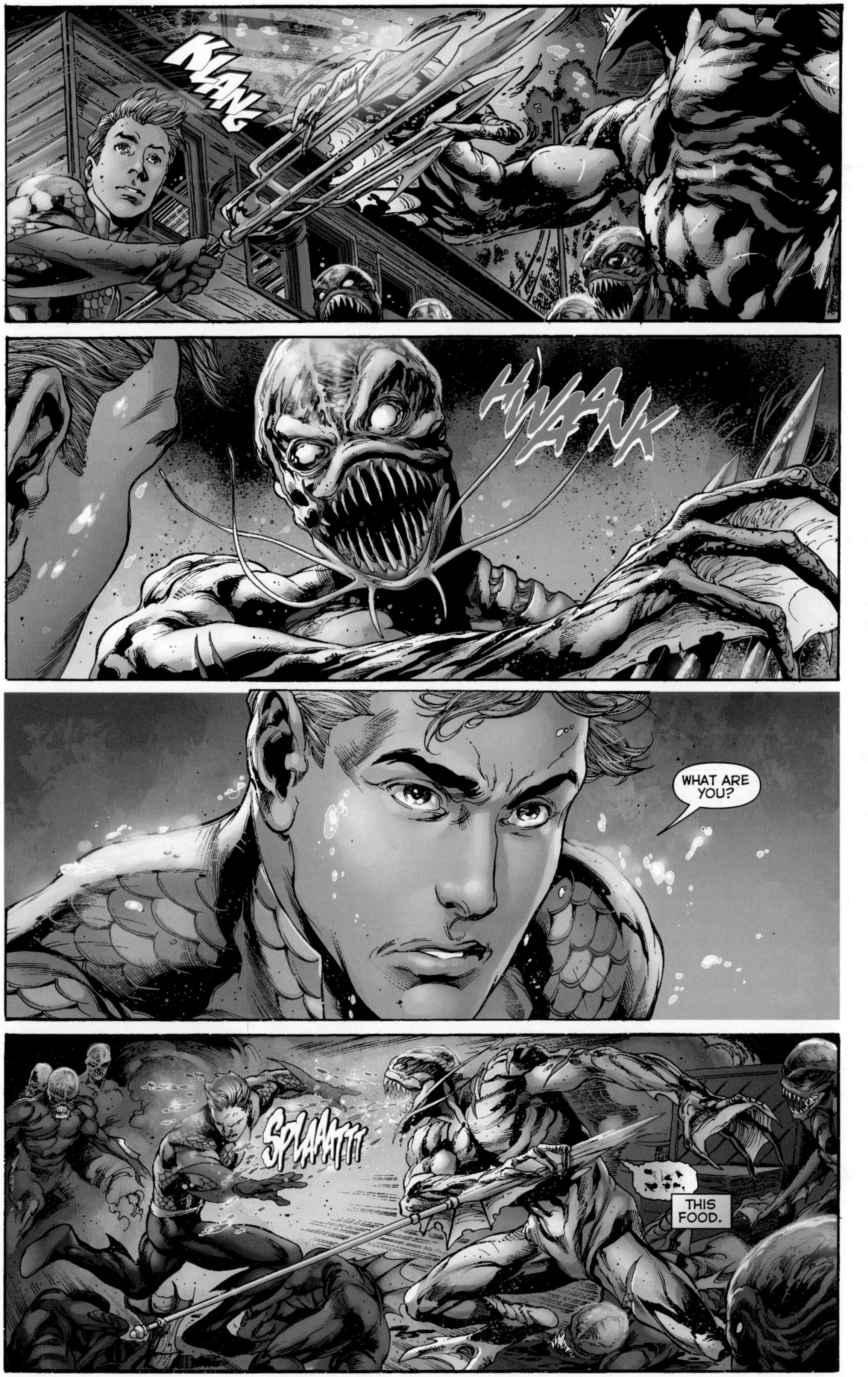
KLANG
HWANK
WHAT ARE YOU?
SPLAAATTT
THIS FOOD.

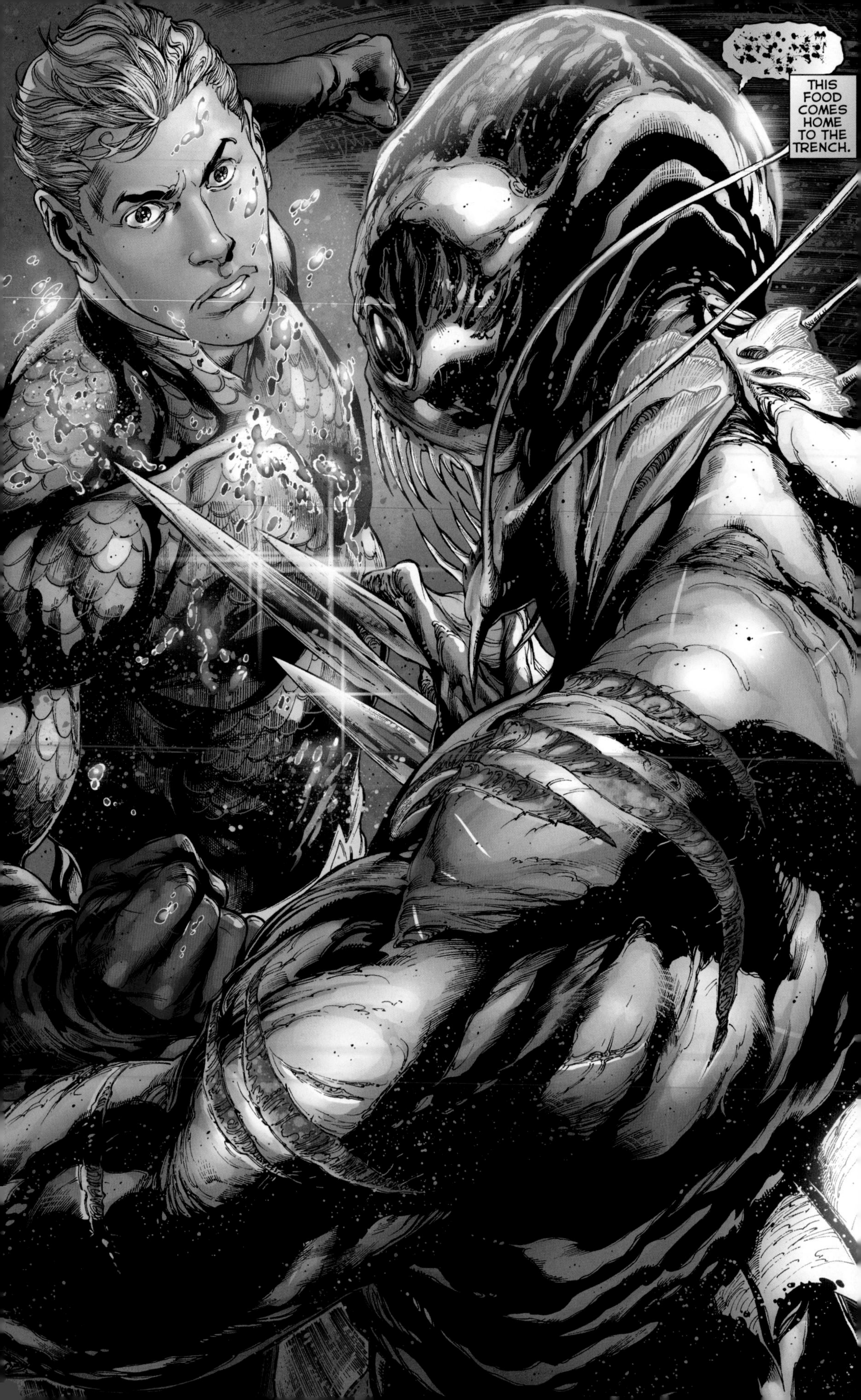
THIS FOOD COMES HOME TO THE TRENCH.

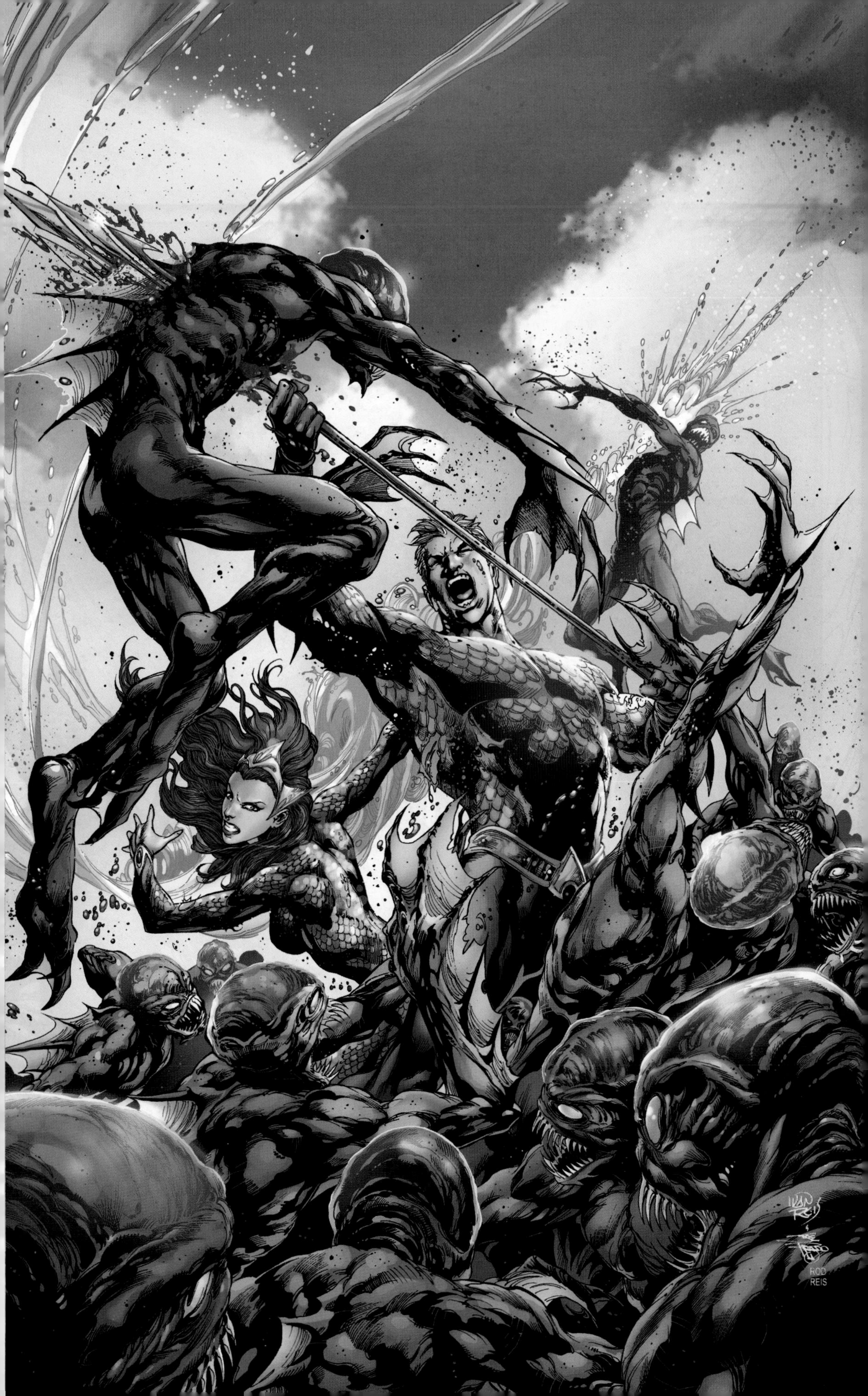
ROD
REIS

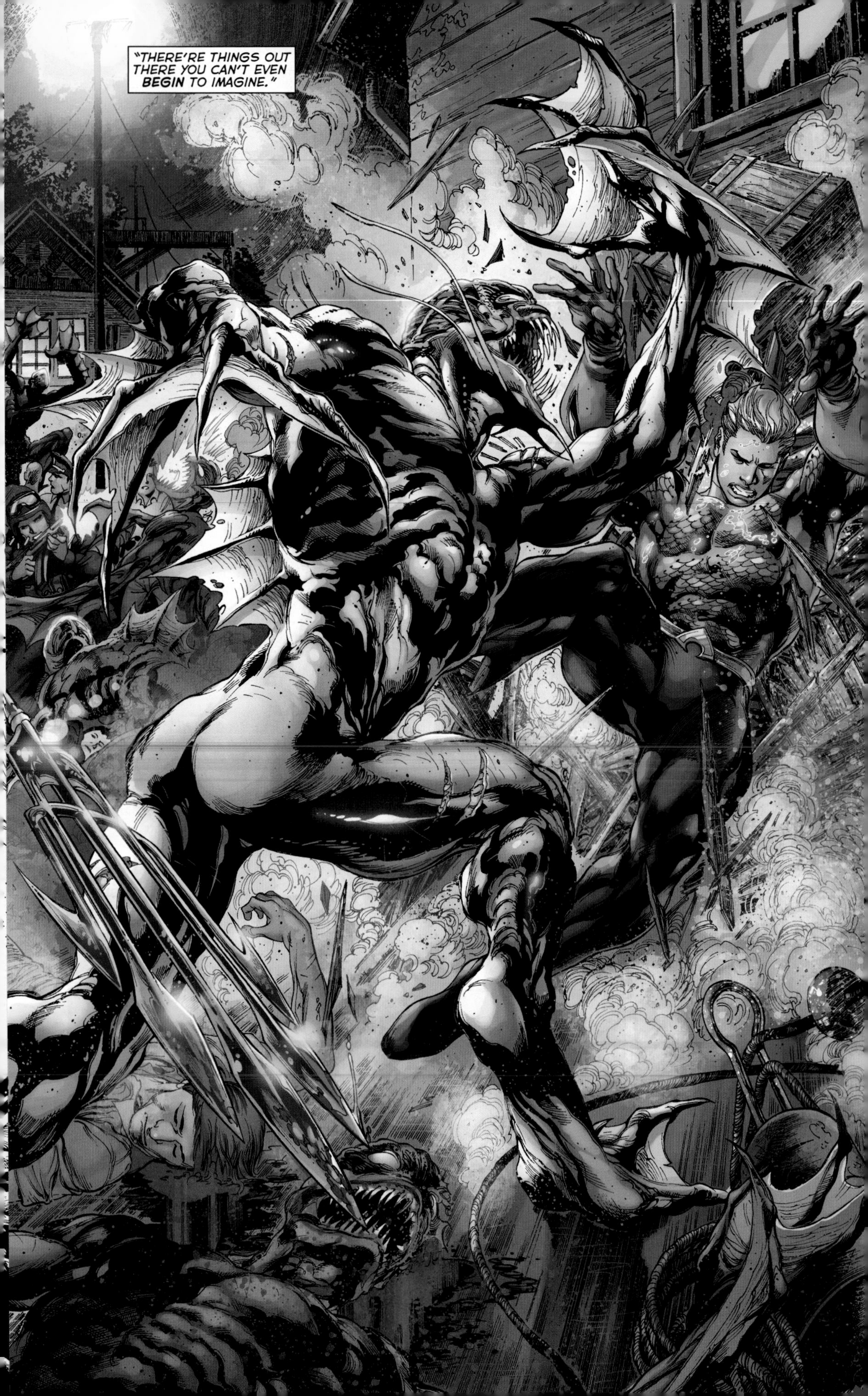
"THERE'RE THINGS OUT THERE YOU CAN'T EVEN BEGIN TO IMAGINE."

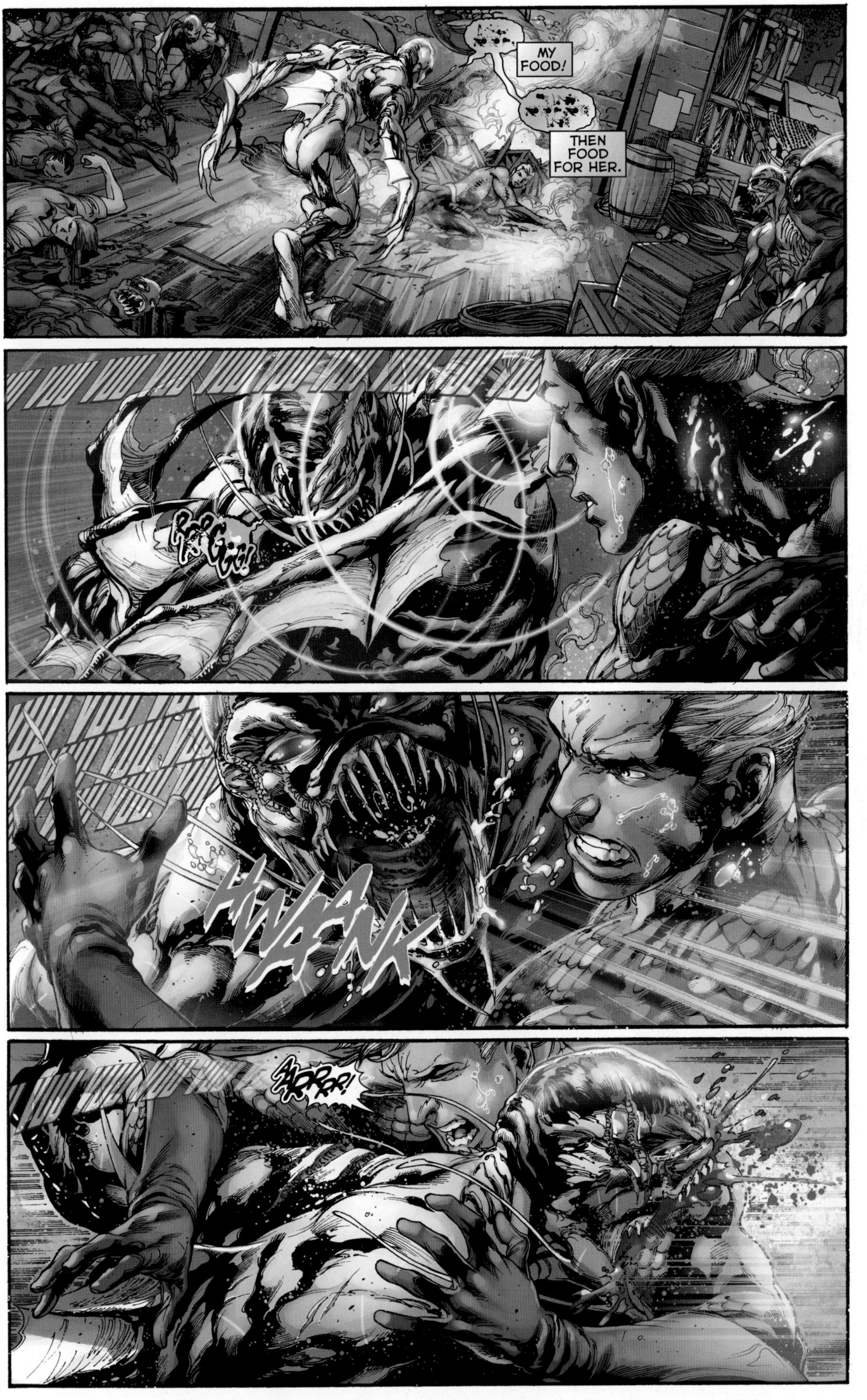

MY FOOD!
THEN FOOD FOR HER.
HWANK
AARRRR!

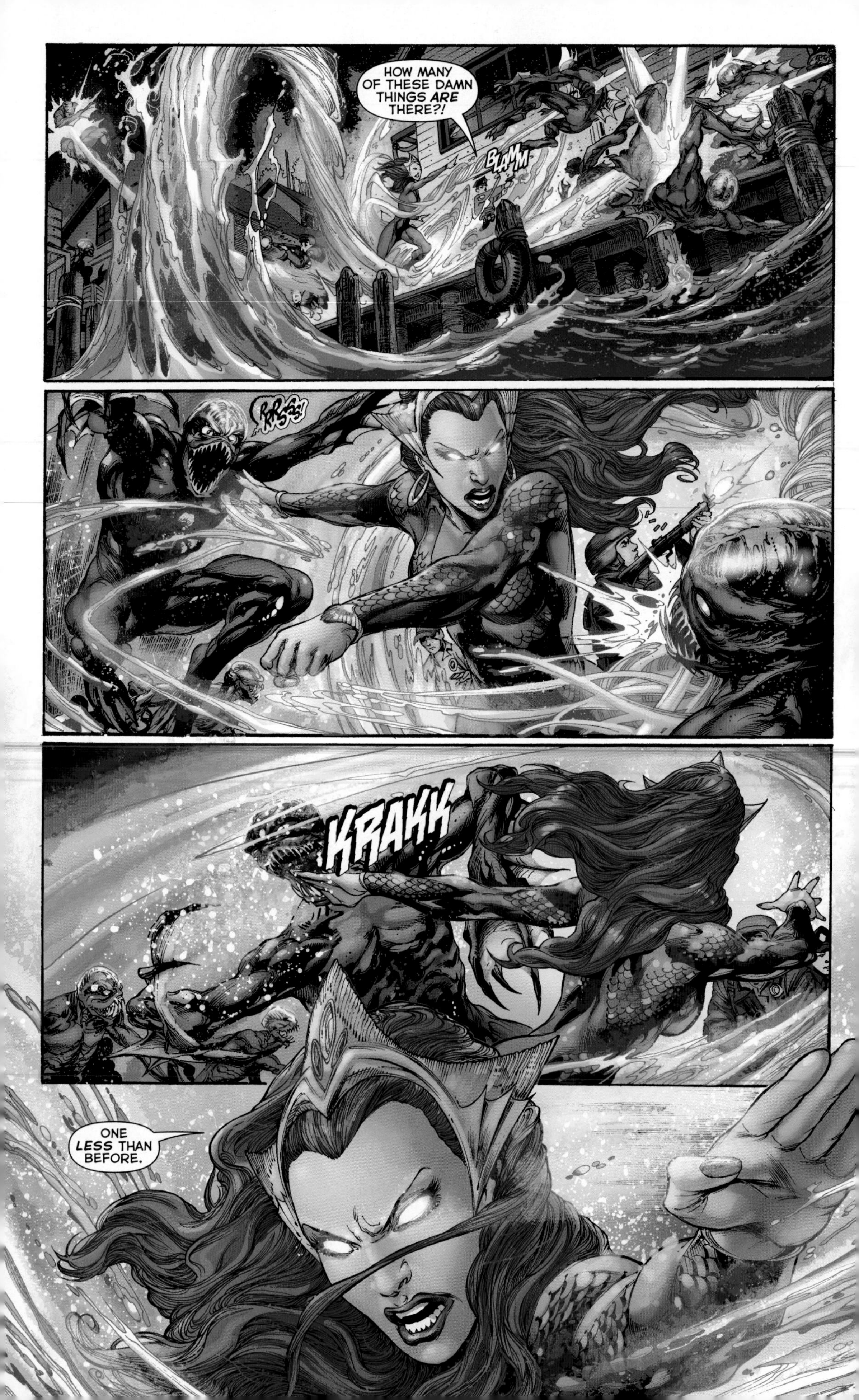
HOW MANY OF THESE DAMN THINGS ARE THERE?!
BLAMM
KRAKK
ONE LESS THAN BEFORE.

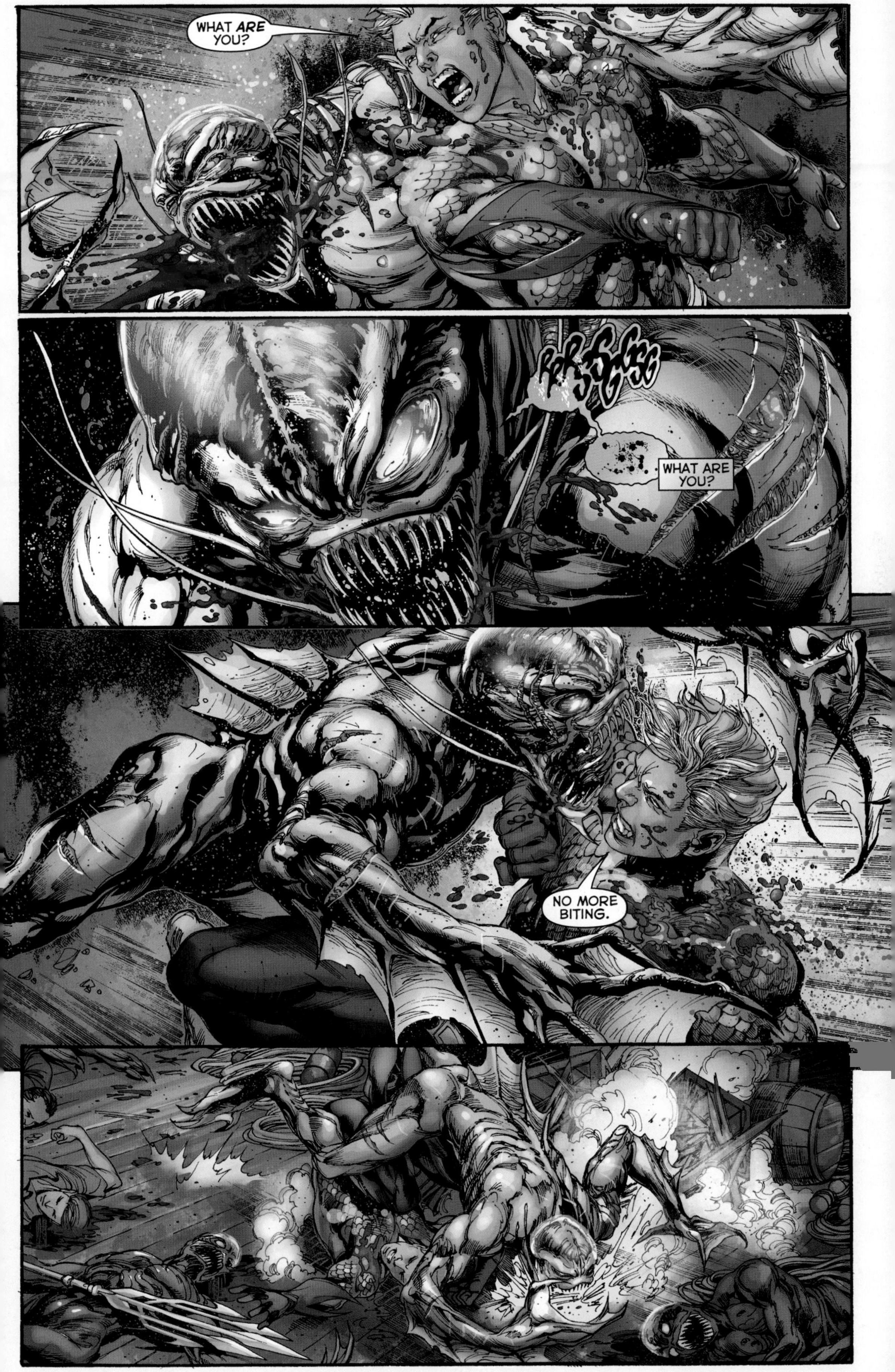
WHAT ARE YOU?
WHAT ARE YOU?
NO MORE BITING.

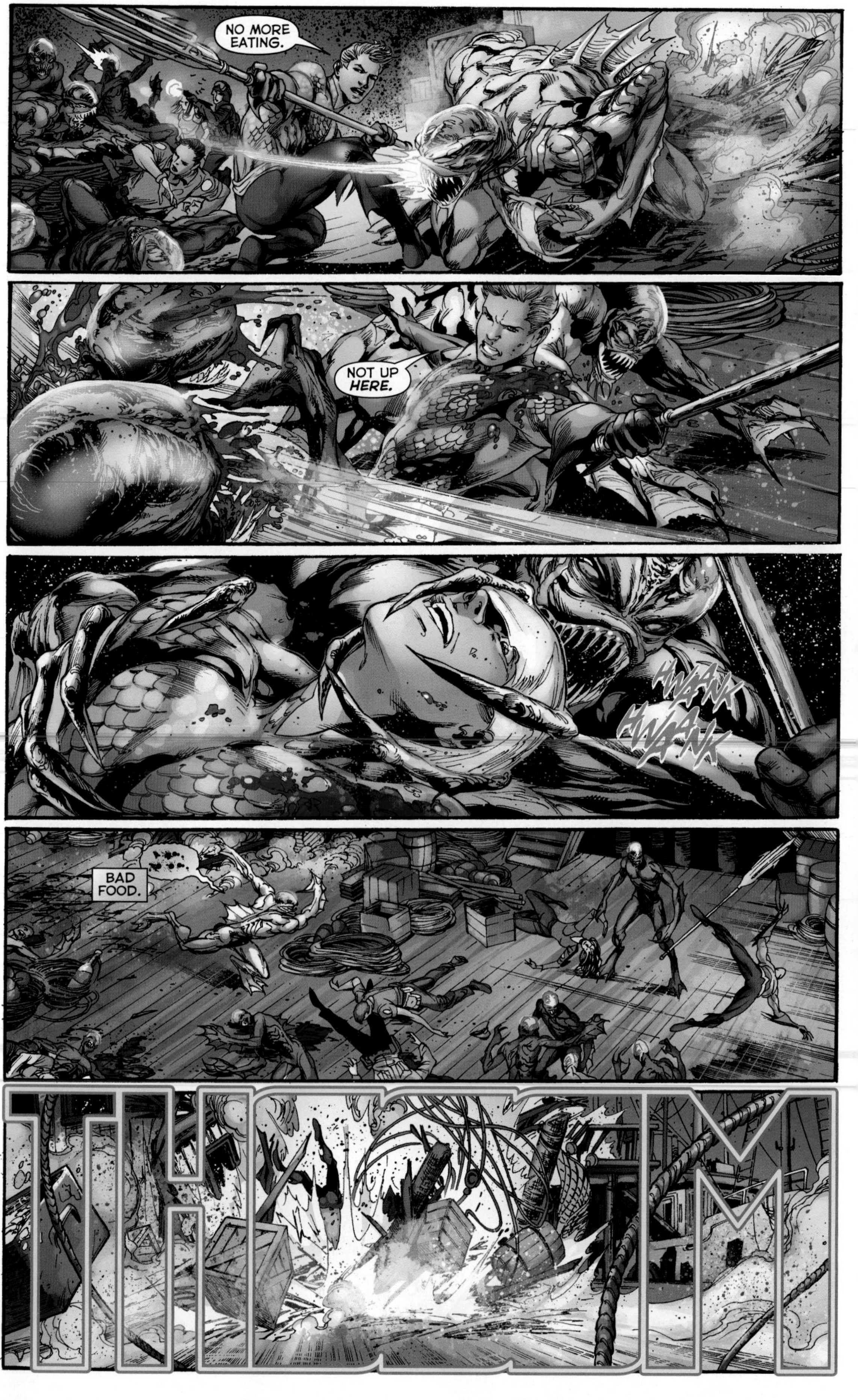
NO MORE EATING.
NOT UP HERE.
HWANK HWANK
BAD FOOD.
THOOM

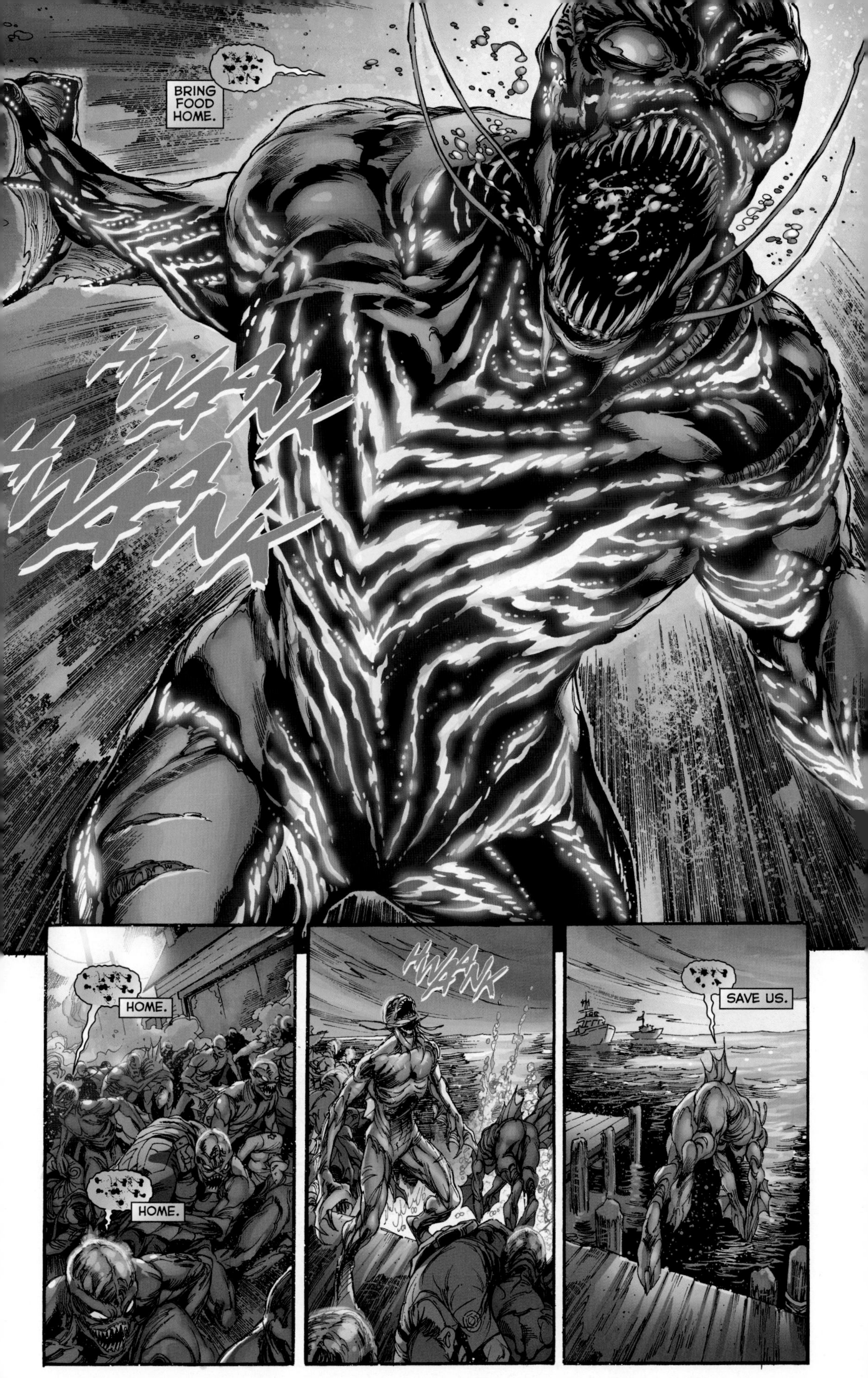
BRING FOOD HOME.
HWANK HWANK
HOME.
HOME.
HWANK
SAVE US.

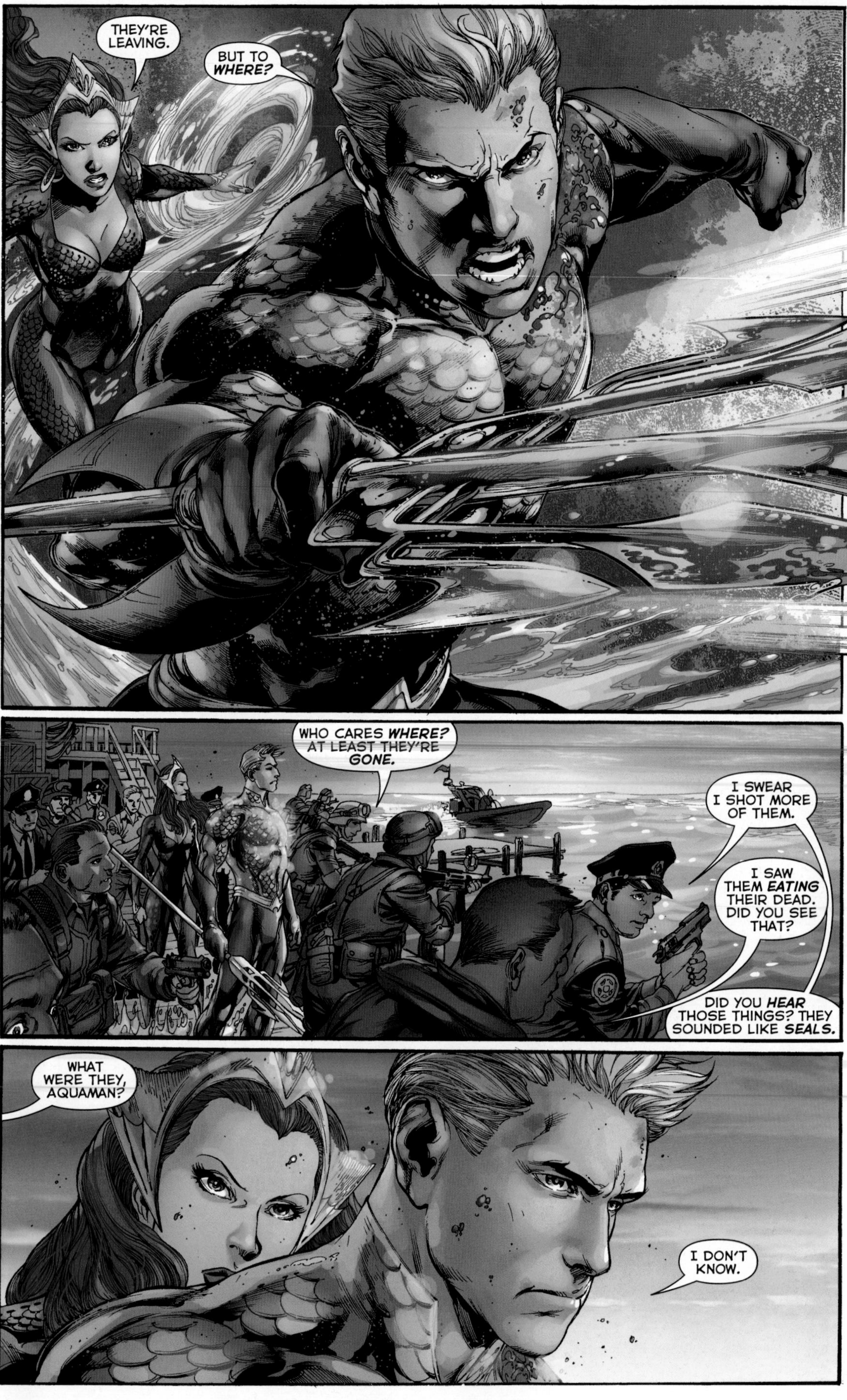
THEY'RE LEAVING.
BUT TO WHERE?
WHO CARES WHERE? AT LEAST THEY'RE GONE.
I SWEAR I SHOT MORE OF THEM.
I SAW THEM EATING THEIR DEAD. DID YOU SEE THAT?
DID YOU HEAR THOSE THINGS? THEY SOUNDED LIKE SEALS.
WHAT WERE THEY, AQUAMAN?
I DON'T KNOW.

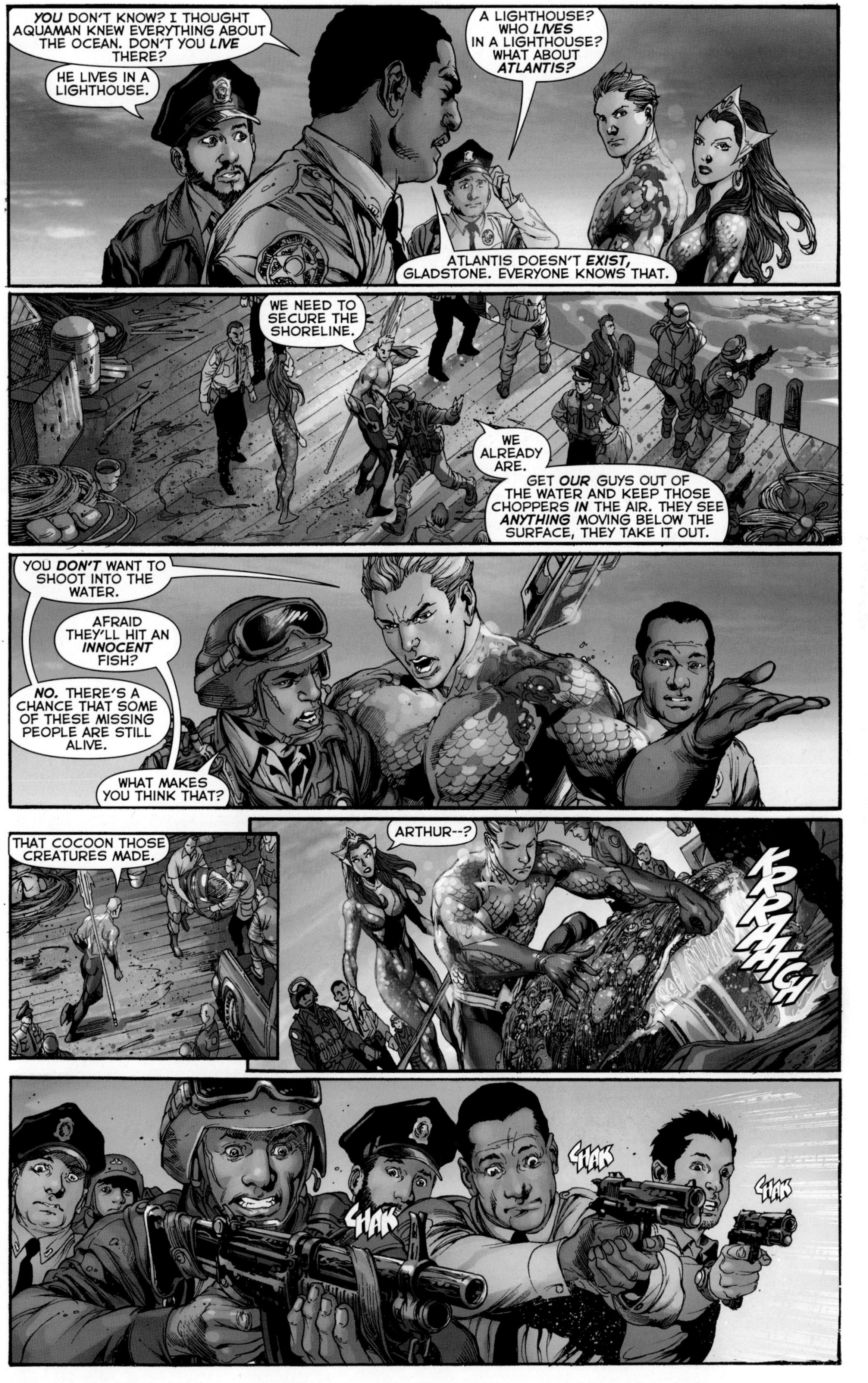

YOU DON'T KNOW? I THOUGHT AQUAMAN KNEW EVERYTHING ABOUT THE OCEAN. DON'T YOU LIVE THERE?
HE LIVES IN A LIGHTHOUSE.
A LIGHTHOUSE? WHO LIVES IN A LIGHTHOUSE? WHAT ABOUT ATLANTIS?
ATLANTIS DOESN'T EXIST, GLADSTONE. EVERYONE KNOWS THAT.
WE NEED TO SECURE THE SHORELINE.
WE ALREADY ARE.
GET OUR GUYS OUT OF THE WATER AND KEEP THOSE CHOPPERS IN THE AIR. THEY SEE ANYTHING MOVING BELOW THE SURFACE, THEY TAKE IT OUT.
YOU DON'T WANT TO SHOOT INTO THE WATER.
AFRAID THEY'LL HIT AN INNOCENT FISH?
NO. THERE'S A CHANCE THAT SOME OF THESE MISSING PEOPLE ARE STILL ALIVE.
WHAT MAKES YOU THINK THAT?
THAT COCOON THOSE CREATURES MADE.
ARTHUR--?
KRAAATCH
CHAK
CHAK
CHAK

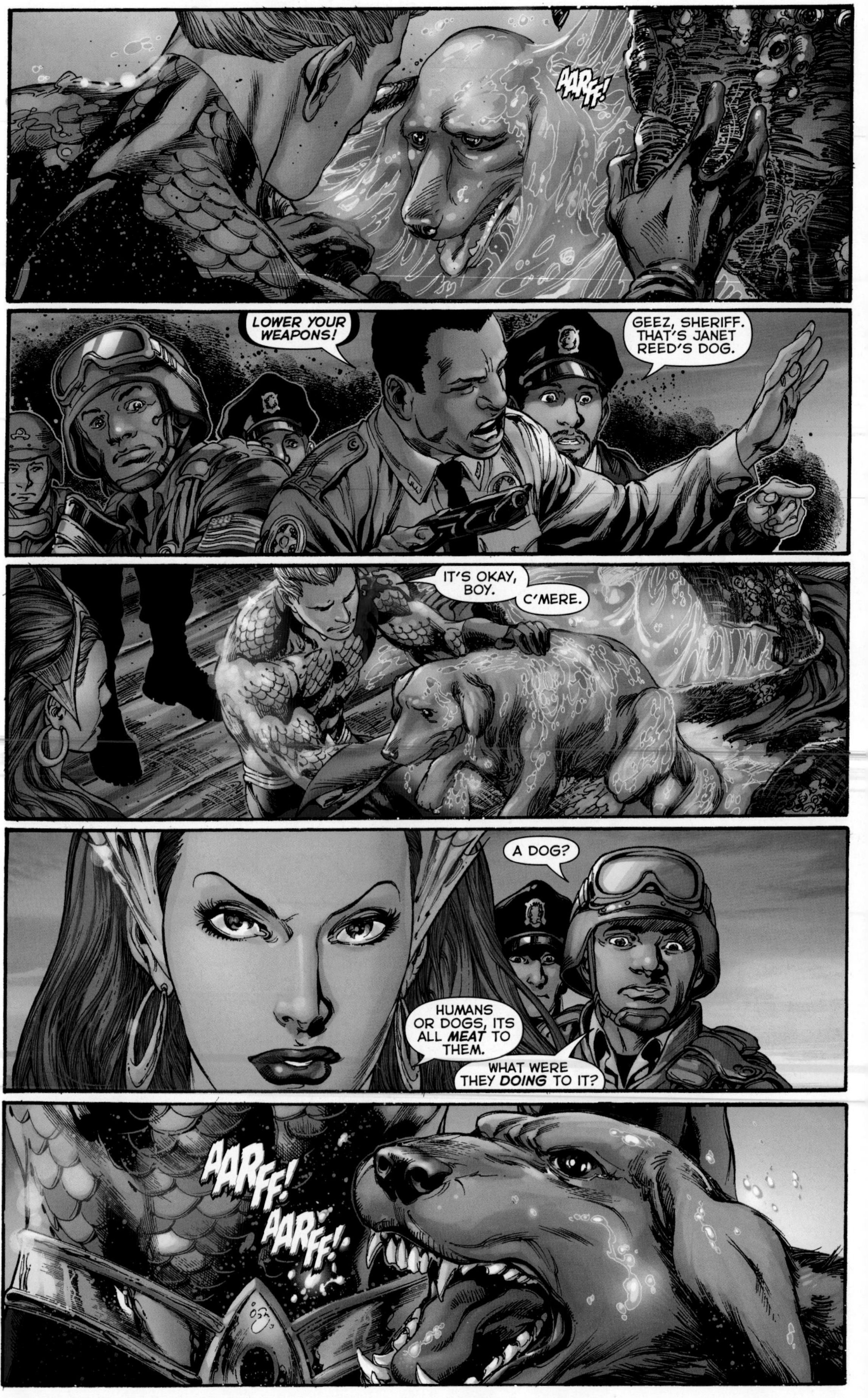
AARFF!
LOWER YOUR WEAPONS!
GEEZ, SHERIFF. THAT'S JANET REED'S DOG.
IT'S OKAY, BOY.
C'MERE.
A DOG?
HUMANS OR DOGS, ITS ALL *MEAT* TO THEM.
WHAT WERE THEY *DOING* TO IT?
AARFF!
AARFF!

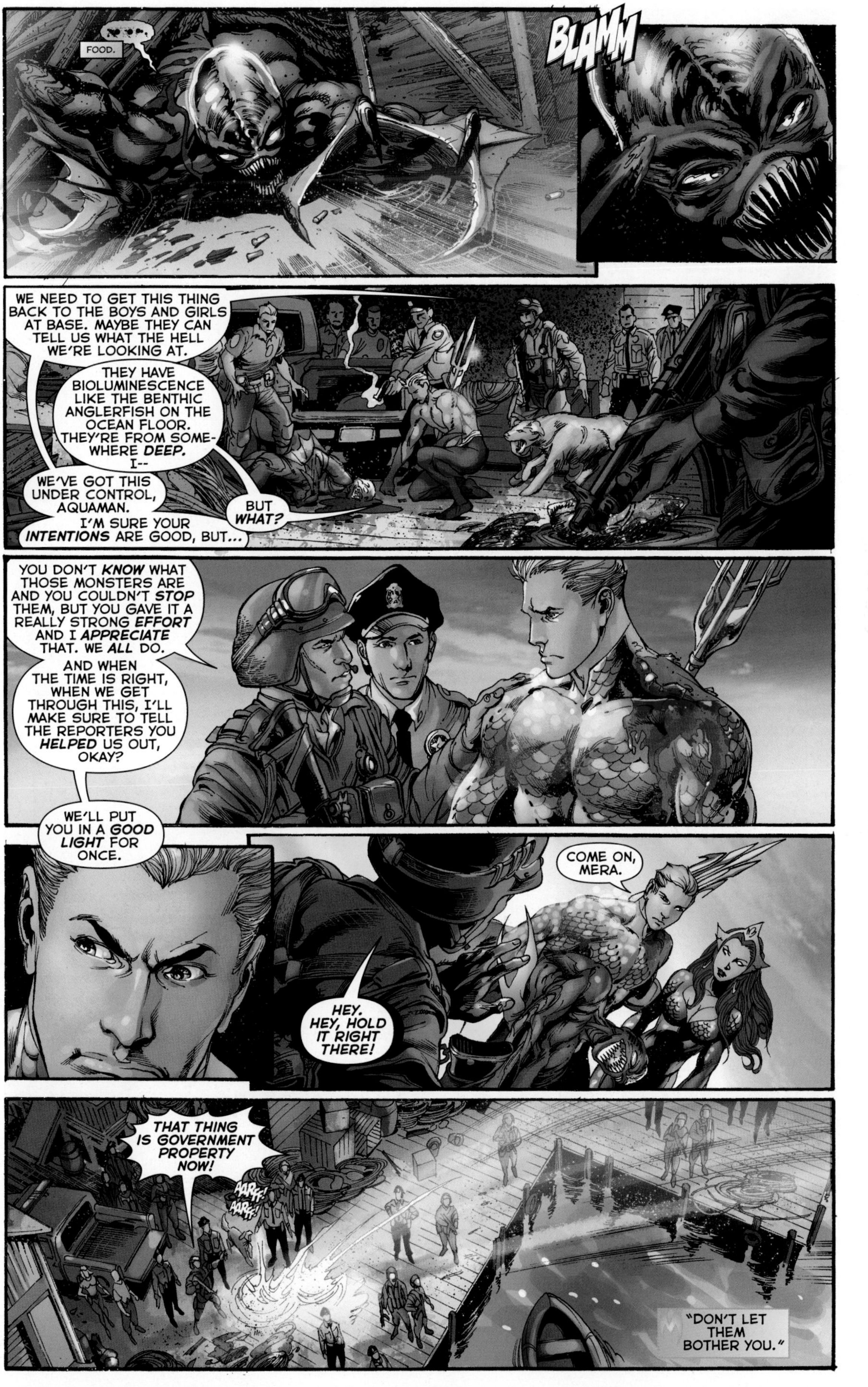
FOOD.
BLAMM
WE NEED TO GET THIS THING BACK TO THE BOYS AND GIRLS AT BASE. MAYBE THEY CAN TELL US WHAT THE HELL WE'RE LOOKING AT.
THEY HAVE BIOLUMINESCENCE LIKE THE BENTHIC ANGLERFISH ON THE OCEAN FLOOR. THEY'RE FROM SOME-WHERE DEEP.
I--
WE'VE GOT THIS UNDER CONTROL, AQUAMAN.
I'M SURE YOUR INTENTIONS ARE GOOD, BUT...
BUT WHAT?
YOU DON'T KNOW WHAT THOSE MONSTERS ARE AND YOU COULDN'T STOP THEM, BUT YOU GAVE IT A REALLY STRONG EFFORT AND I APPRECIATE THAT. WE ALL DO.
AND WHEN THE TIME IS RIGHT, WHEN WE GET THROUGH THIS, I'LL MAKE SURE TO TELL THE REPORTERS YOU HELPED US OUT, OKAY?
WE'LL PUT YOU IN A GOOD LIGHT FOR ONCE.
COME ON, MERA.
HEY. HEY, HOLD IT RIGHT THERE!
THAT THING IS GOVERNMENT PROPERTY NOW!
AARF! AARF!
"DON'T LET THEM BOTHER YOU."

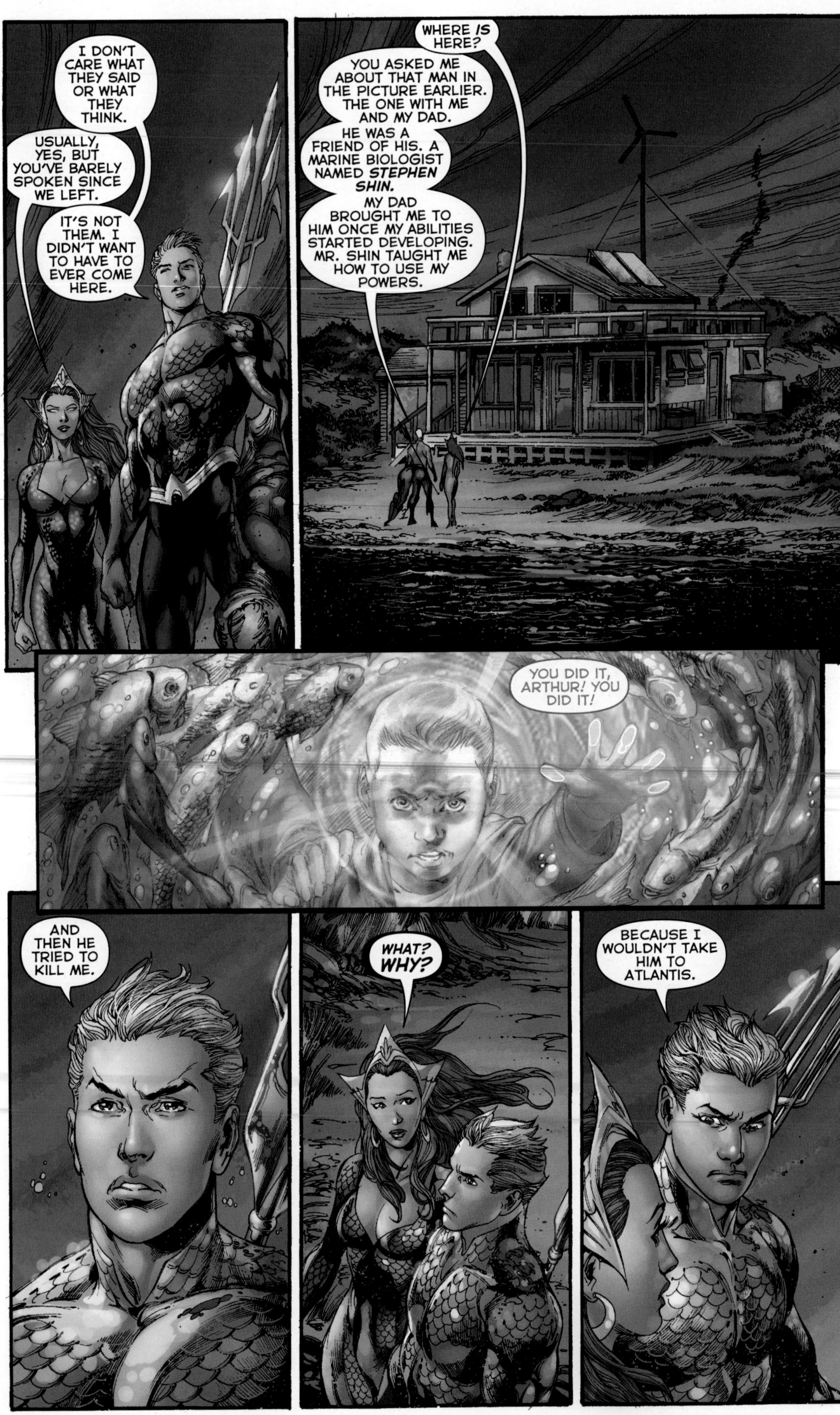
I DON'T CARE WHAT THEY SAID OR WHAT THEY THINK.
USUALLY, YES, BUT YOU'VE BARELY SPOKEN SINCE WE LEFT.
IT'S NOT THEM. I DIDN'T WANT TO HAVE TO EVER COME HERE.
WHERE *IS* HERE?
YOU ASKED ME ABOUT THAT MAN IN THE PICTURE EARLIER. THE ONE WITH ME AND MY DAD.
HE WAS A FRIEND OF HIS. A MARINE BIOLOGIST NAMED ***STEPHEN SHIN.***
MY DAD BROUGHT ME TO HIM ONCE MY ABILITIES STARTED DEVELOPING. MR. SHIN TAUGHT ME HOW TO USE MY POWERS.
YOU DID IT, ARTHUR*!* YOU DID IT*!*
AND THEN HE TRIED TO KILL ME.
WHAT? WHY?
BECAUSE I WOULDN'T TAKE HIM TO ATLANTIS.

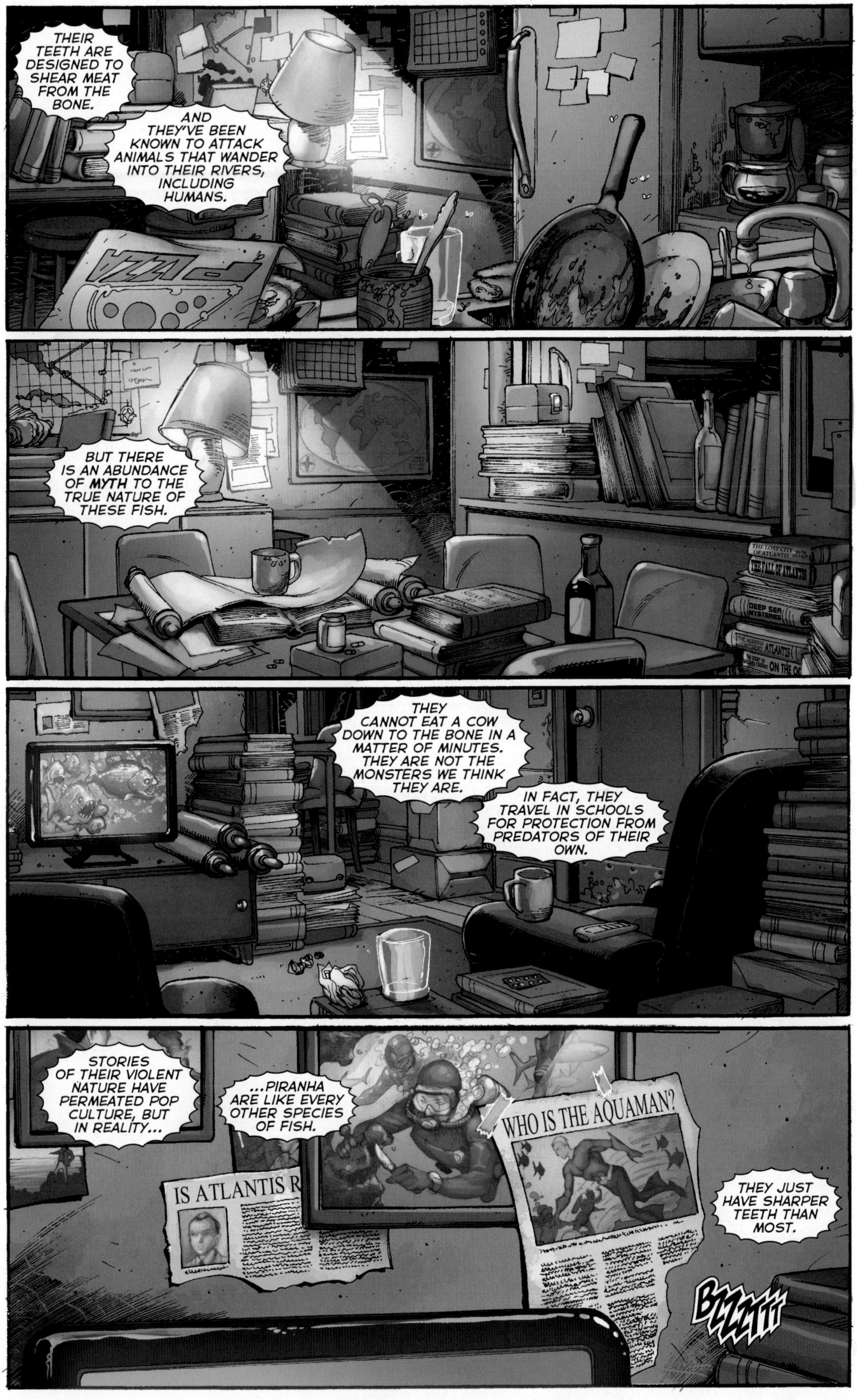
THEIR TEETH ARE DESIGNED TO SHEAR MEAT FROM THE BONE.
AND THEY'VE BEEN KNOWN TO ATTACK ANIMALS THAT WANDER INTO THEIR RIVERS, INCLUDING HUMANS.
BUT THERE IS AN ABUNDANCE OF MYTH TO THE TRUE NATURE OF THESE FISH.
THE LOST CITY OF ATLANTIS
THE FALL OF ATLANTIS
DEEP SEA MYSTERIES
THEY CANNOT EAT A COW DOWN TO THE BONE IN A MATTER OF MINUTES. THEY ARE NOT THE MONSTERS WE THINK THEY ARE.
IN FACT, THEY TRAVEL IN SCHOOLS FOR PROTECTION FROM PREDATORS OF THEIR OWN.
STORIES OF THEIR VIOLENT NATURE HAVE PERMEATED POP CULTURE, BUT IN REALITY...
...PIRANHA ARE LIKE EVERY OTHER SPECIES OF FISH.
IS ATLANTIS R
WHO IS THE AQUAMAN?
THEY JUST HAVE SHARPER TEETH THAN MOST.
BZZZTTT

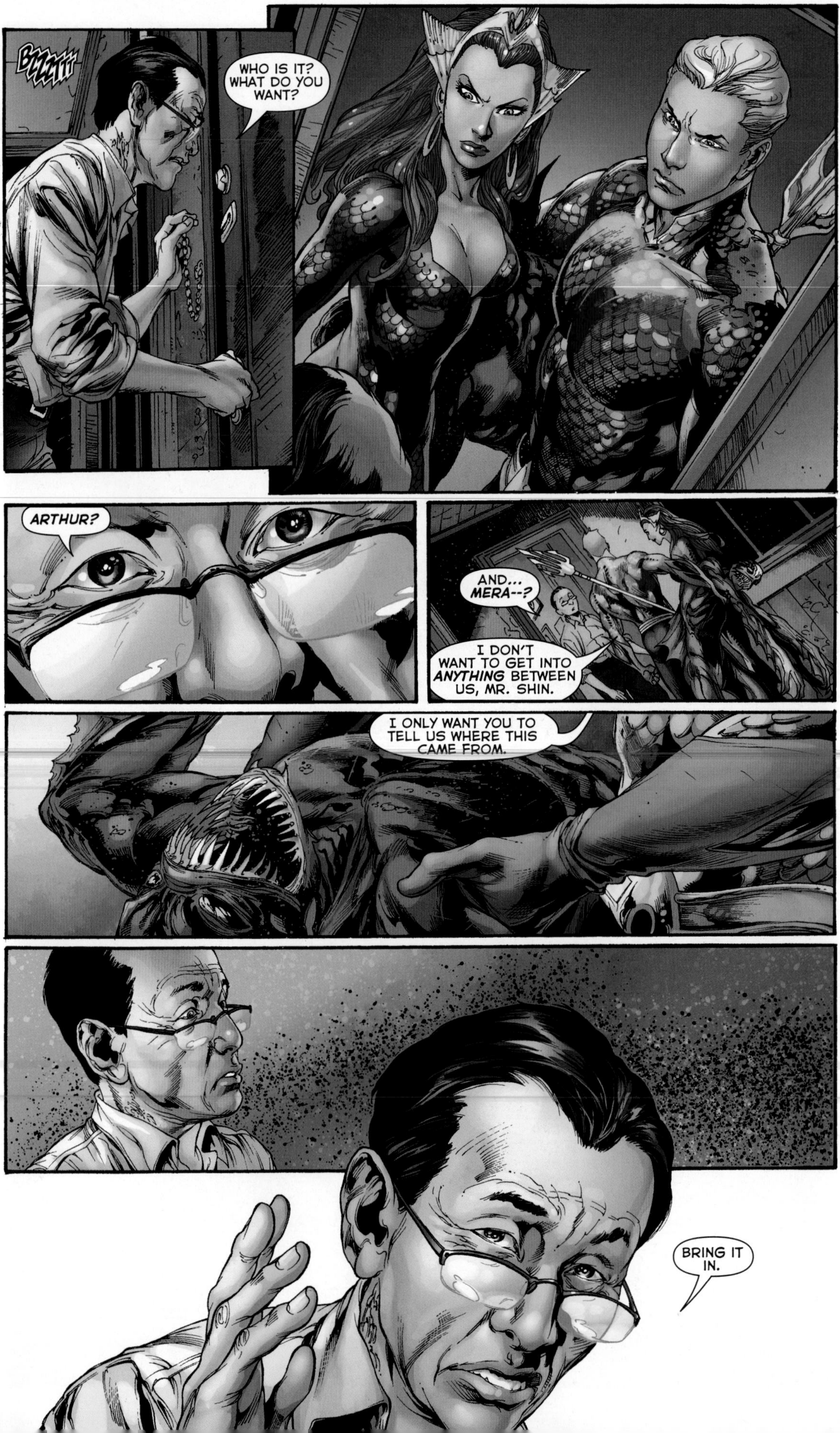
BZZZTTT
WHO IS IT? WHAT DO YOU WANT?
ARTHUR?
AND... MERA--?
I DON'T WANT TO GET INTO ANYTHING BETWEEN US, MR. SHIN.
I ONLY WANT YOU TO TELL US WHERE THIS CAME FROM.
BRING IT IN.

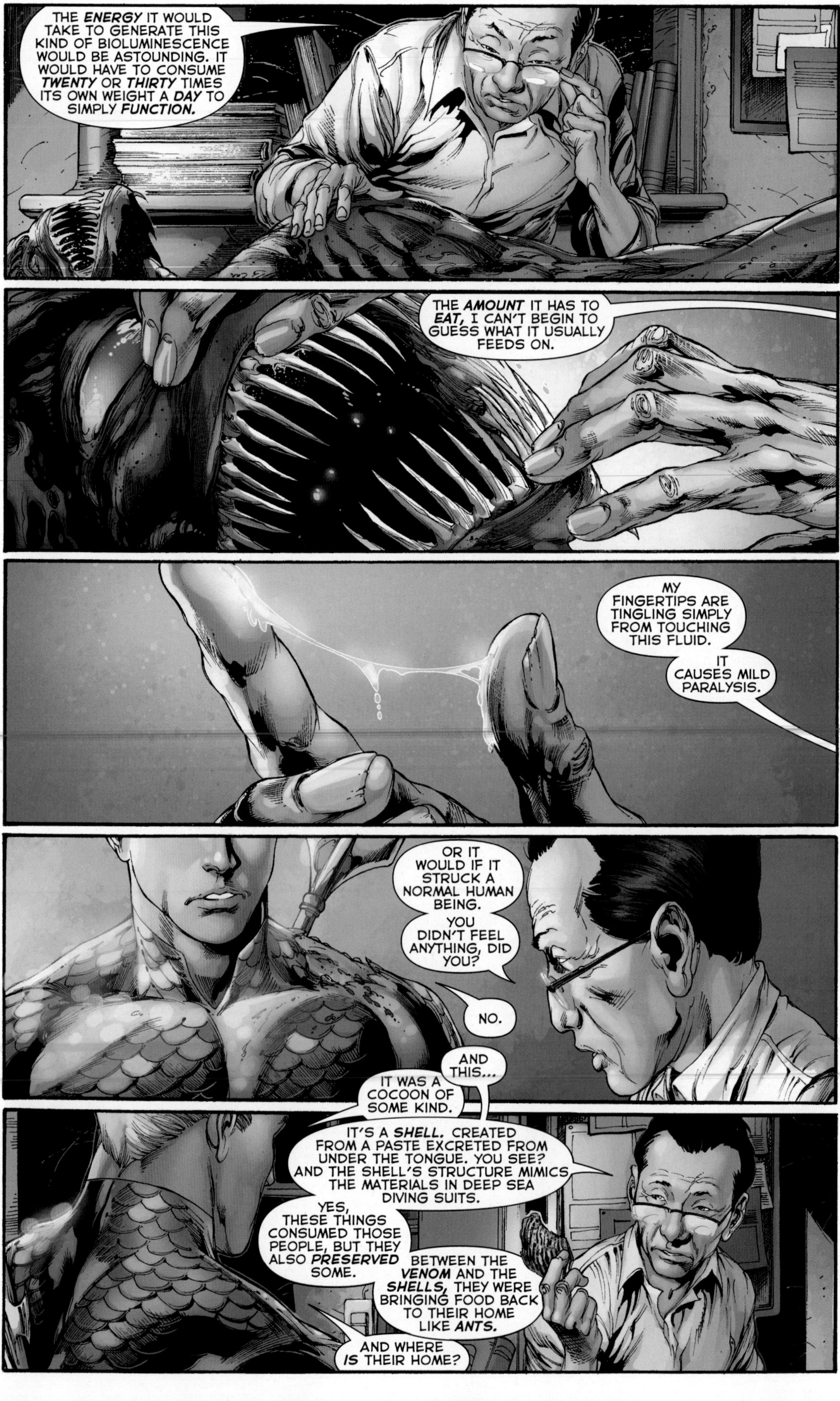
THE ENERGY IT WOULD TAKE TO GENERATE THIS KIND OF BIOLUMINESCENCE WOULD BE ASTOUNDING. IT WOULD HAVE TO CONSUME TWENTY OR THIRTY TIMES ITS OWN WEIGHT A DAY TO SIMPLY FUNCTION.
THE AMOUNT IT HAS TO EAT, I CAN'T BEGIN TO GUESS WHAT IT USUALLY FEEDS ON.
MY FINGERTIPS ARE TINGLING SIMPLY FROM TOUCHING THIS FLUID.
IT CAUSES MILD PARALYSIS.
OR IT WOULD IF IT STRUCK A NORMAL HUMAN BEING.
YOU DIDN'T FEEL ANYTHING, DID YOU?
NO.
AND THIS...
IT WAS A COCOON OF SOME KIND.
IT'S A SHELL. CREATED FROM A PASTE EXCRETED FROM UNDER THE TONGUE. YOU SEE? AND THE SHELL'S STRUCTURE MIMICS THE MATERIALS IN DEEP SEA DIVING SUITS.
YES, THESE THINGS CONSUMED THOSE PEOPLE, BUT THEY ALSO PRESERVED SOME.
BETWEEN THE VENOM AND THE SHELLS, THEY WERE BRINGING FOOD BACK TO THEIR HOME LIKE ANTS.
AND WHERE IS THEIR HOME?

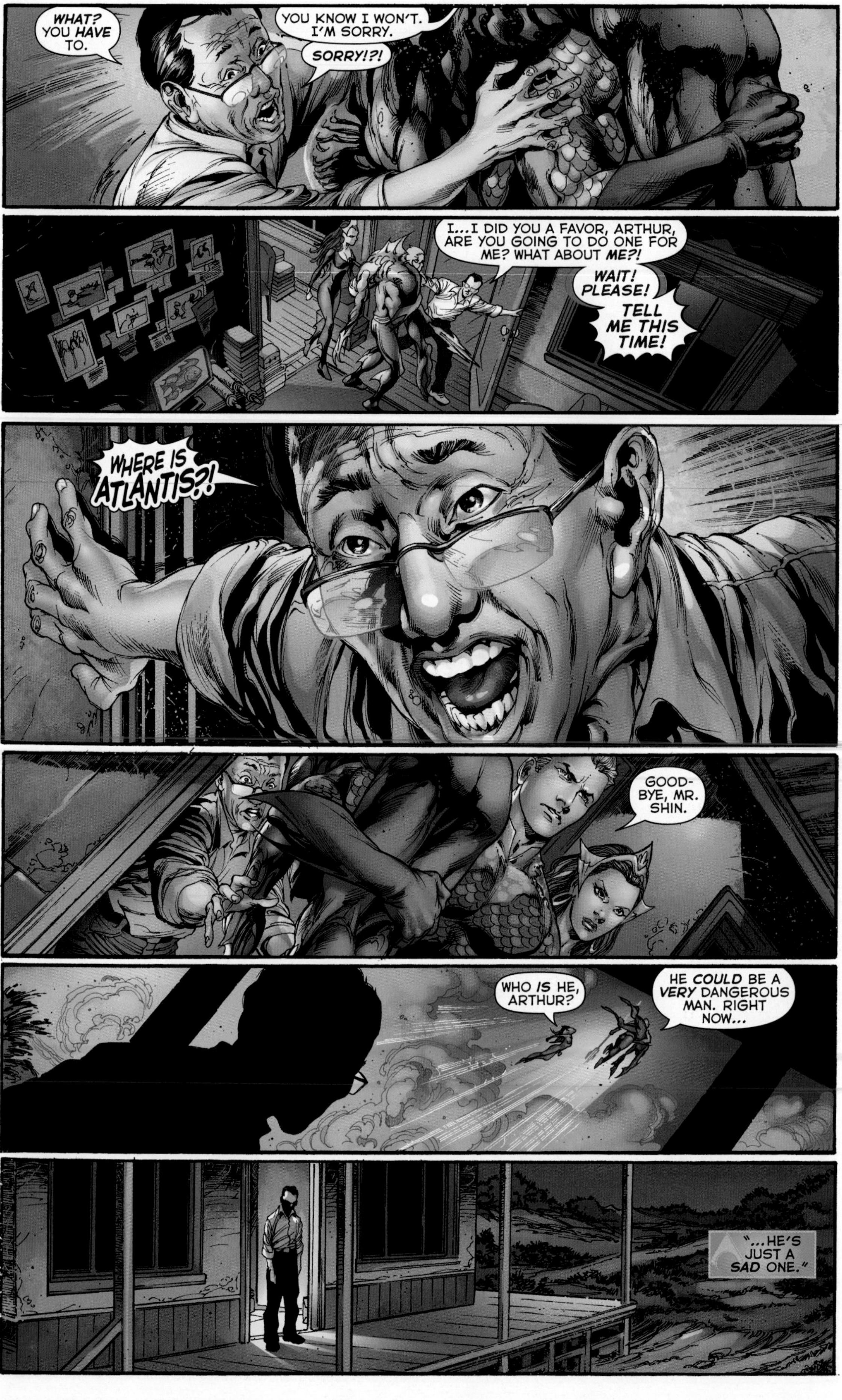
WHAT? YOU HAVE TO.
YOU KNOW I WON'T. I'M SORRY.
SORRY!?!
I...I DID YOU A FAVOR, ARTHUR, ARE YOU GOING TO DO ONE FOR ME? WHAT ABOUT ME?!
WAIT! PLEASE!
TELL ME THIS TIME!
WHERE IS ATLANTIS?!
GOOD-BYE, MR. SHIN.
WHO IS HE, ARTHUR?
HE COULD BE A VERY DANGEROUS MAN. RIGHT NOW...
"...HE'S JUST A SAD ONE."

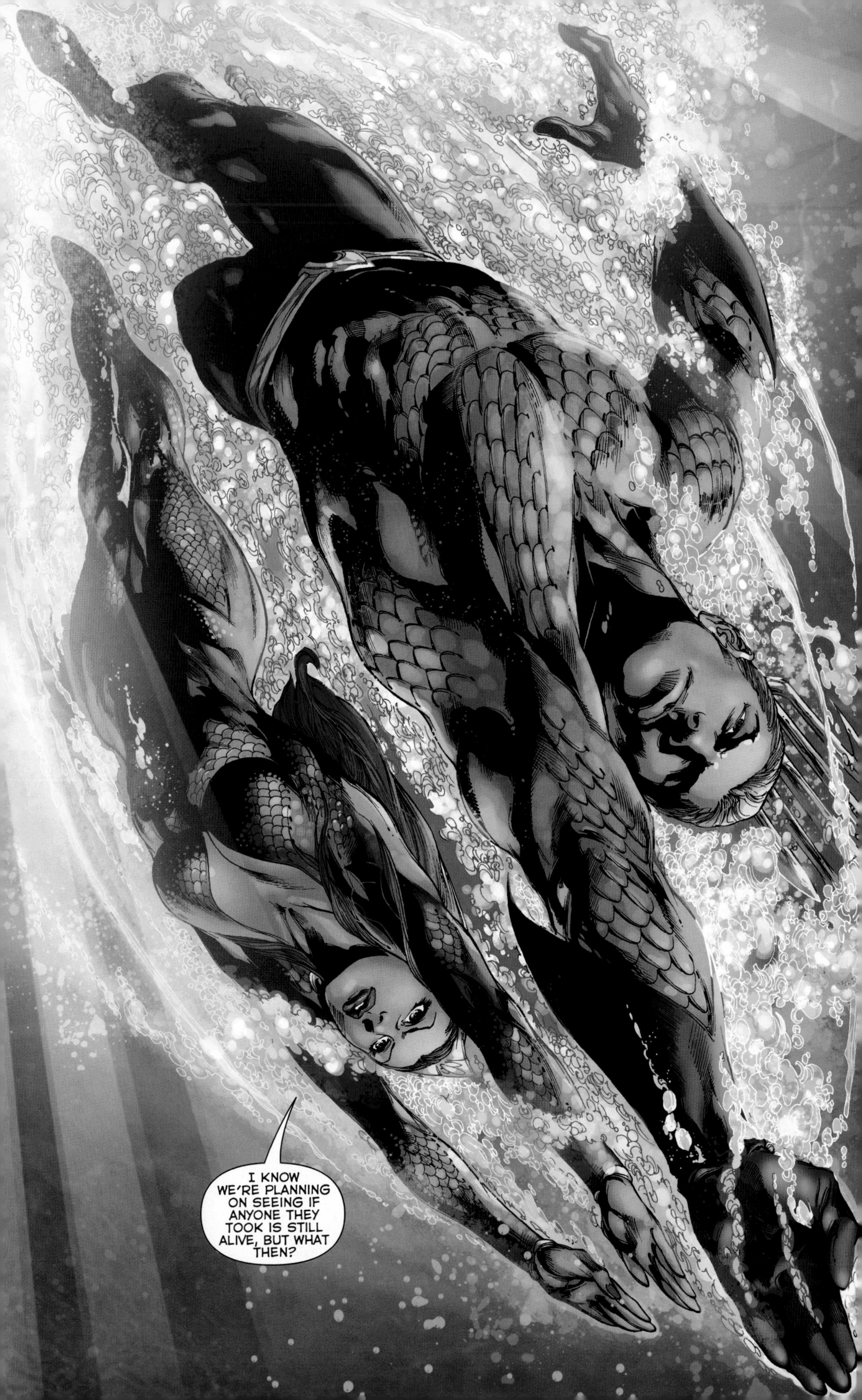
I KNOW WE'RE PLANNING ON SEEING IF ANYONE THEY TOOK IS STILL ALIVE, BUT WHAT THEN?

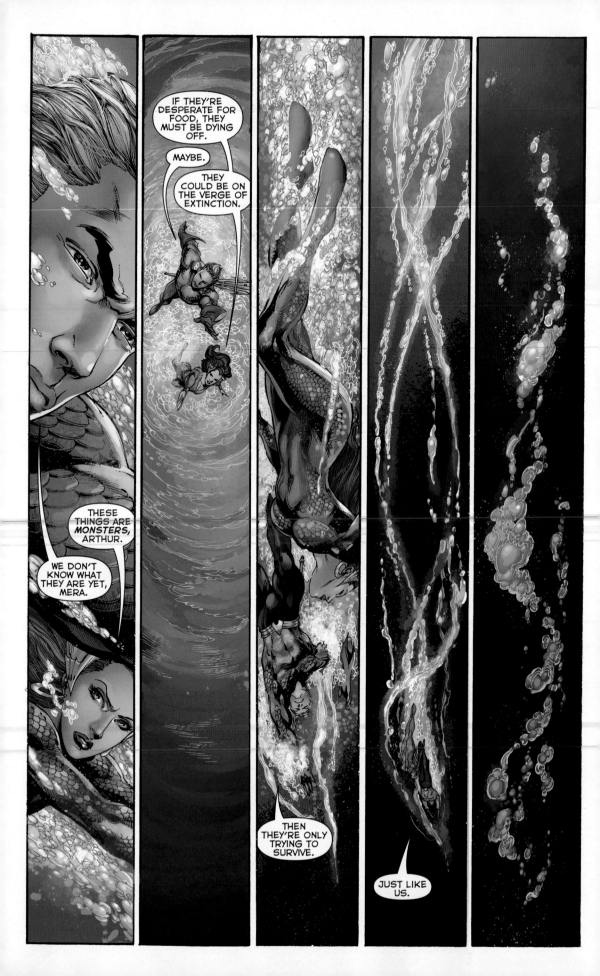

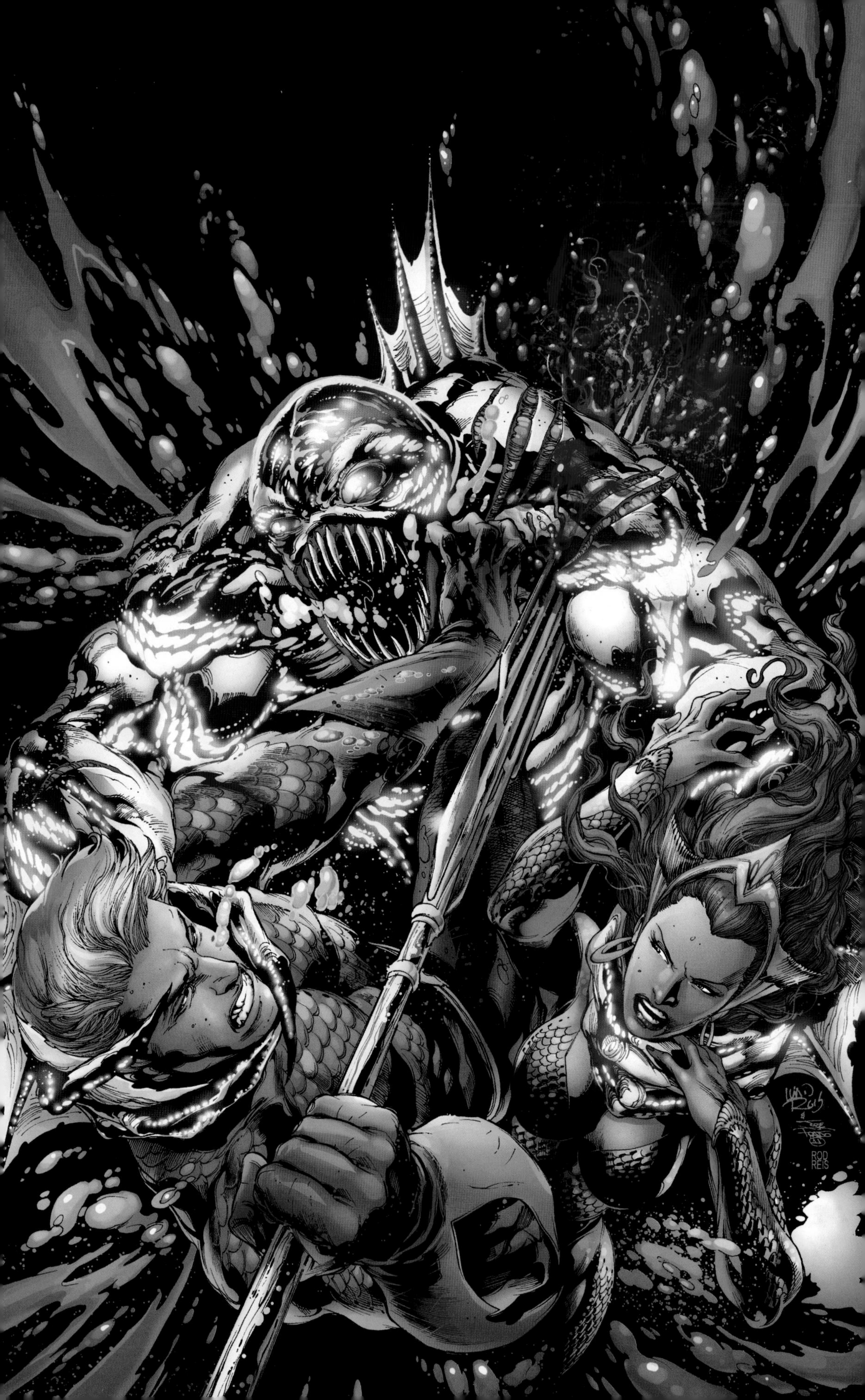
ROD
REIS

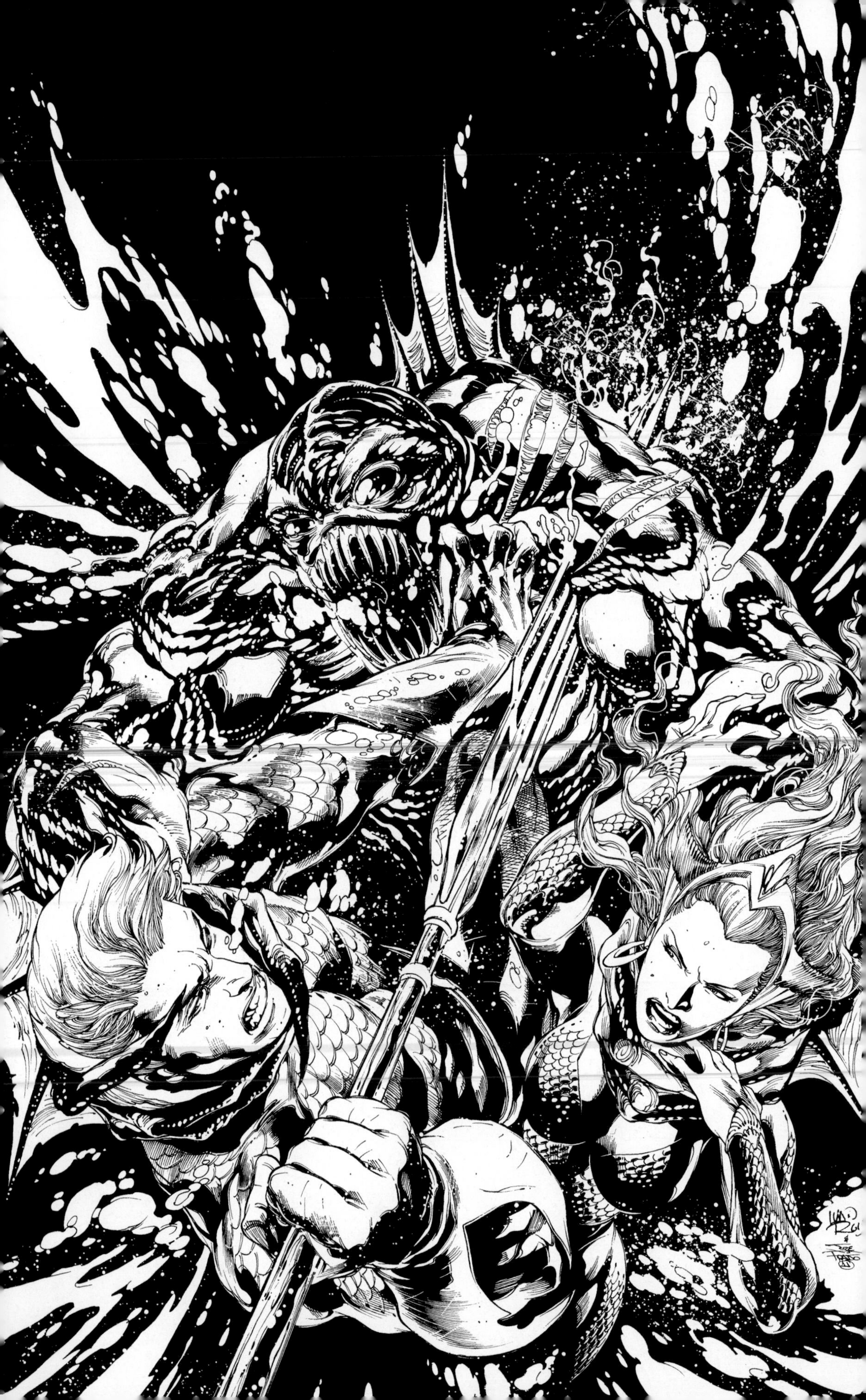

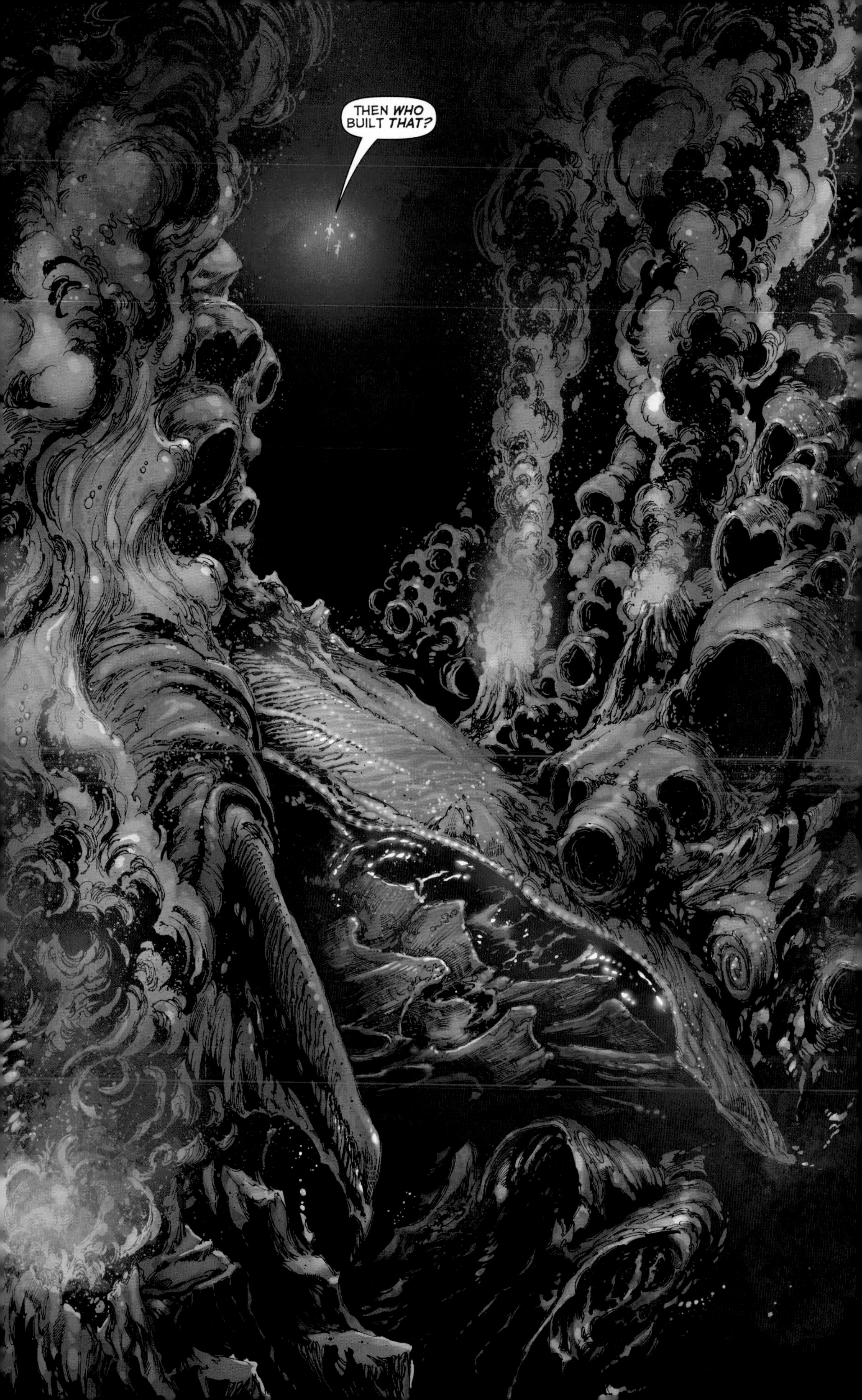
THEN *WHO* BUILT *THAT?*

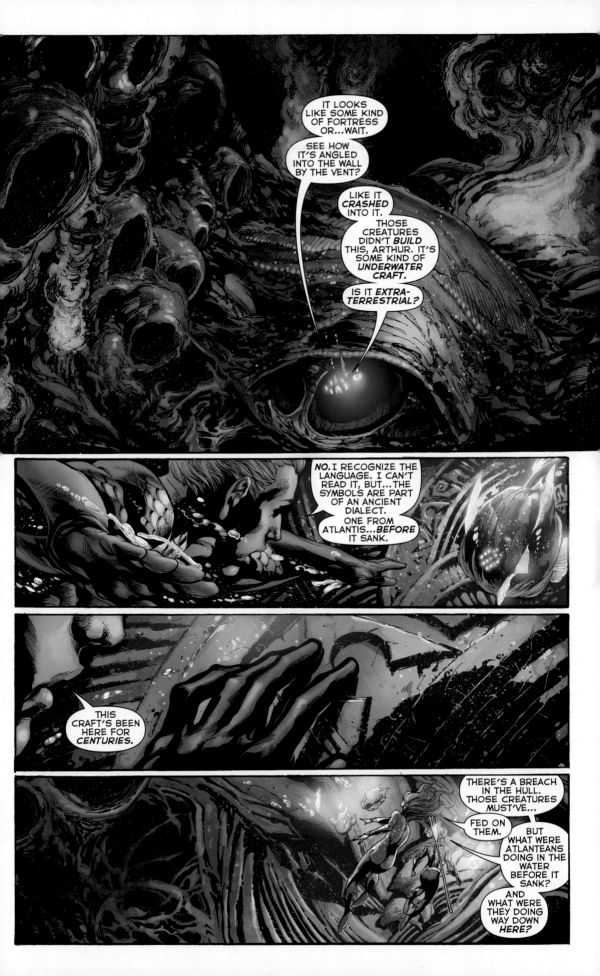

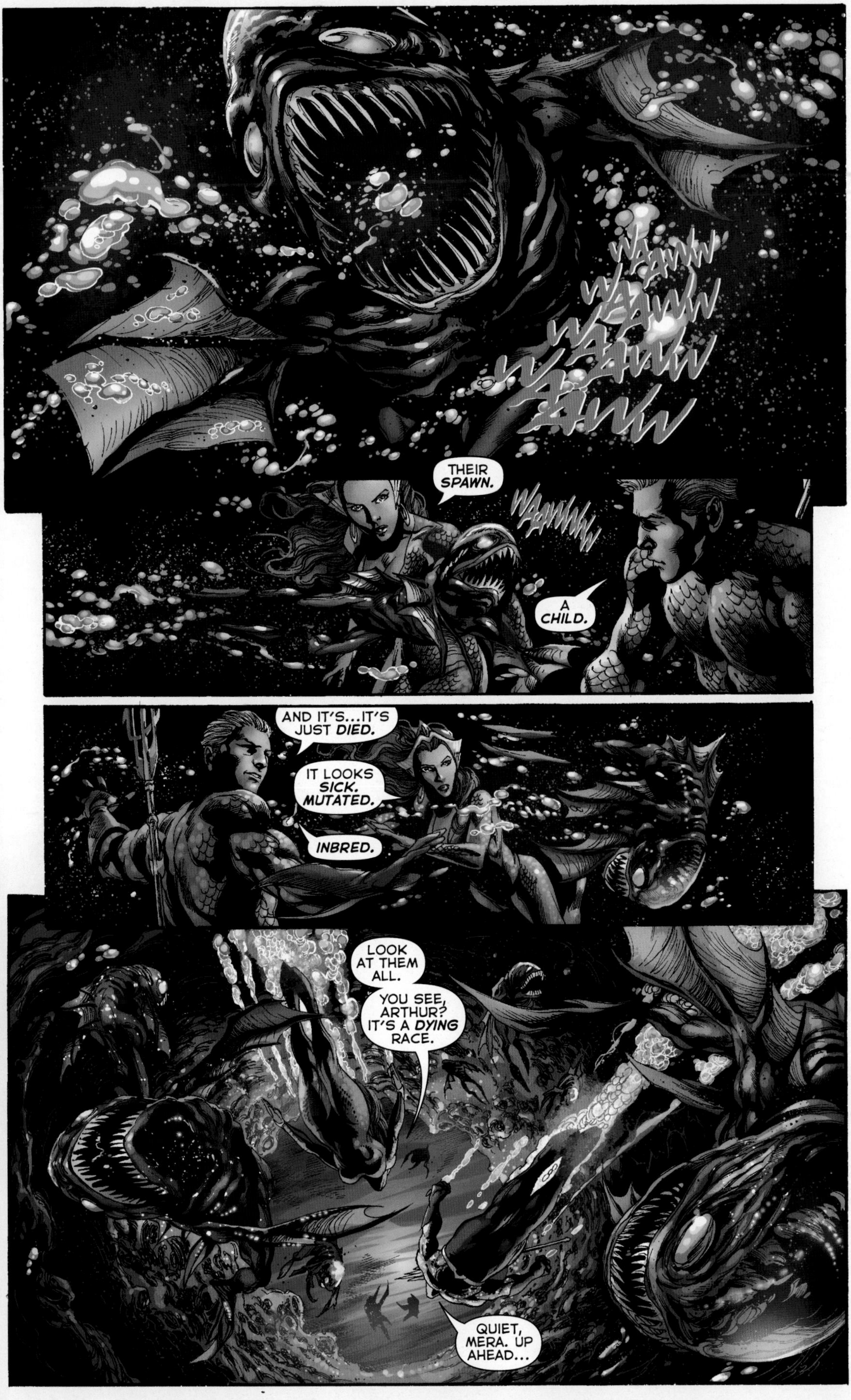
WAAWW WAAWW WAAWW WAAWW
THEIR SPAWN.
WAAWWW
A CHILD.
AND IT'S...IT'S JUST DIED.
IT LOOKS SICK. MUTATED.
INBRED.
LOOK AT THEM ALL.
YOU SEE, ARTHUR? IT'S A DYING RACE.
QUIET, MERA. UP AHEAD...

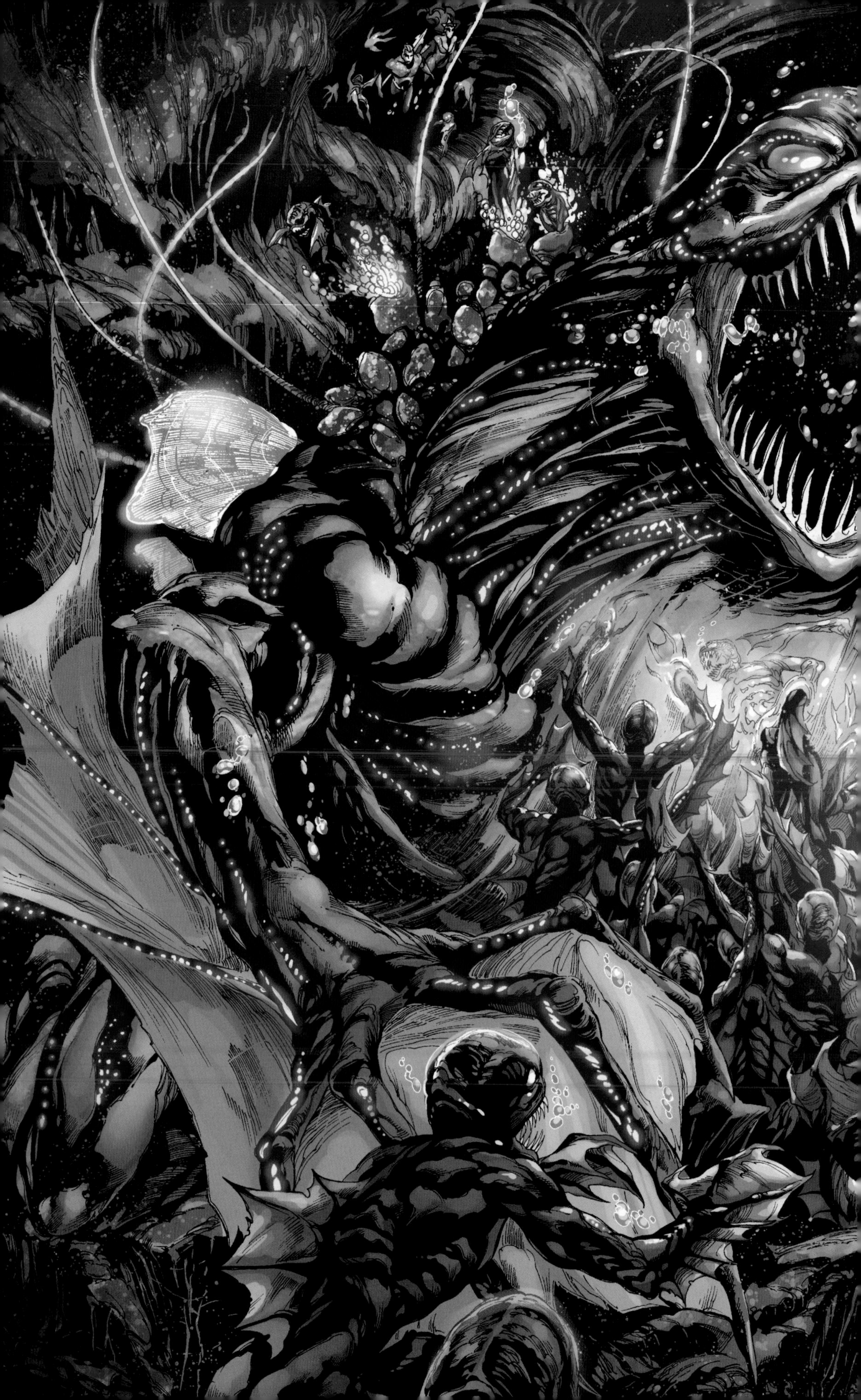

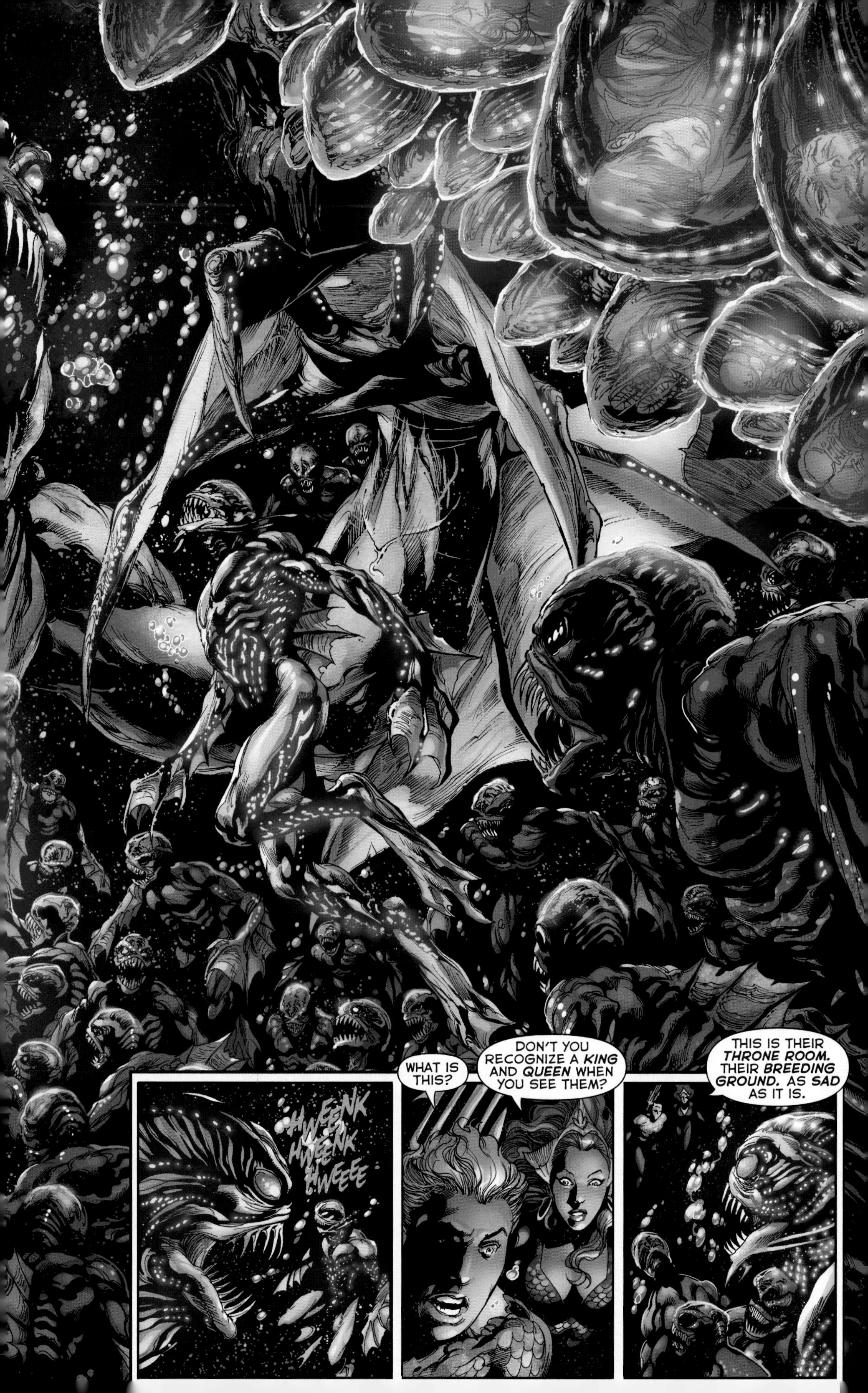
HWEENK
HWEENK
HWEEE
WHAT IS THIS?
DON'T YOU RECOGNIZE A *KING* AND *QUEEN* WHEN YOU SEE THEM?
THIS IS THEIR *THRONE ROOM.* THEIR *BREEDING GROUND.* AS *SAD* AS IT IS.

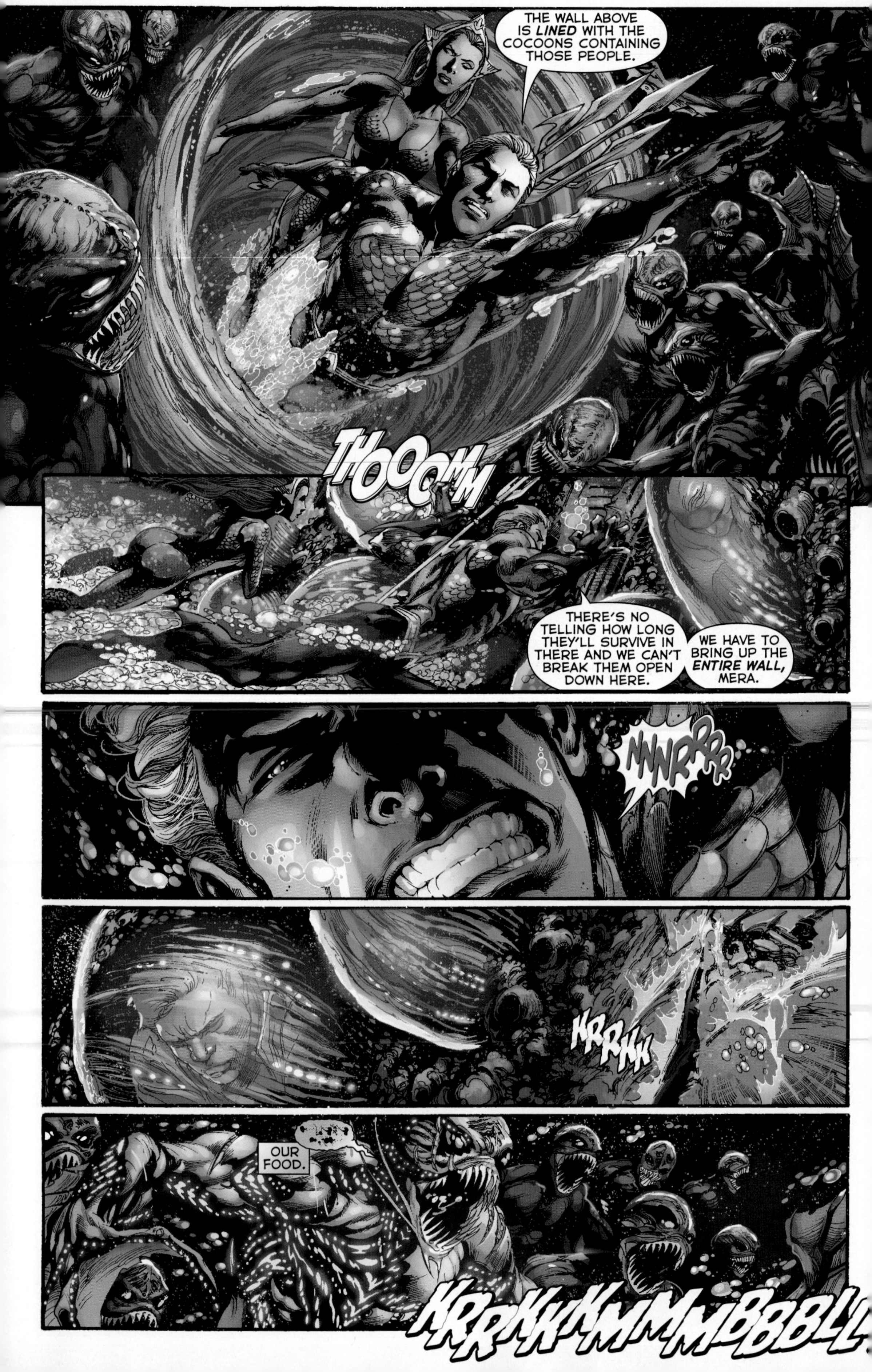
THE WALL ABOVE IS *LINED* WITH THE COCOONS CONTAINING THOSE PEOPLE.
THOOOMM
THERE'S NO TELLING HOW LONG THEY'LL SURVIVE IN THERE AND WE CAN'T BREAK THEM OPEN DOWN HERE.
WE HAVE TO BRING UP THE *ENTIRE WALL,* MERA.
NNNRRRR
KRRKK
OUR FOOD.
KRRKKMMMBBBLL

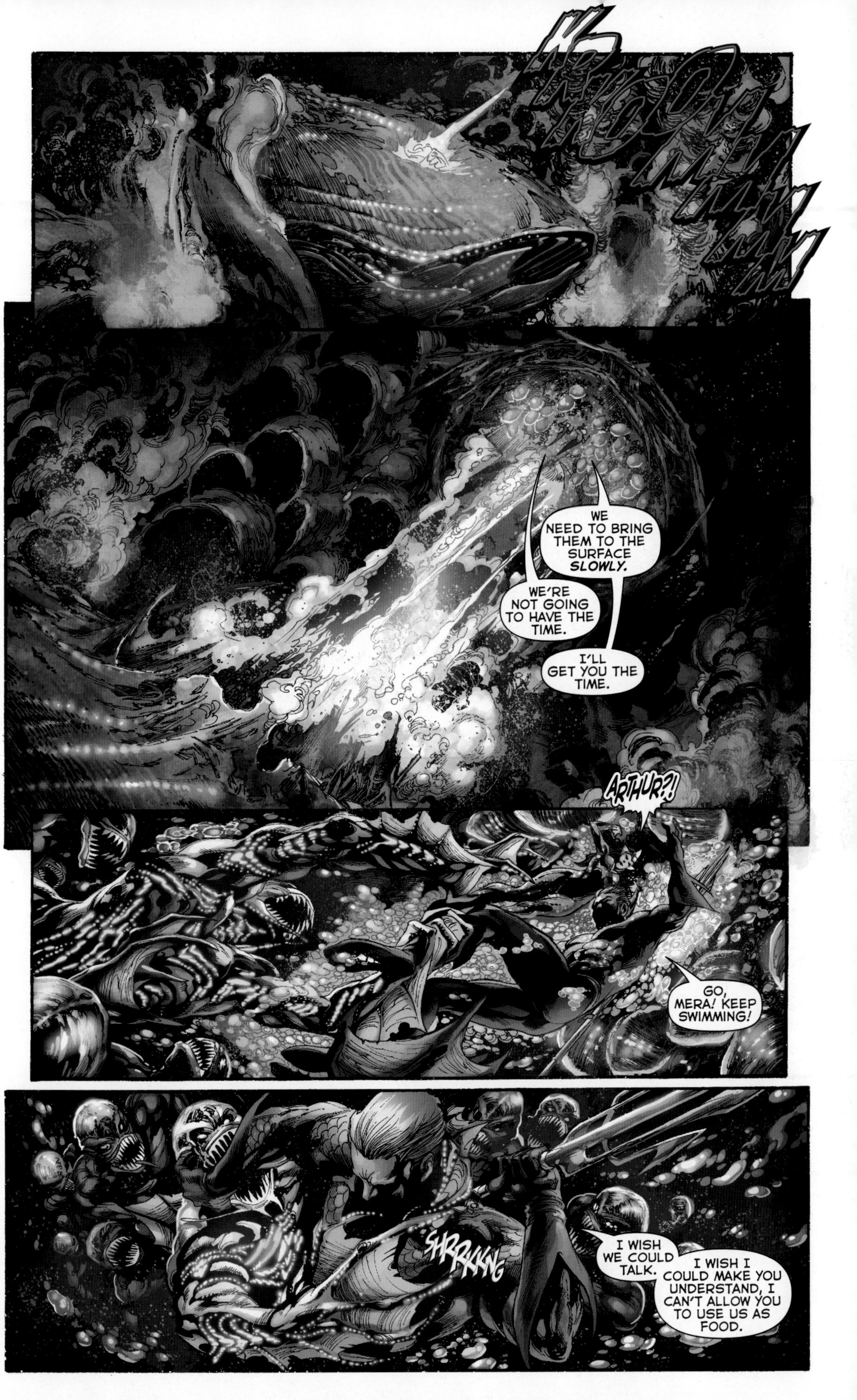
WE NEED TO BRING THEM TO THE SURFACE *SLOWLY.*
WE'RE NOT GOING TO HAVE THE TIME.
I'LL GET YOU THE TIME.
ARTHUR?!
GO, MERA! KEEP SWIMMING!
I WISH WE COULD TALK.
I WISH I COULD MAKE YOU UNDERSTAND, I CAN'T ALLOW YOU TO USE US AS FOOD.

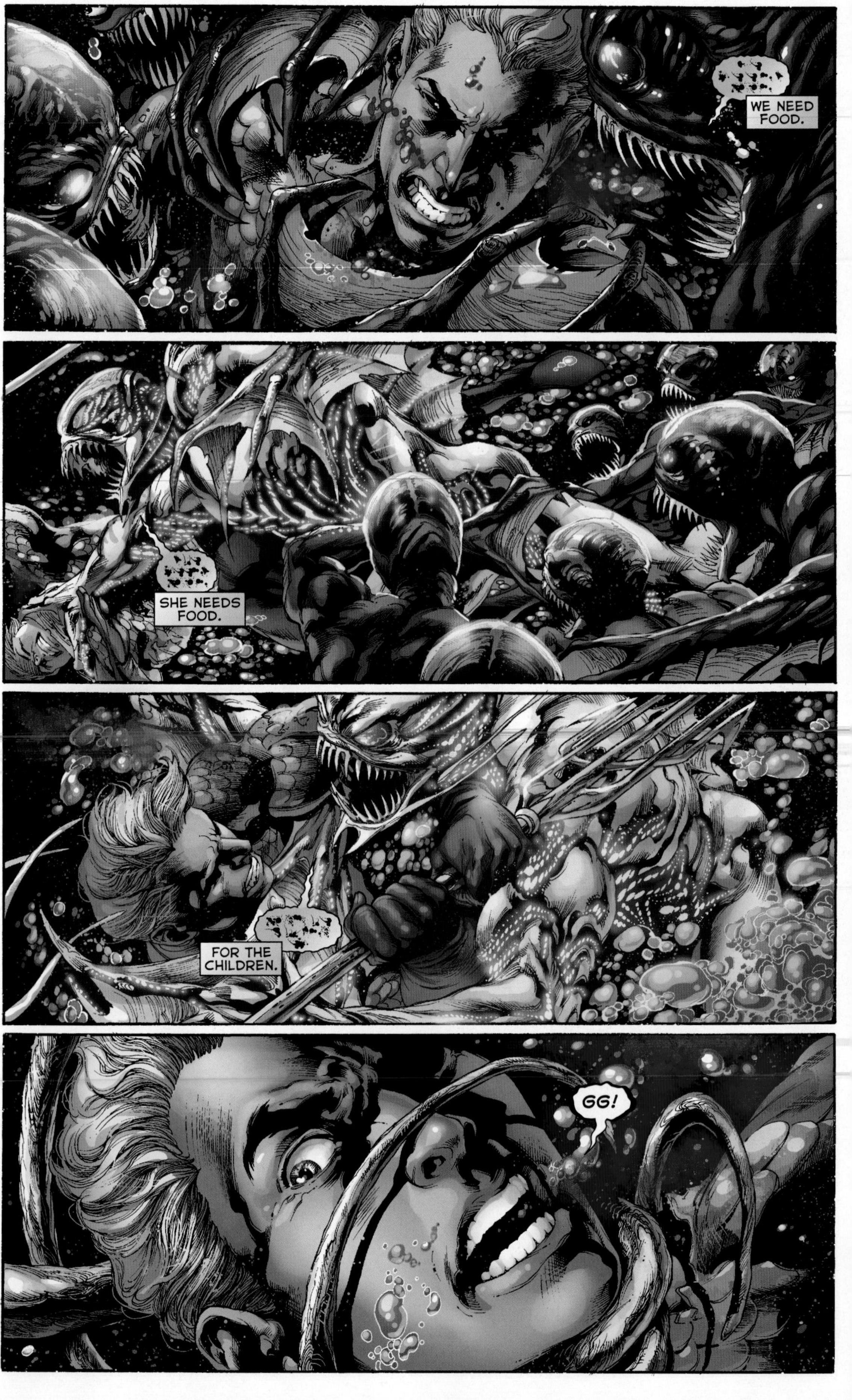
WE NEED FOOD.
SHE NEEDS FOOD.
FOR THE CHILDREN.
GG!

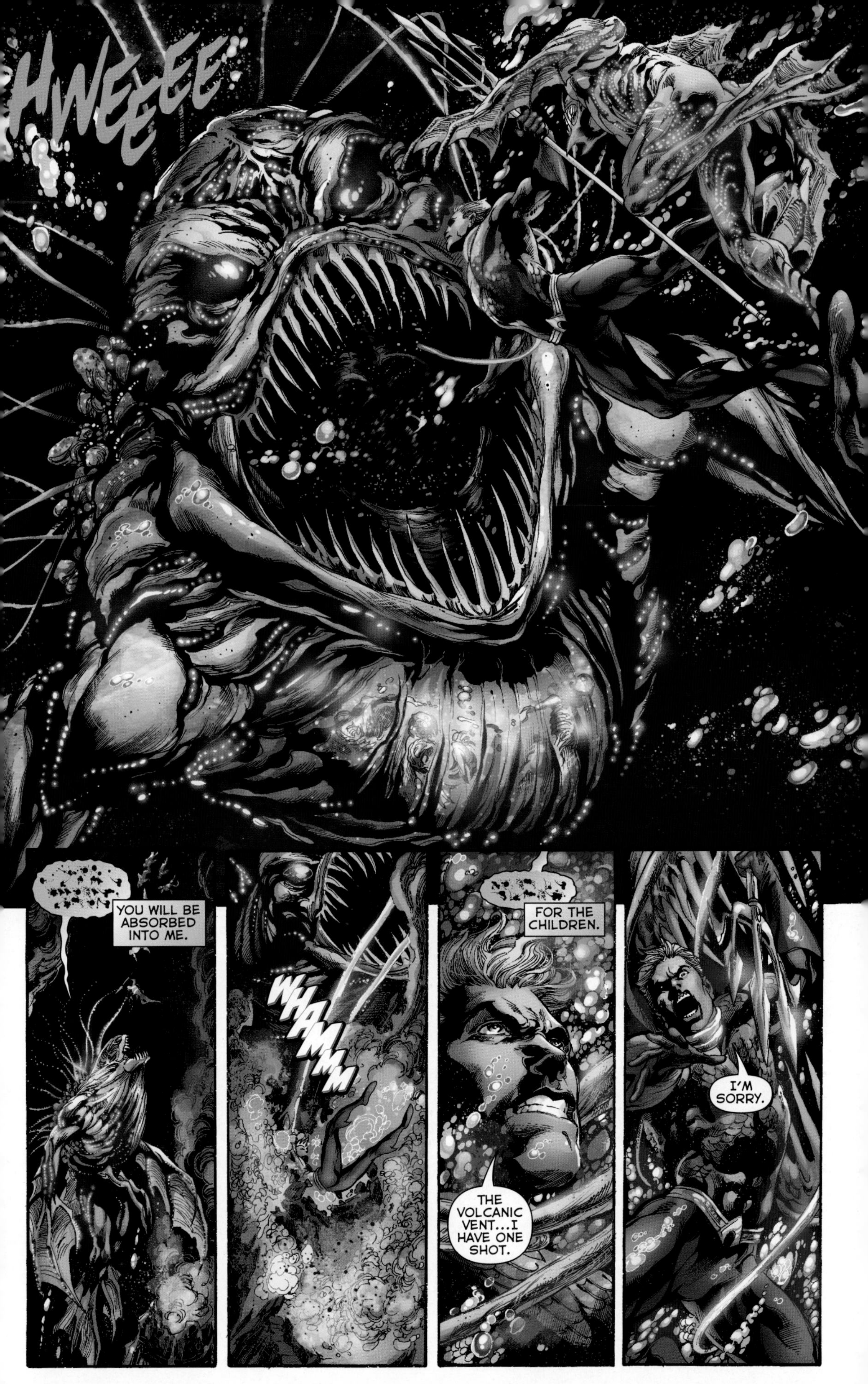
HWEEEE
YOU WILL BE ABSORBED INTO ME.
WHAMMM
FOR THE CHILDREN.
THE VOLCANIC VENT...I HAVE ONE SHOT.
I'M SORRY.

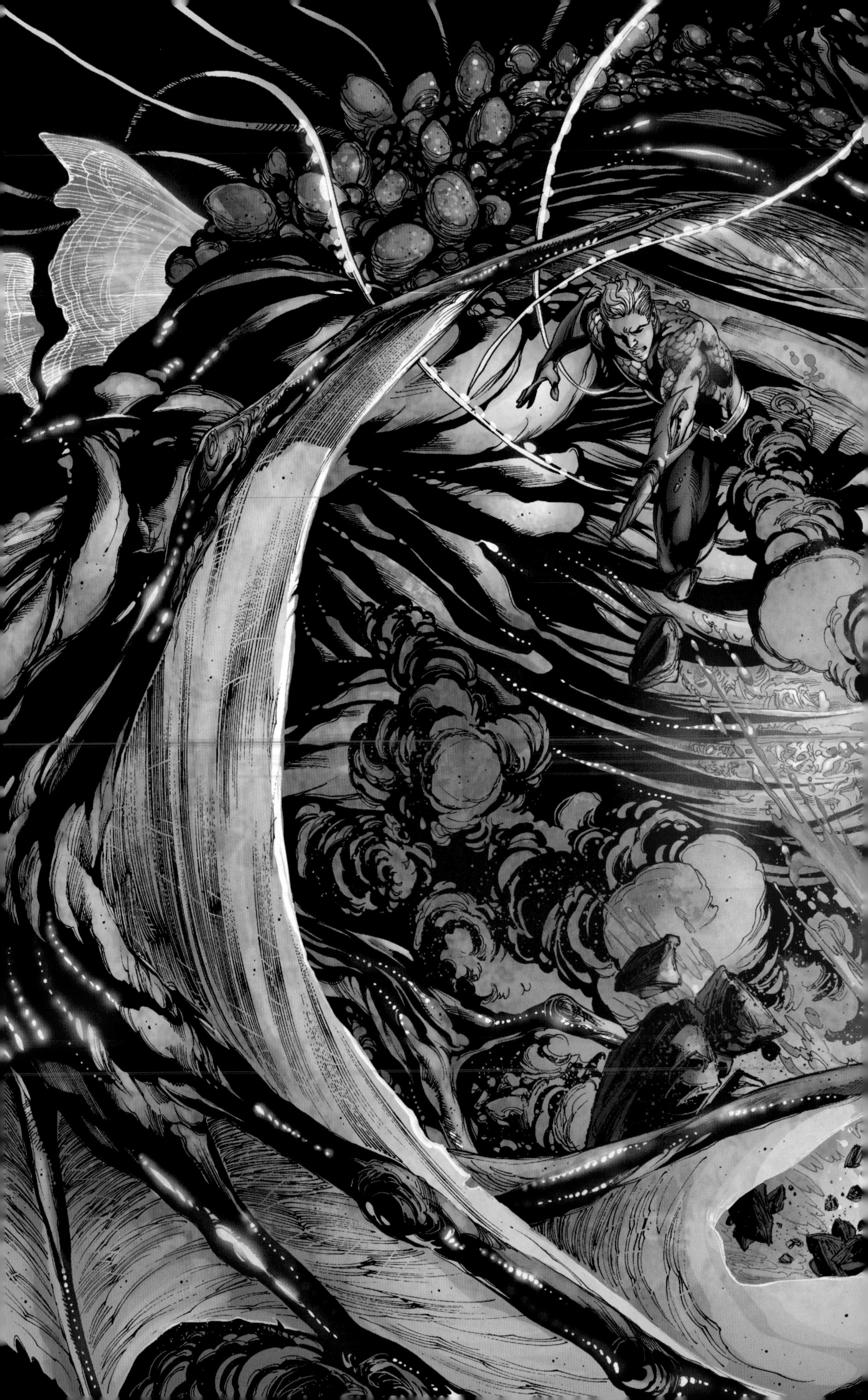

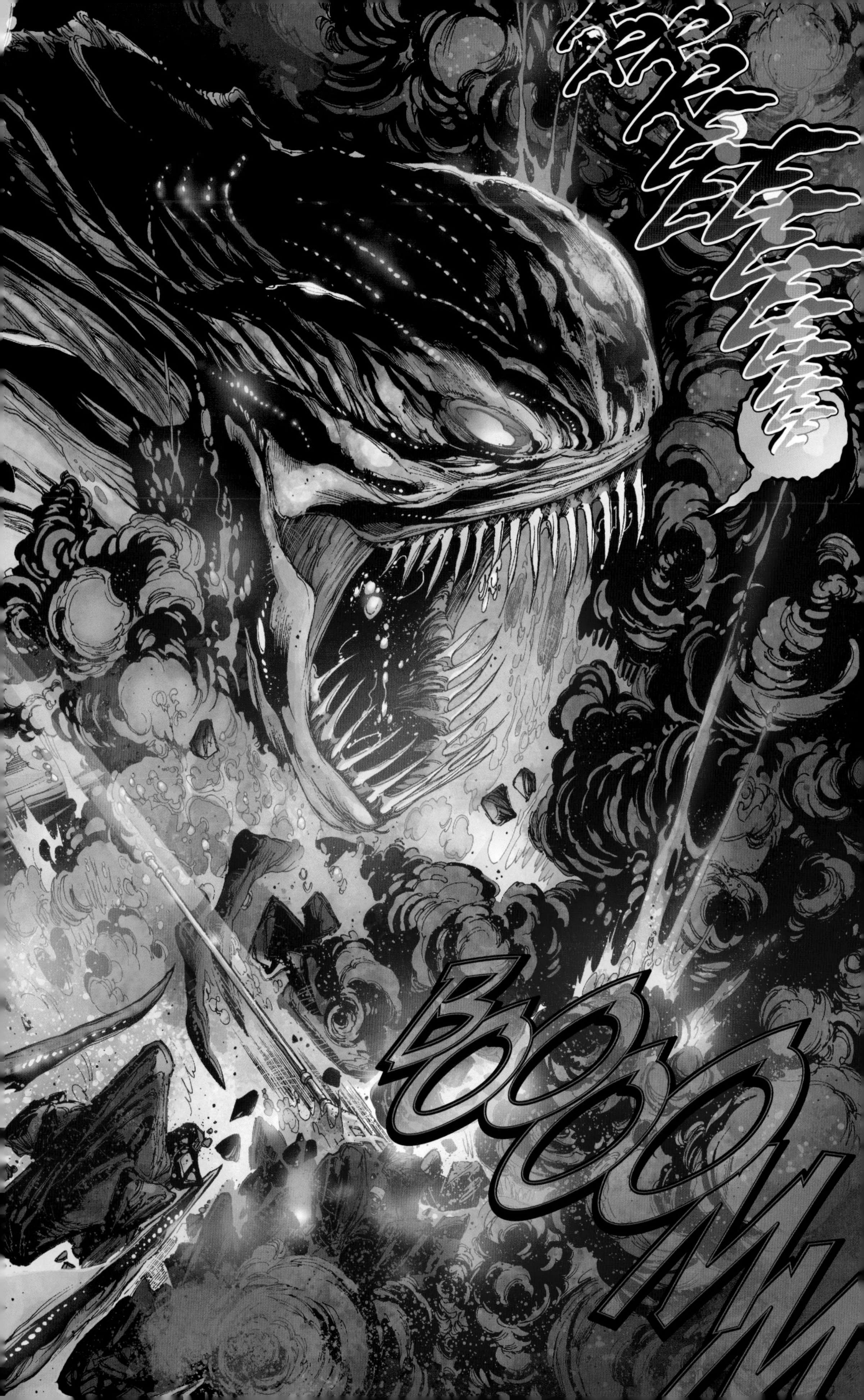
BOOOOMMM

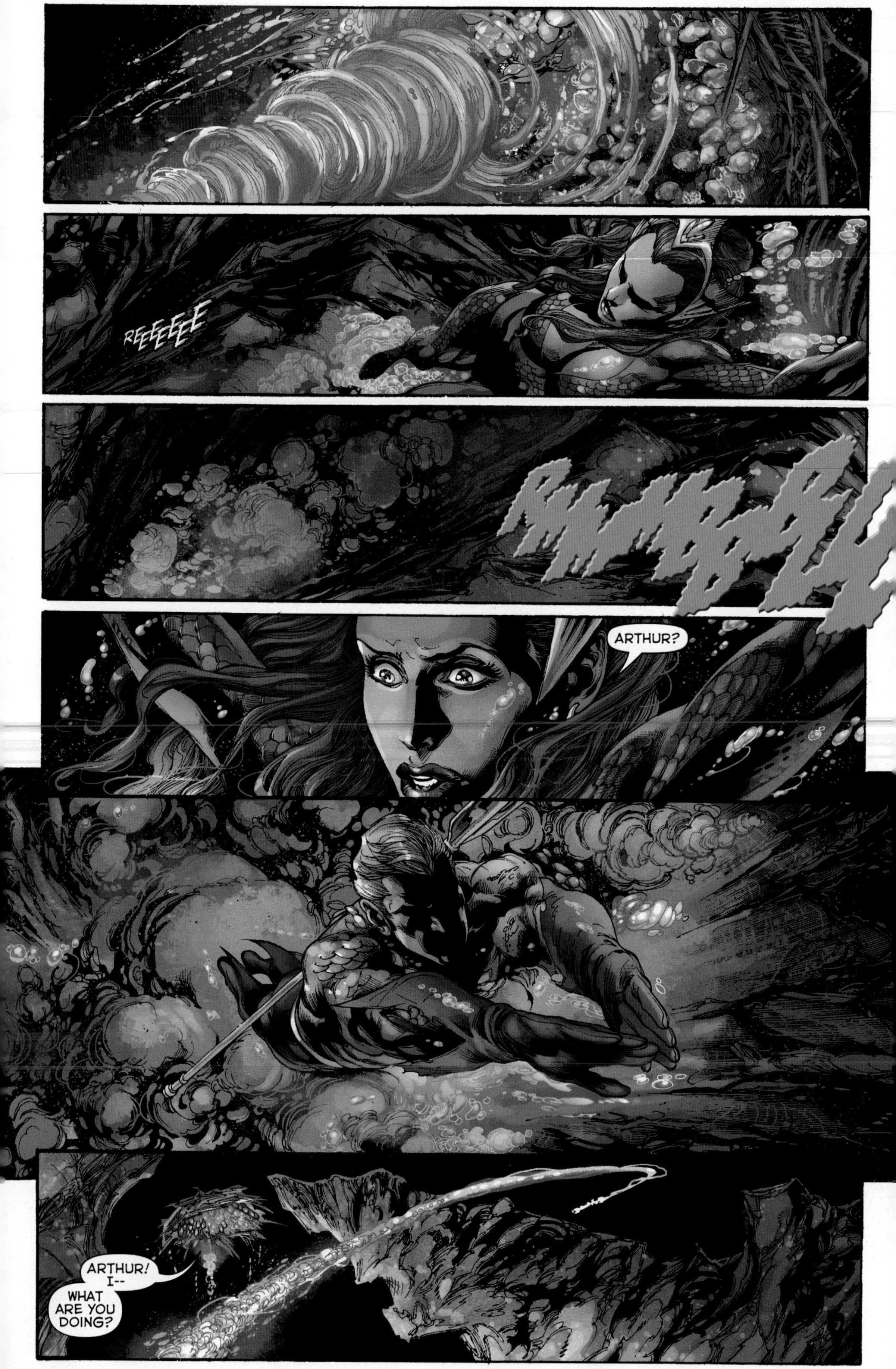
REEEEEEEE
ARTHUR?
ARTHUR! I-- WHAT ARE YOU DOING?

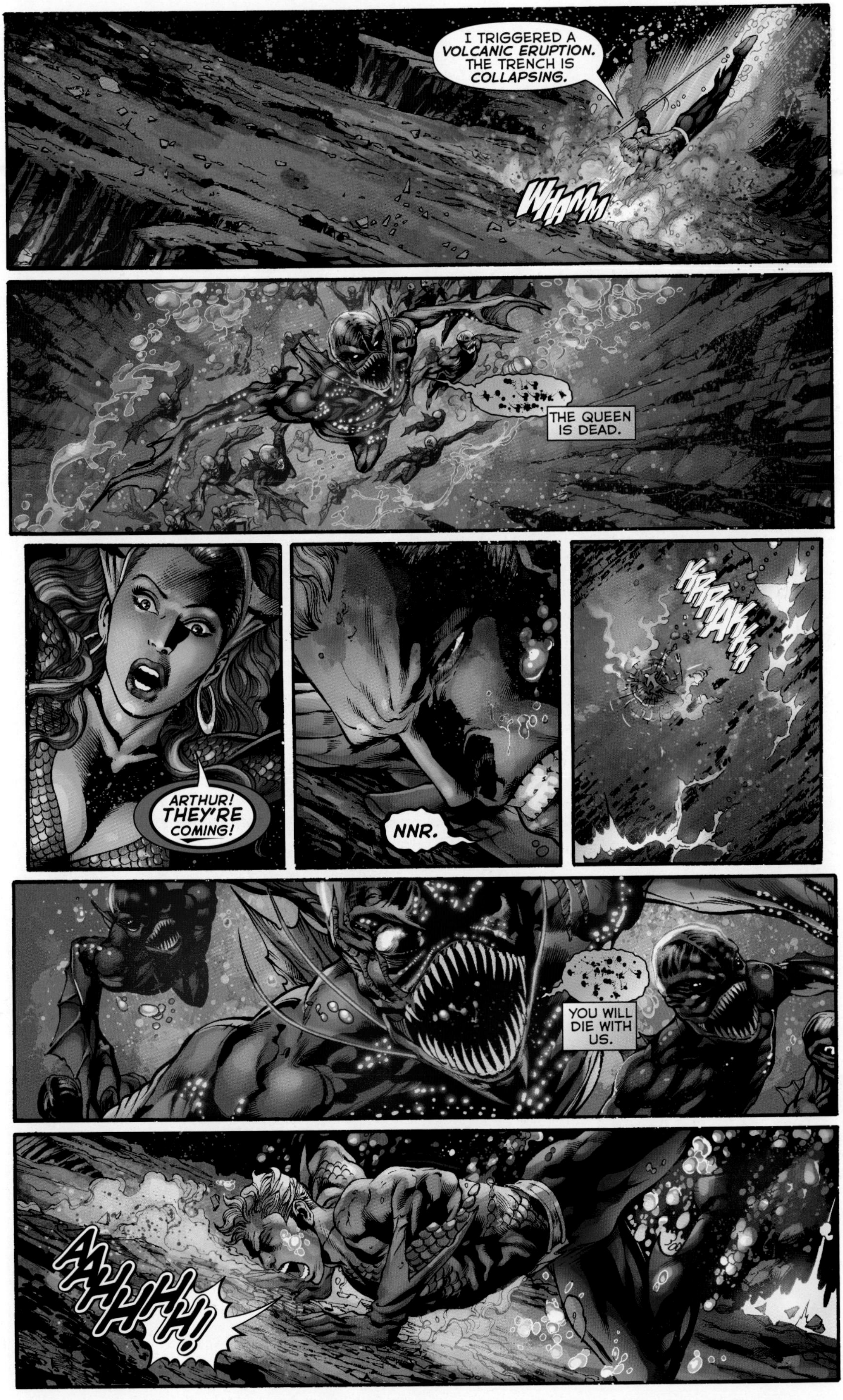
I TRIGGERED A VOLCANIC ERUPTION. THE TRENCH IS COLLAPSING.
WHAMM
THE QUEEN IS DEAD.
ARTHUR! THEY'RE COMING!
NNR.
KRRAKKK
YOU WILL DIE WITH US.
AAAHHH!

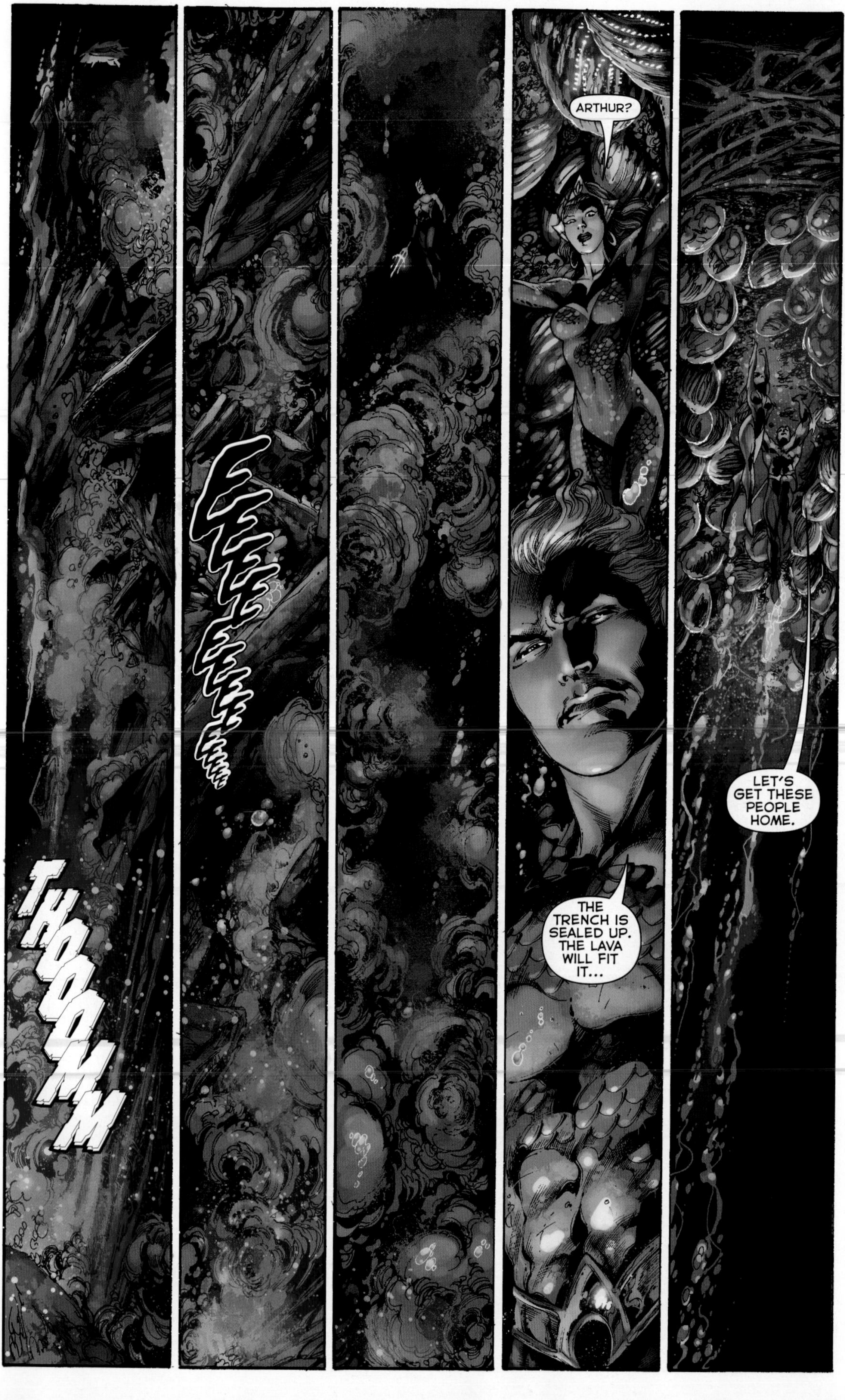
THOOMM
EEEEEEEEEEEEEEE
ARTHUR?
THE TRENCH IS SEALED UP. THE LAVA WILL FIT IT...
LET'S GET THESE PEOPLE HOME.

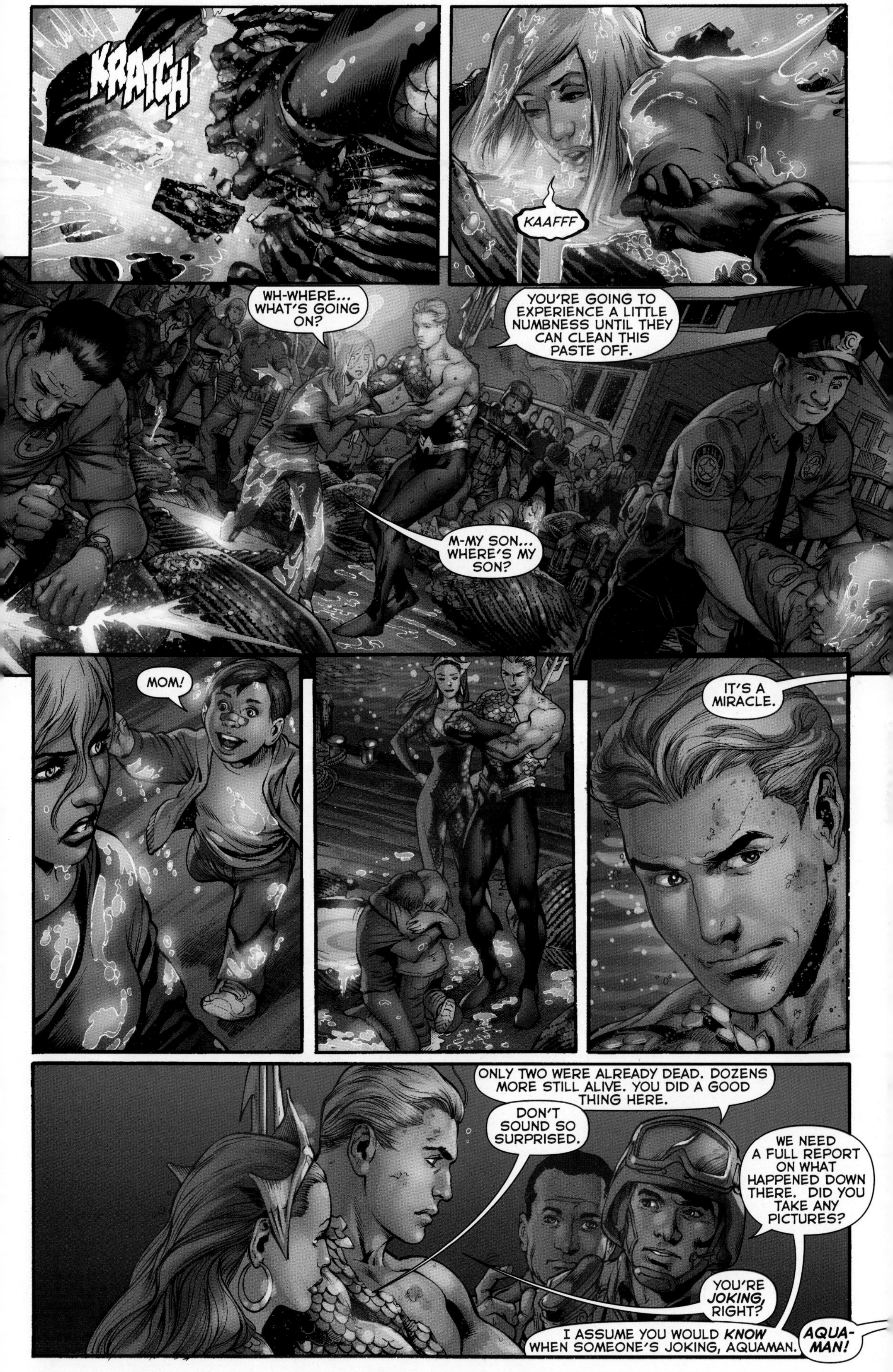
KRATCH
KAAFFF
WH-WHERE... WHAT'S GOING ON?
YOU'RE GOING TO EXPERIENCE A LITTLE NUMBNESS UNTIL THEY CAN CLEAN THIS PASTE OFF.
M-MY SON... WHERE'S MY SON?
MOM!
IT'S A MIRACLE.
ONLY TWO WERE ALREADY DEAD. DOZENS MORE STILL ALIVE. YOU DID A GOOD THING HERE.
DON'T SOUND SO SURPRISED.
WE NEED A FULL REPORT ON WHAT HAPPENED DOWN THERE. DID YOU TAKE ANY PICTURES?
YOU'RE JOKING, RIGHT?
I ASSUME YOU WOULD KNOW WHEN SOMEONE'S JOKING, AQUAMAN.
AQUA-MAN!

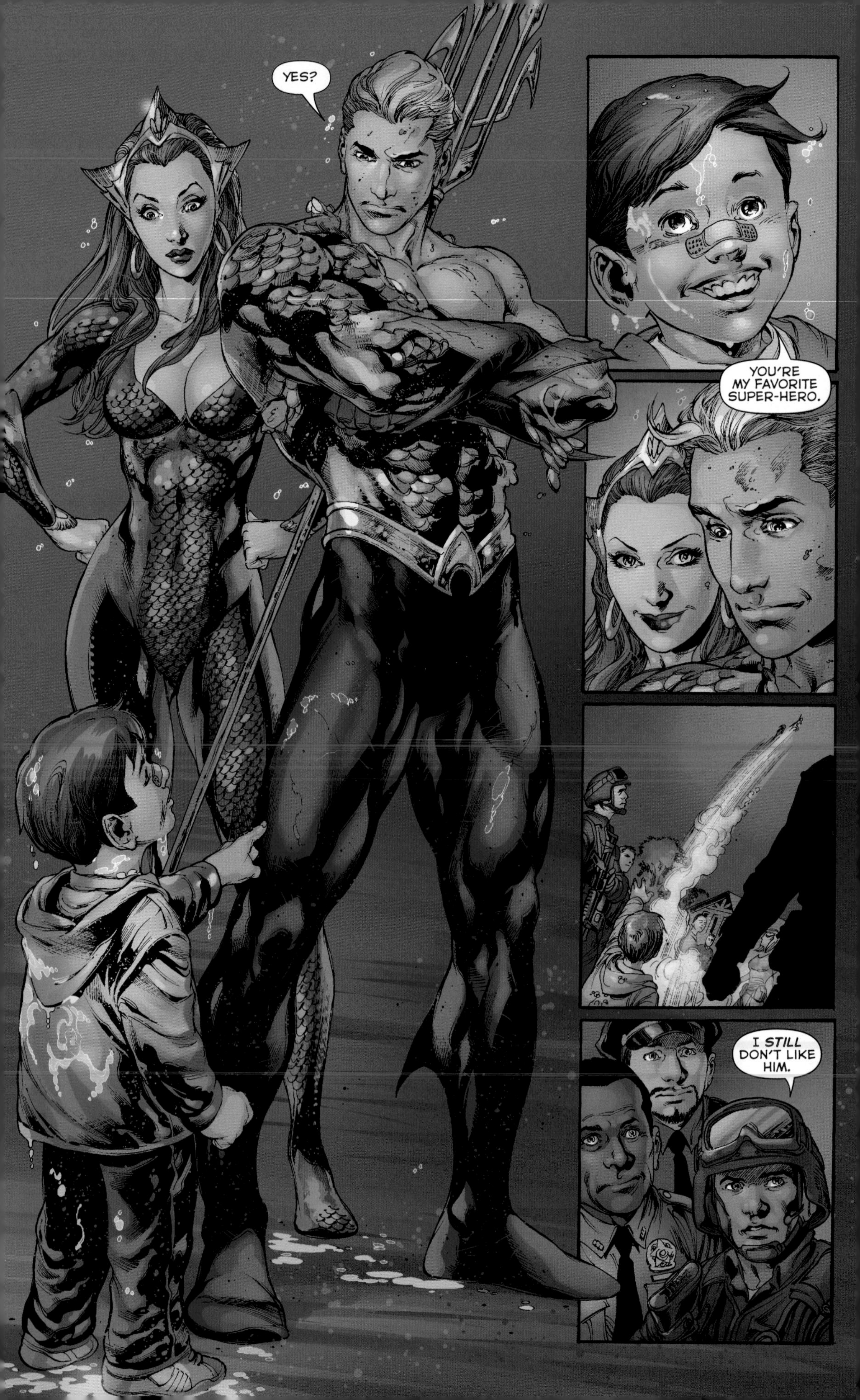

YES?
YOU'RE MY FAVORITE SUPER-HERO.
I *STILL* DON'T LIKE HIM.

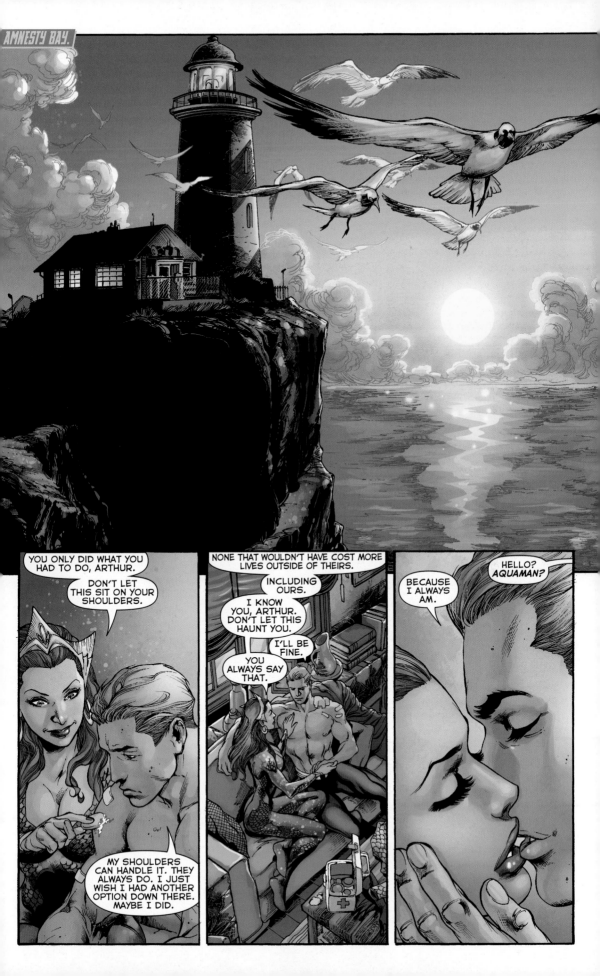

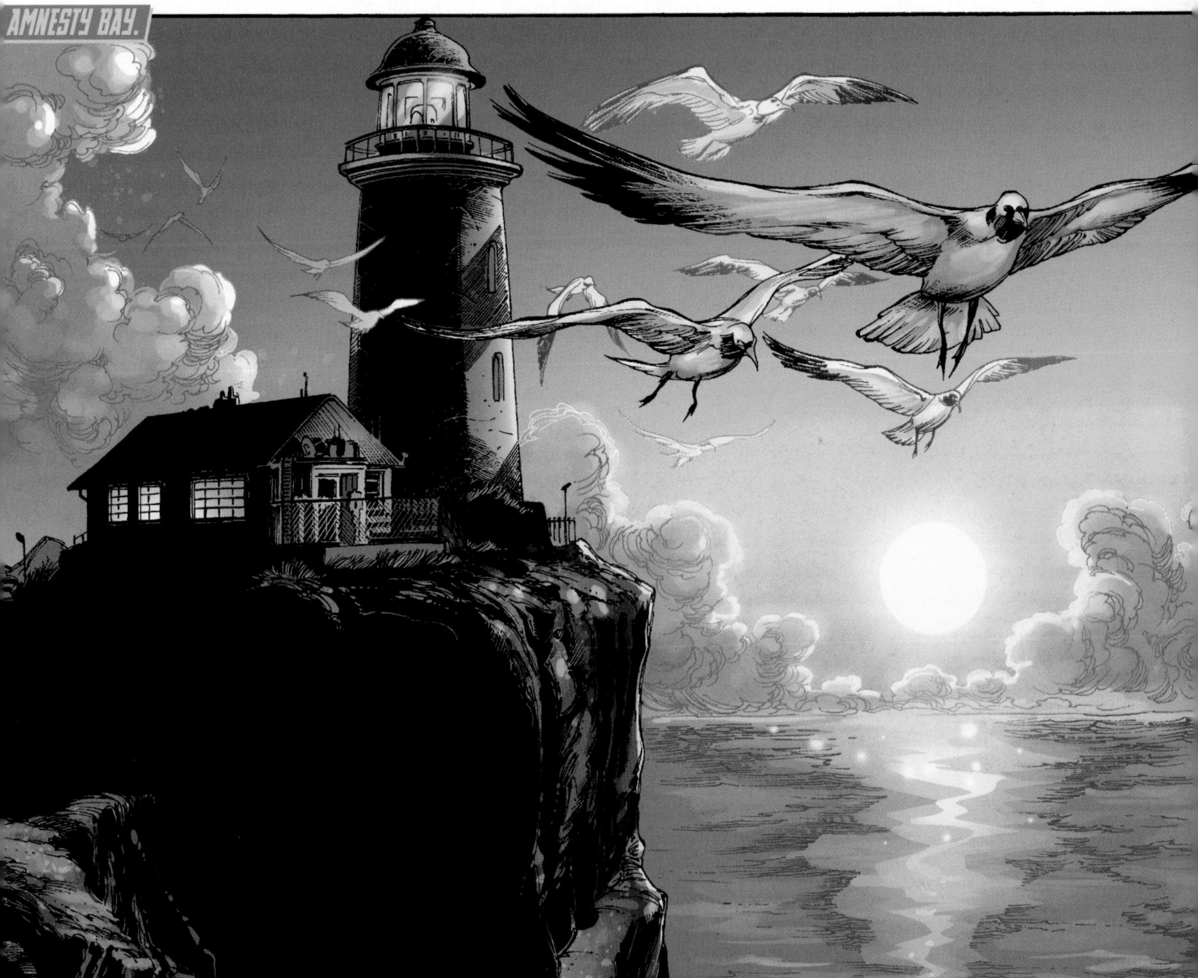
AMNESTY BAY.
YOU ONLY DID WHAT YOU HAD TO DO, ARTHUR.
DON'T LET THIS SIT ON YOUR SHOULDERS.
MY SHOULDERS CAN HANDLE IT. THEY ALWAYS DO. I JUST WISH I HAD ANOTHER OPTION DOWN THERE. MAYBE I DID.
NONE THAT WOULDN'T HAVE COST MORE LIVES OUTSIDE OF THEIRS.
INCLUDING OURS.
I KNOW YOU, ARTHUR. DON'T LET THIS HAUNT YOU.
I'LL BE FINE.
YOU ALWAYS SAY THAT.
BECAUSE I ALWAYS AM.
HELLO? *AQUAMAN?*

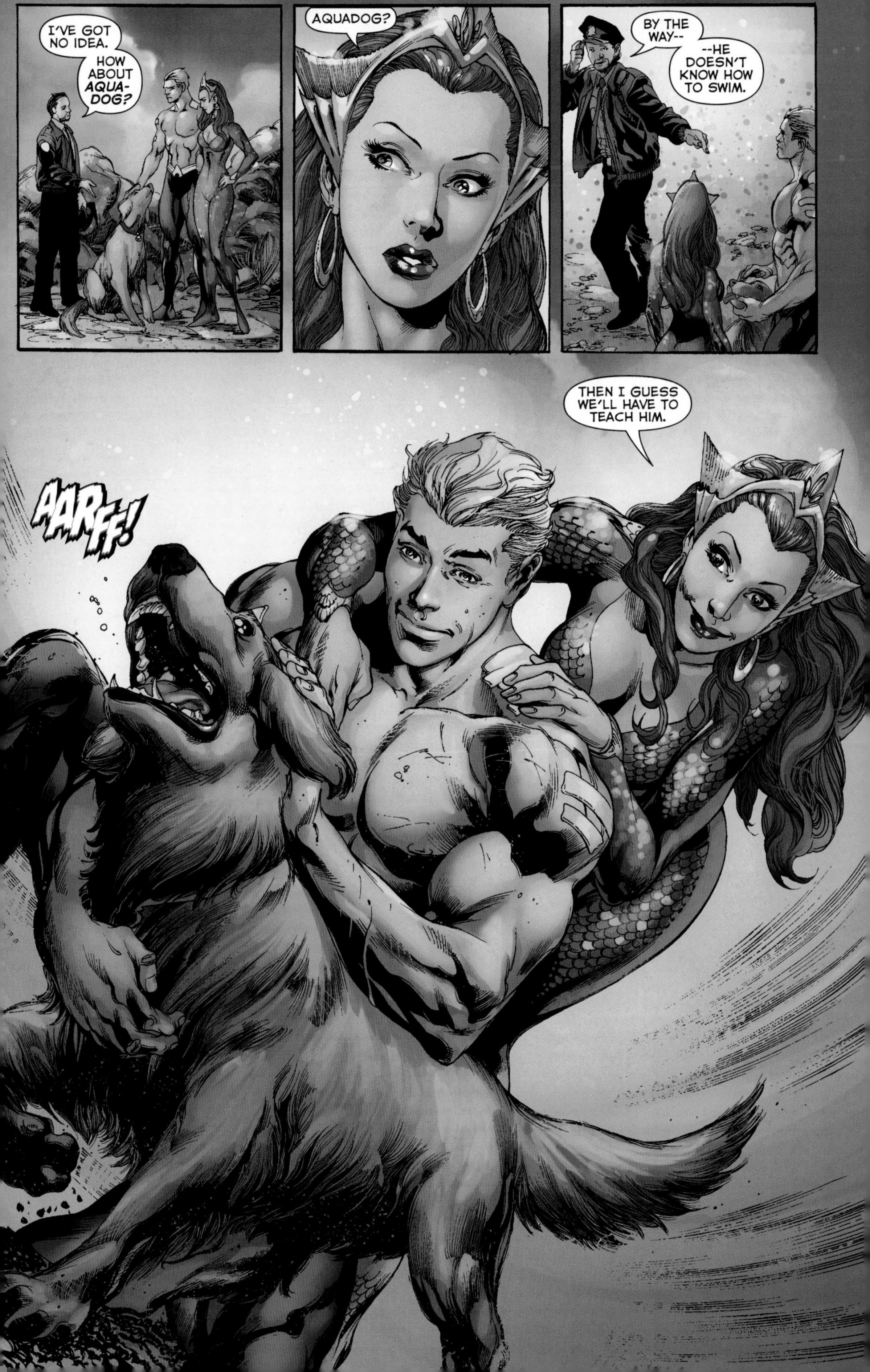
I'VE GOT NO IDEA.
HOW ABOUT *AQUA-DOG?*
AQUADOG?
BY THE WAY--
--HE DOESN'T KNOW HOW TO SWIM.
THEN I GUESS WE'LL HAVE TO TEACH HIM.
AARFF!

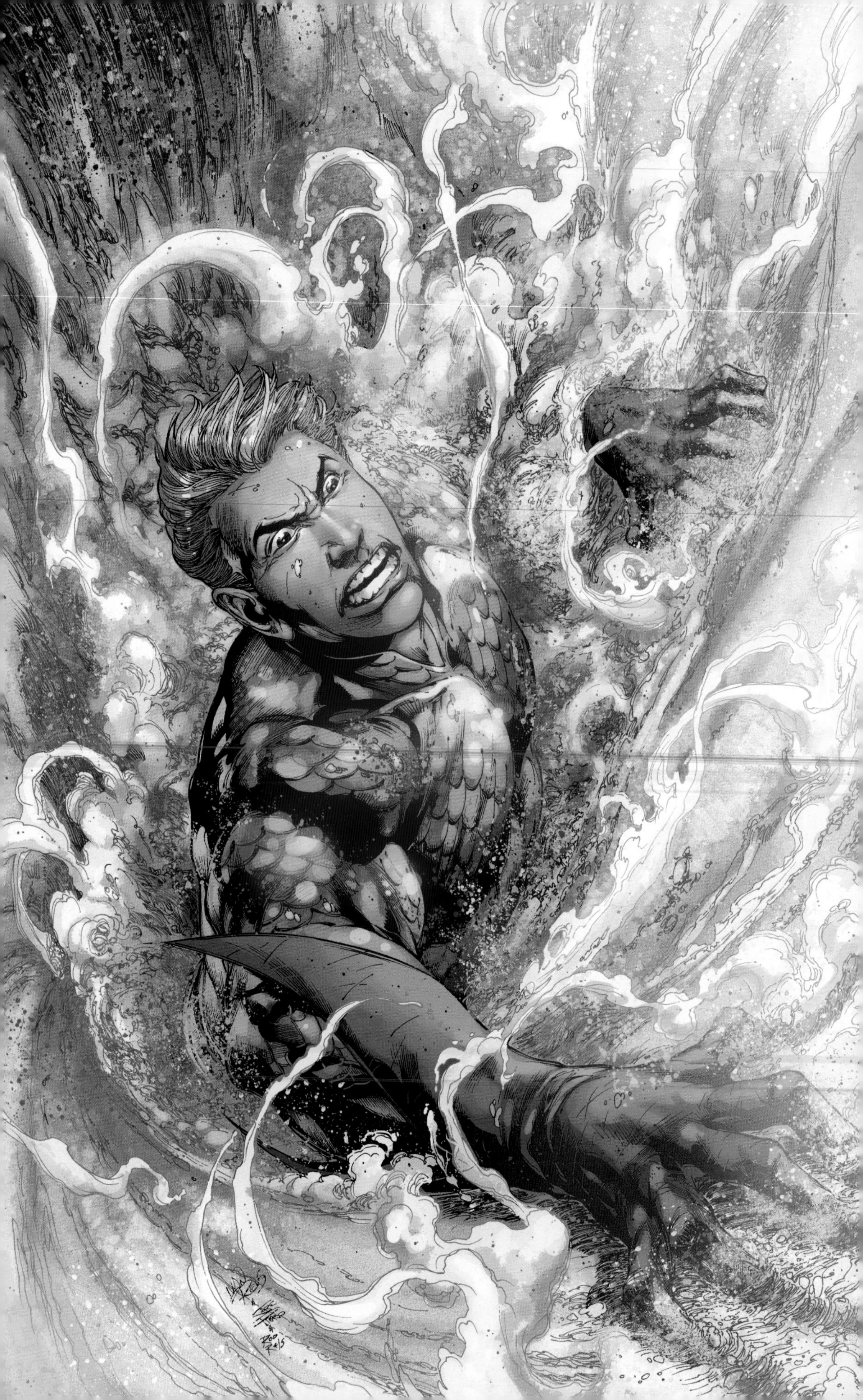

THOOMM

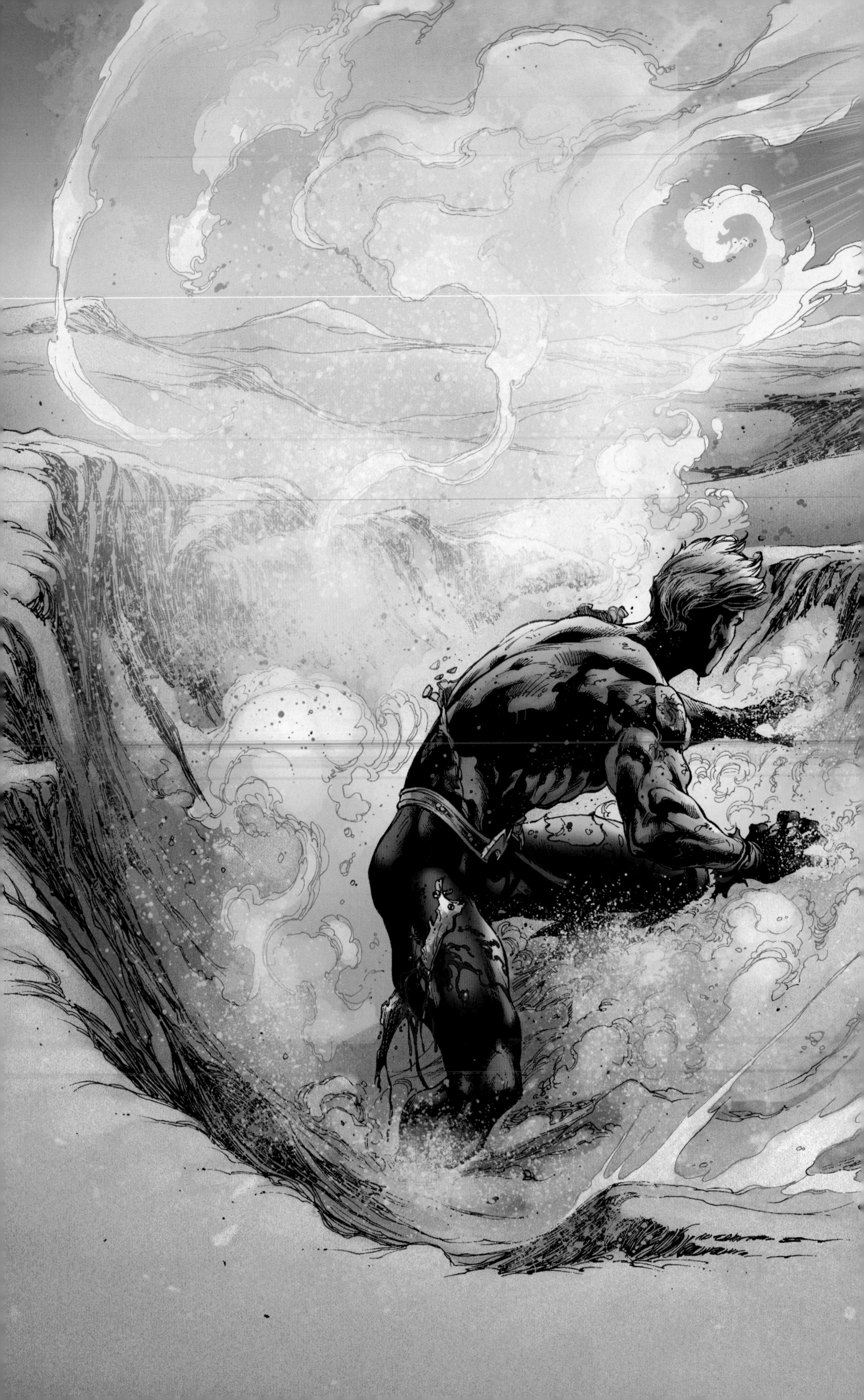

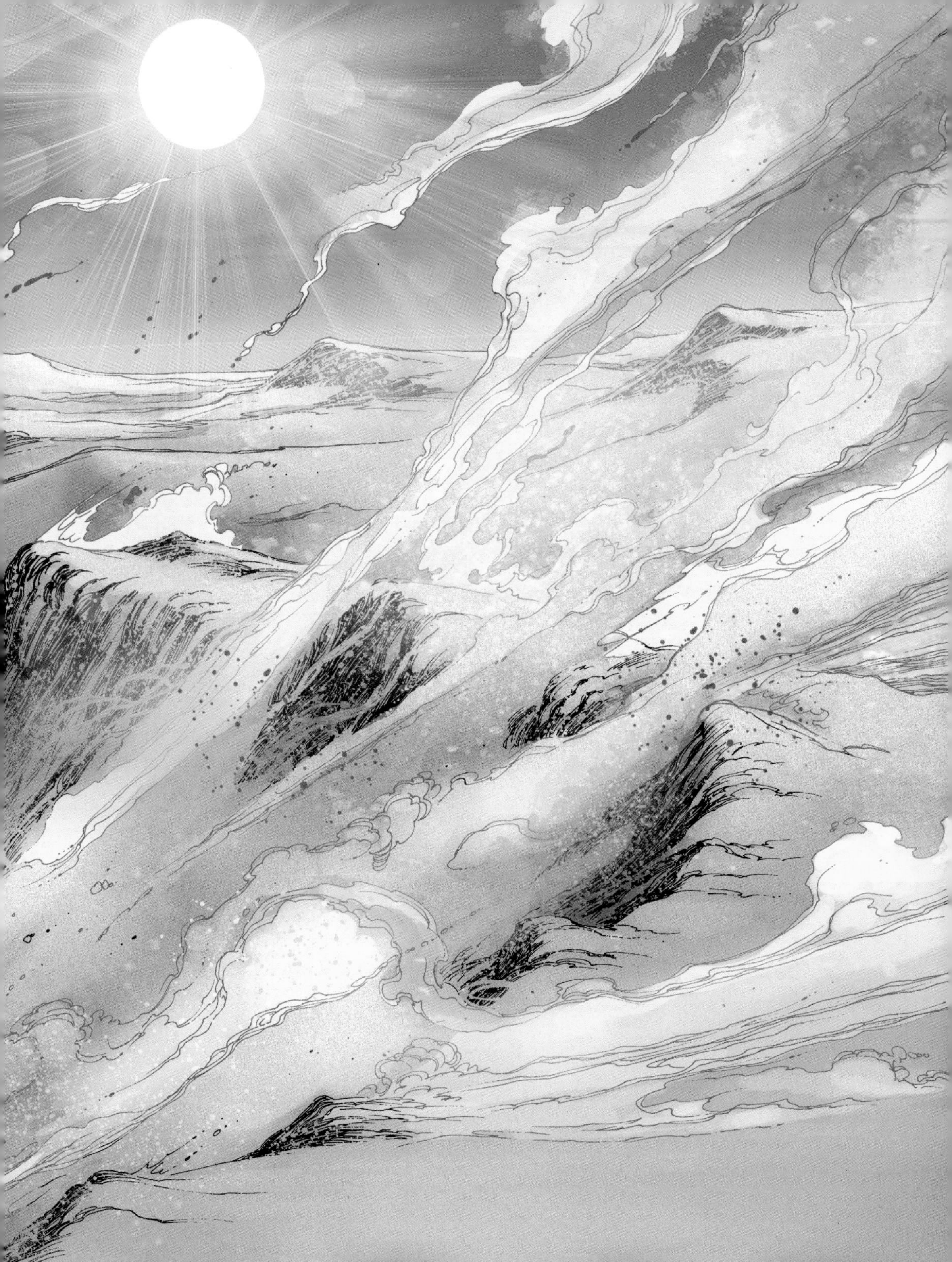

L·O·S·T

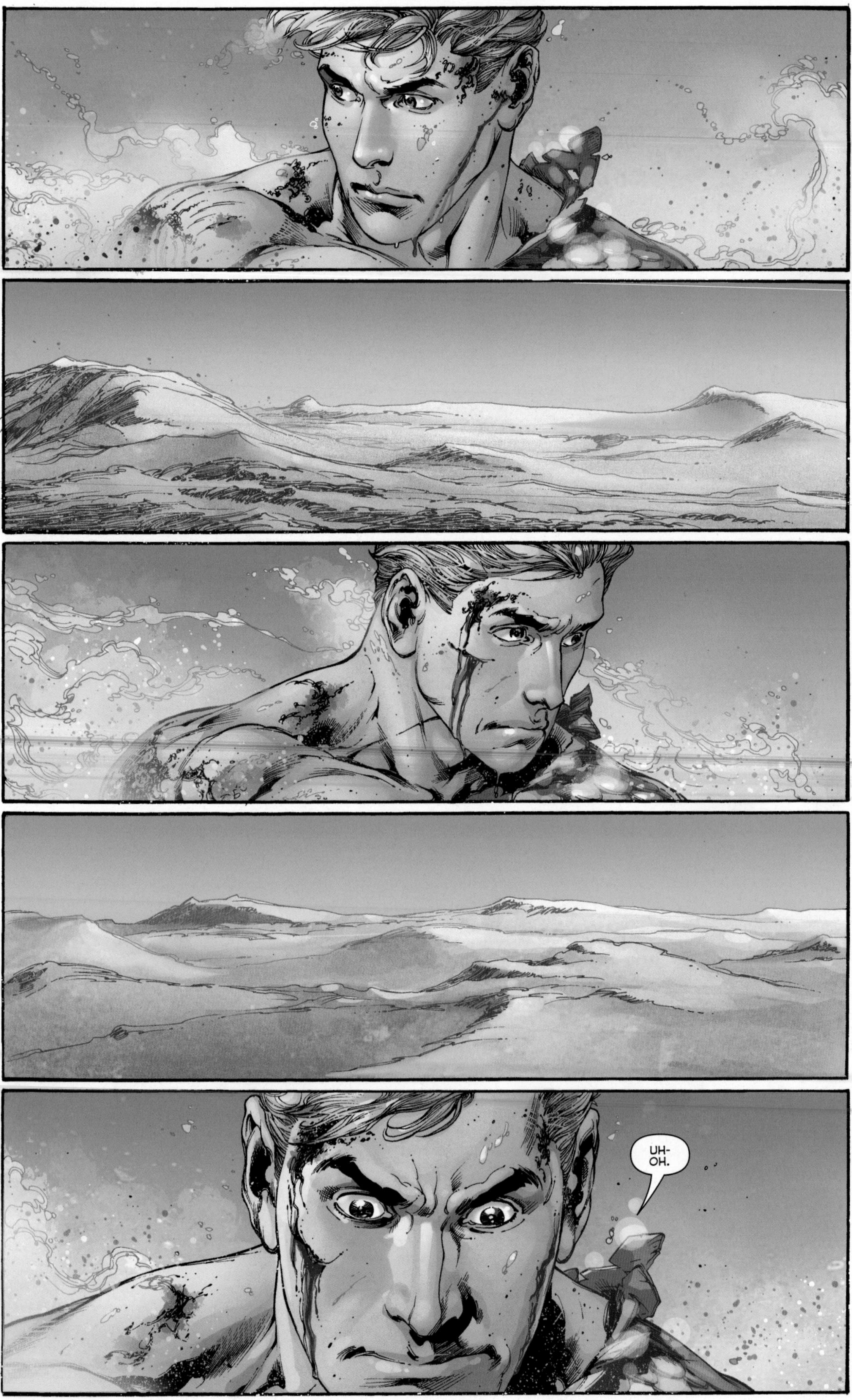
UH-
OH.

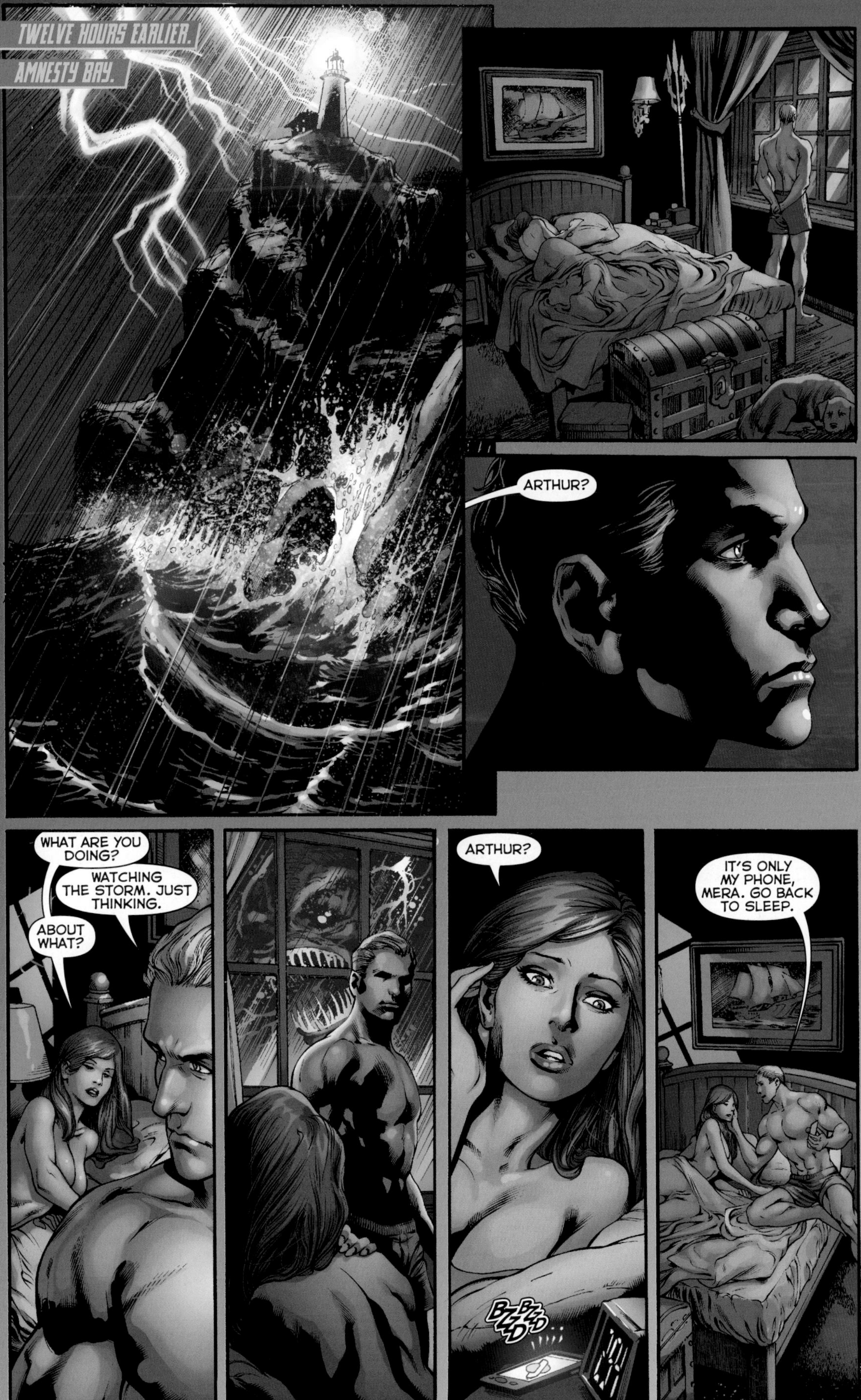
TWELVE HOURS EARLIER.
AMNESTY BAY.
ARTHUR?
WHAT ARE YOU DOING?
WATCHING THE STORM. JUST THINKING.
ABOUT WHAT?
ARTHUR?
BZZD BZZD
IT'S ONLY MY PHONE, MERA. GO BACK TO SLEEP.

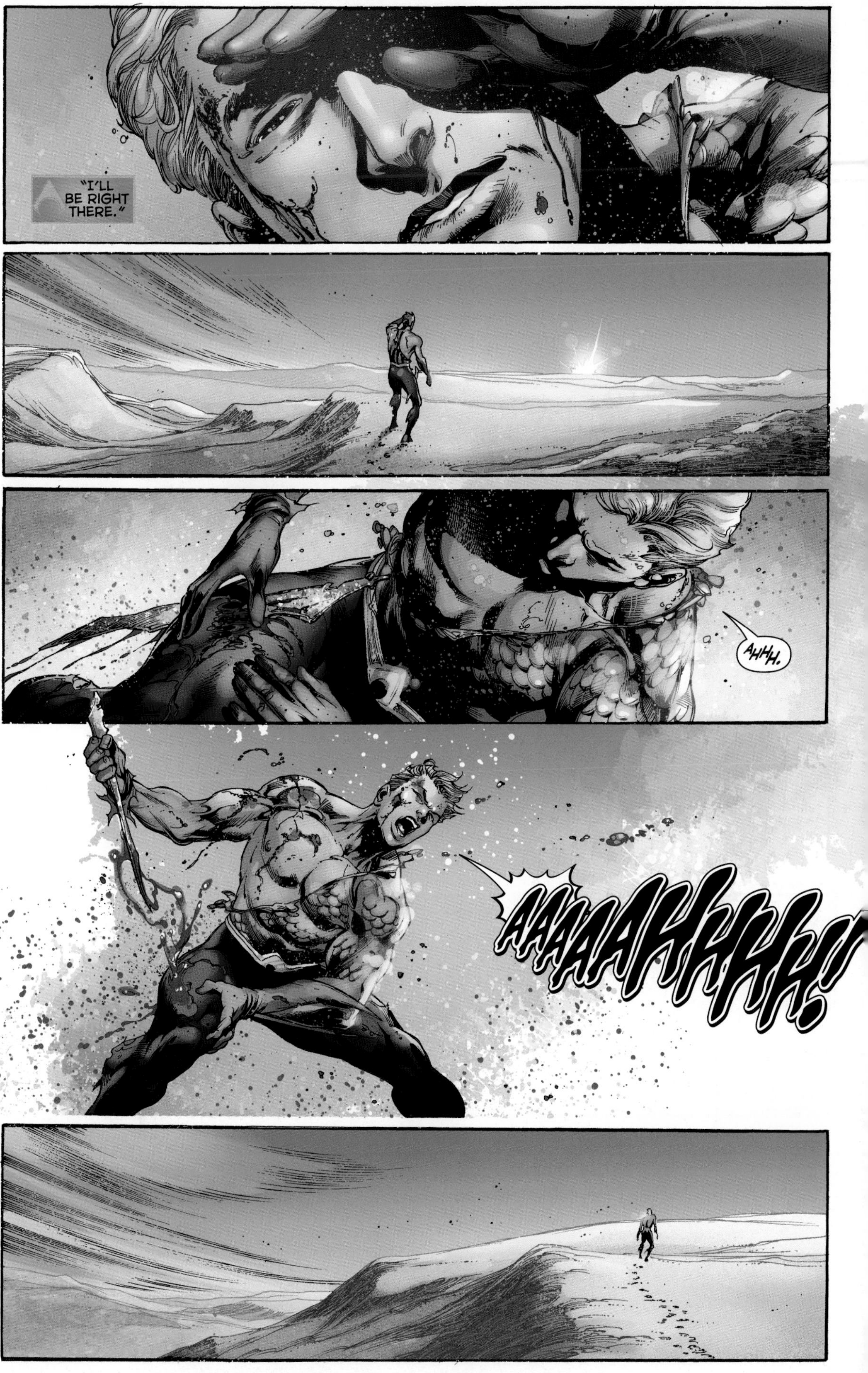
"I'LL BE RIGHT THERE."
AHHH.
AAAAAHHHHH!

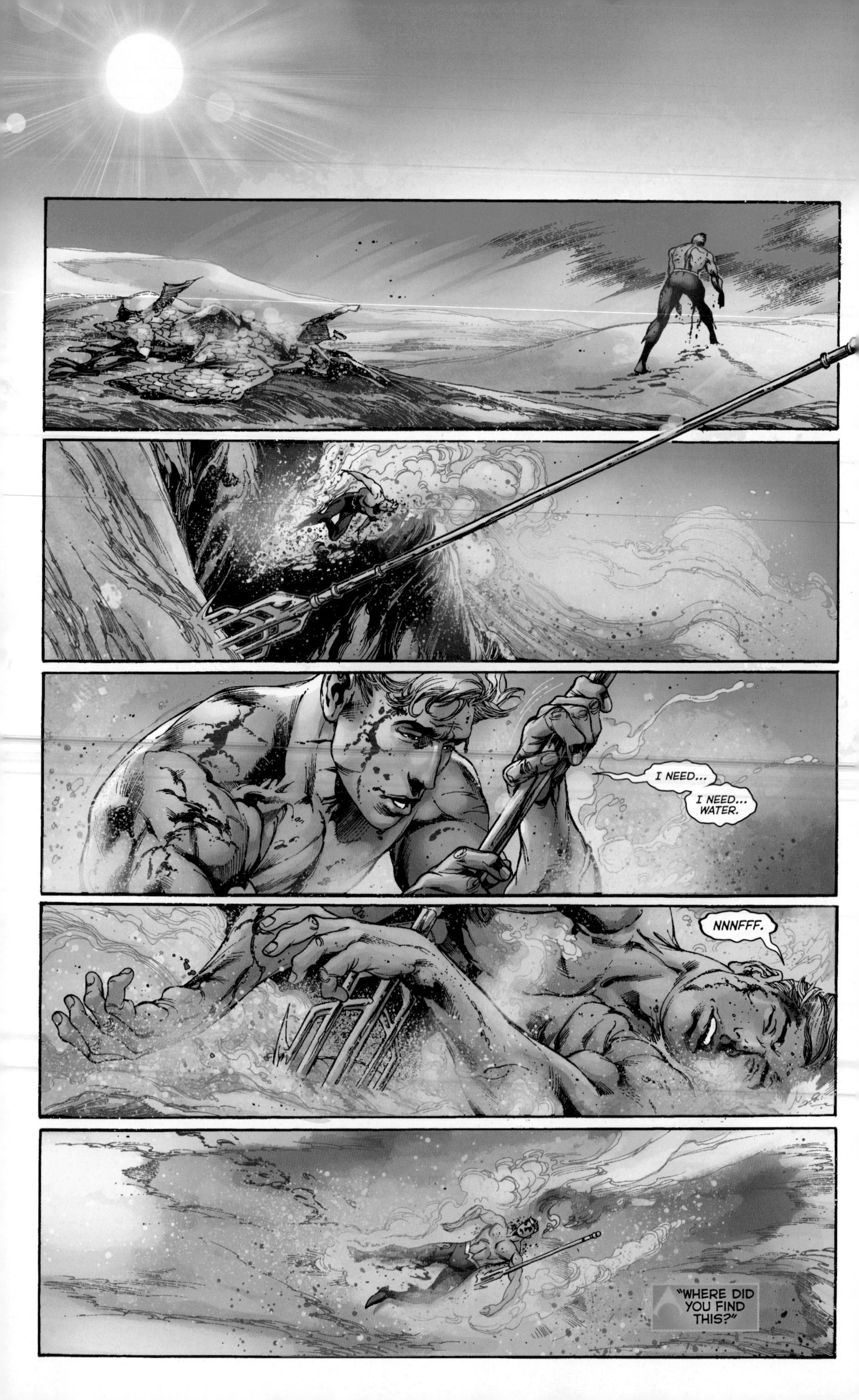
I NEED... I NEED... WATER.
NNNFFF.
"WHERE DID YOU FIND THIS?"

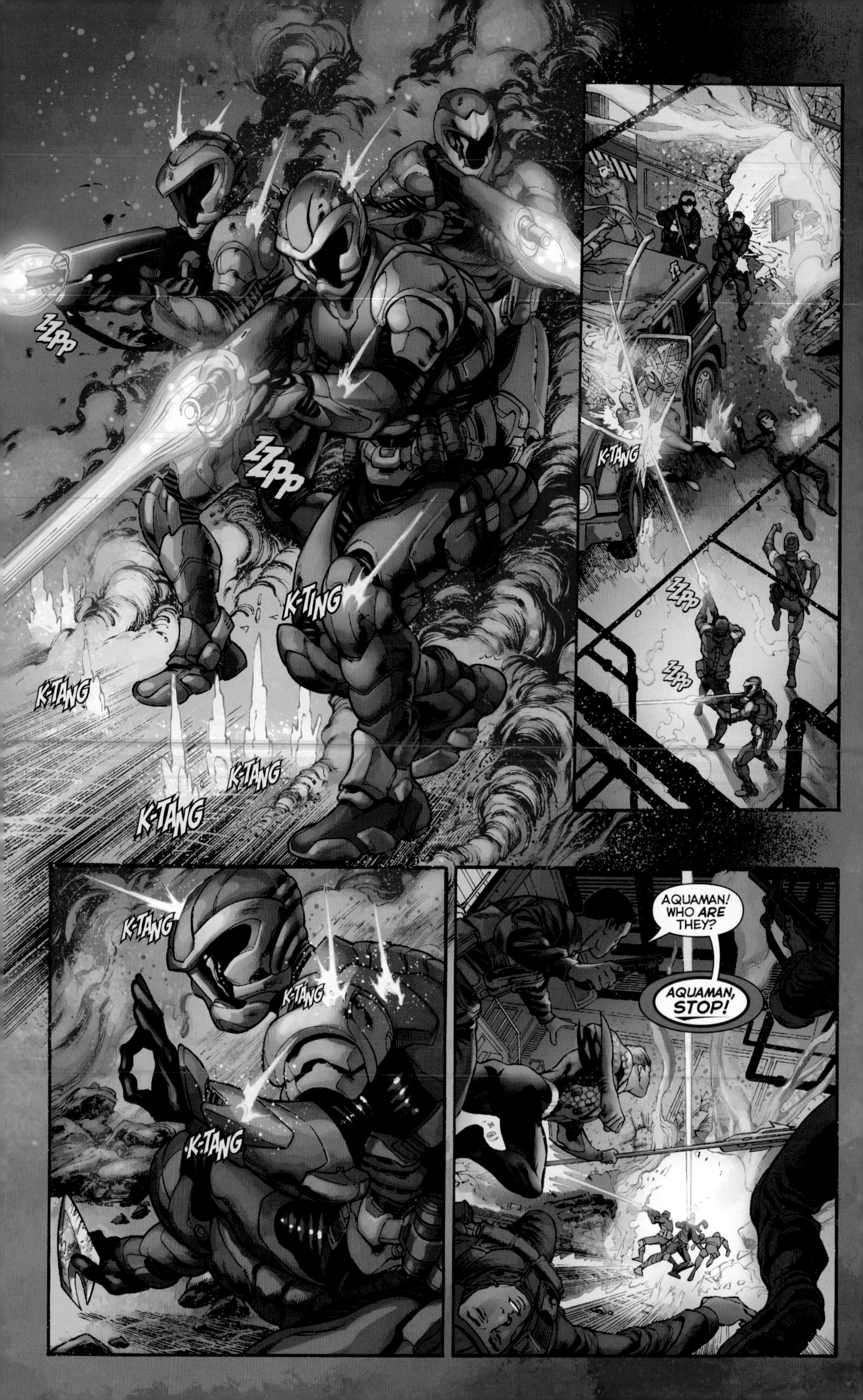
ZZPP
ZZPP
K-TING
K-TANG
K-TANG
K-TANG
K-TANG
ZZPP
ZZPP
K-TANG
K-TANG
K-TANG
AQUAMAN! WHO ARE THEY?
AQUAMAN, STOP!

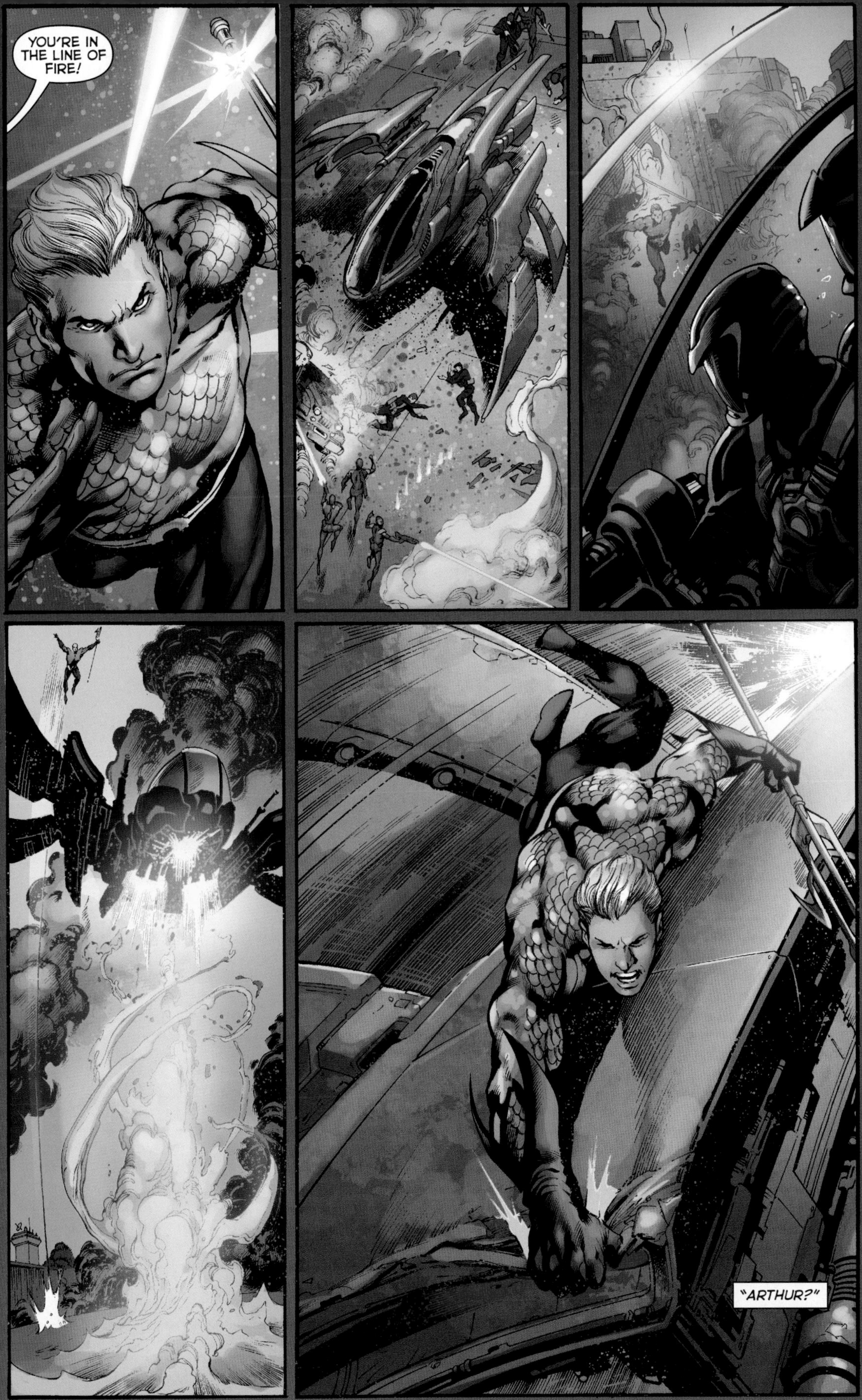
YOU'RE IN THE LINE OF FIRE!
"ARTHUR?"

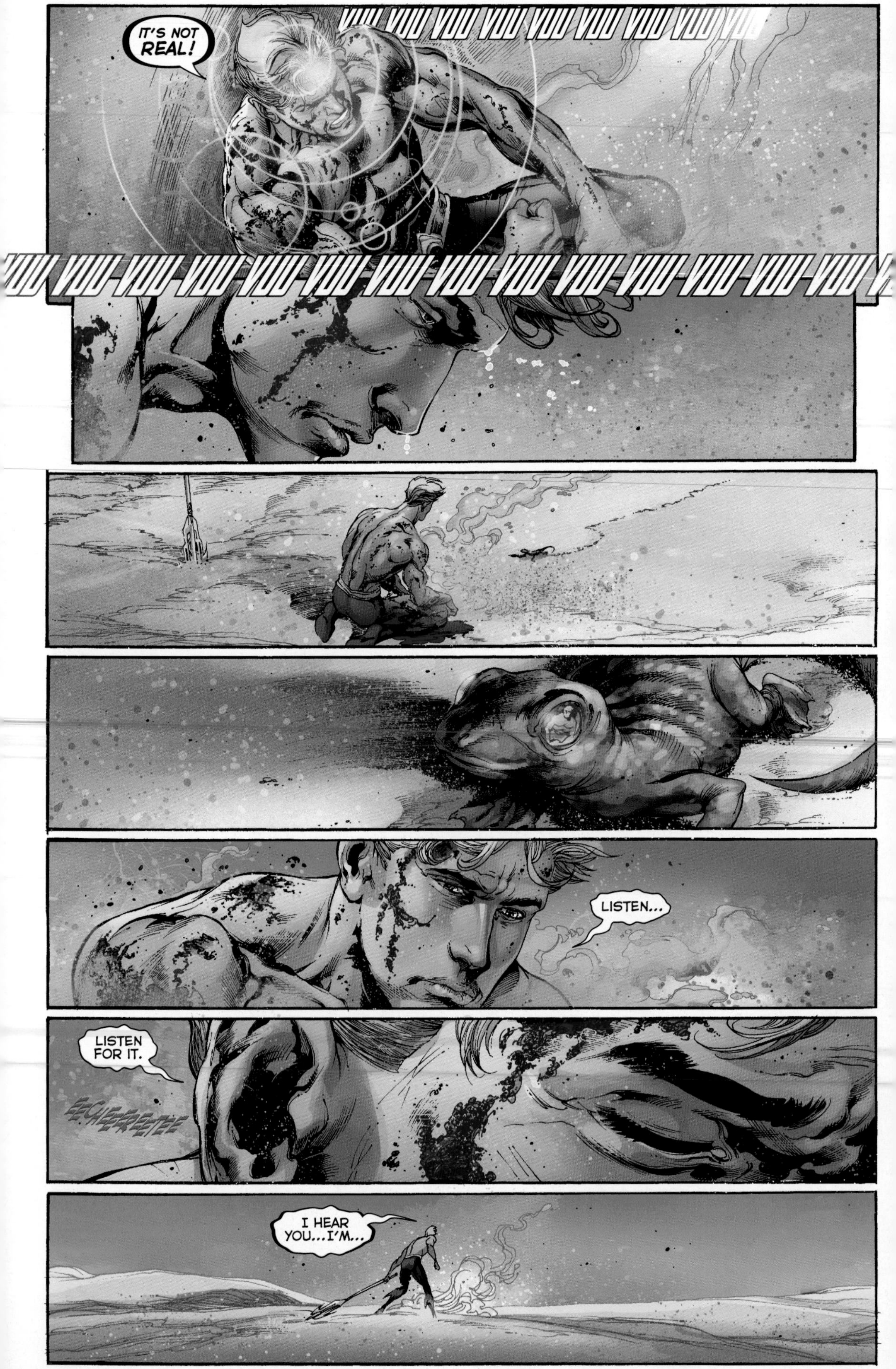
IT'S NOT REAL!
VUU VUU VUU VUU VUU VUU VUU VUU VUU
VUU VUU VUU VUU VUU VUU VUU VUU VUU VUU VUU VUU VUU
LISTEN...
LISTEN FOR IT.
I HEAR YOU...I'M...

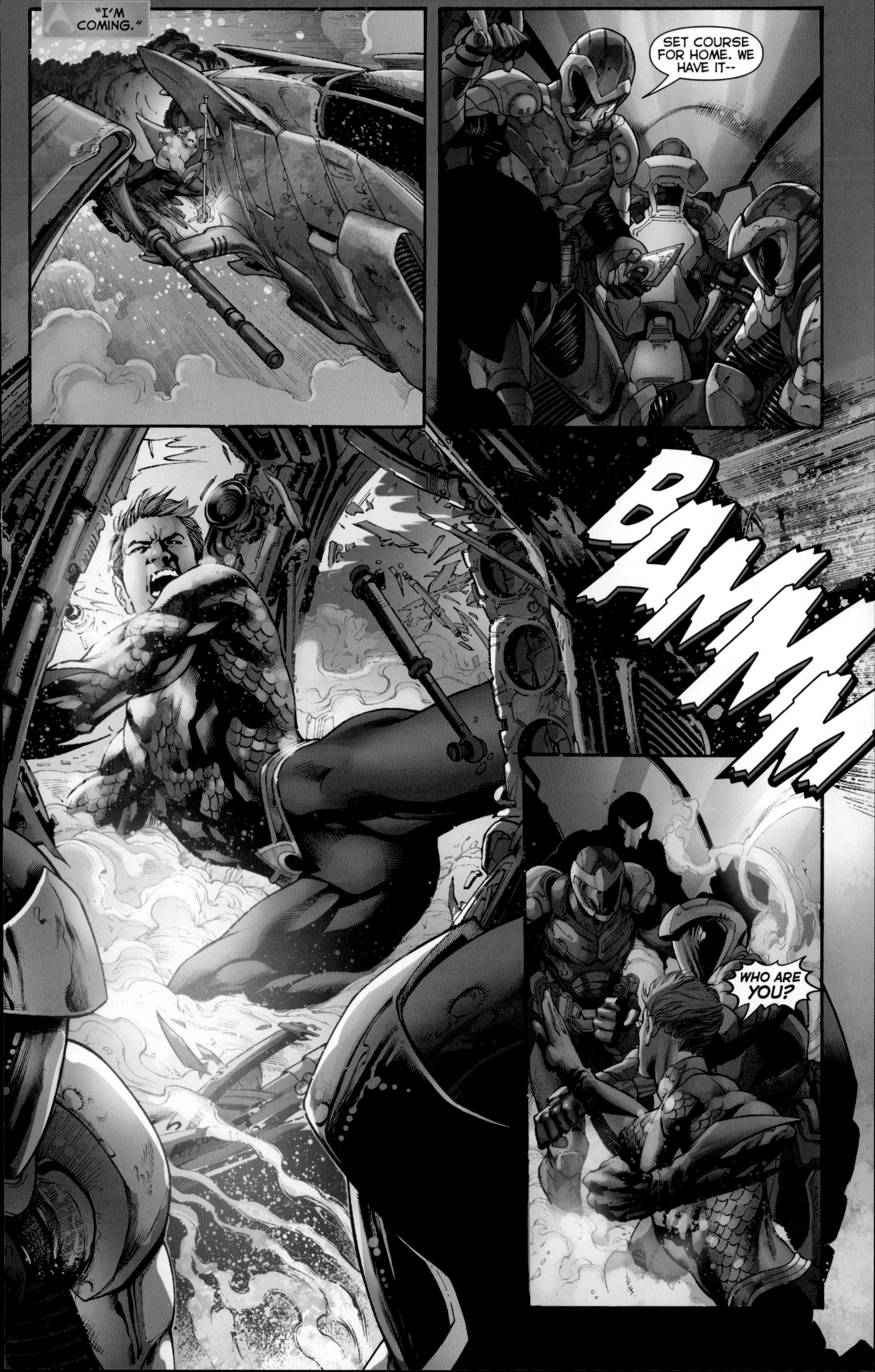
"I'M COMING."
SET COURSE FOR HOME. WE HAVE IT--
BAMMM
WHO ARE YOU?

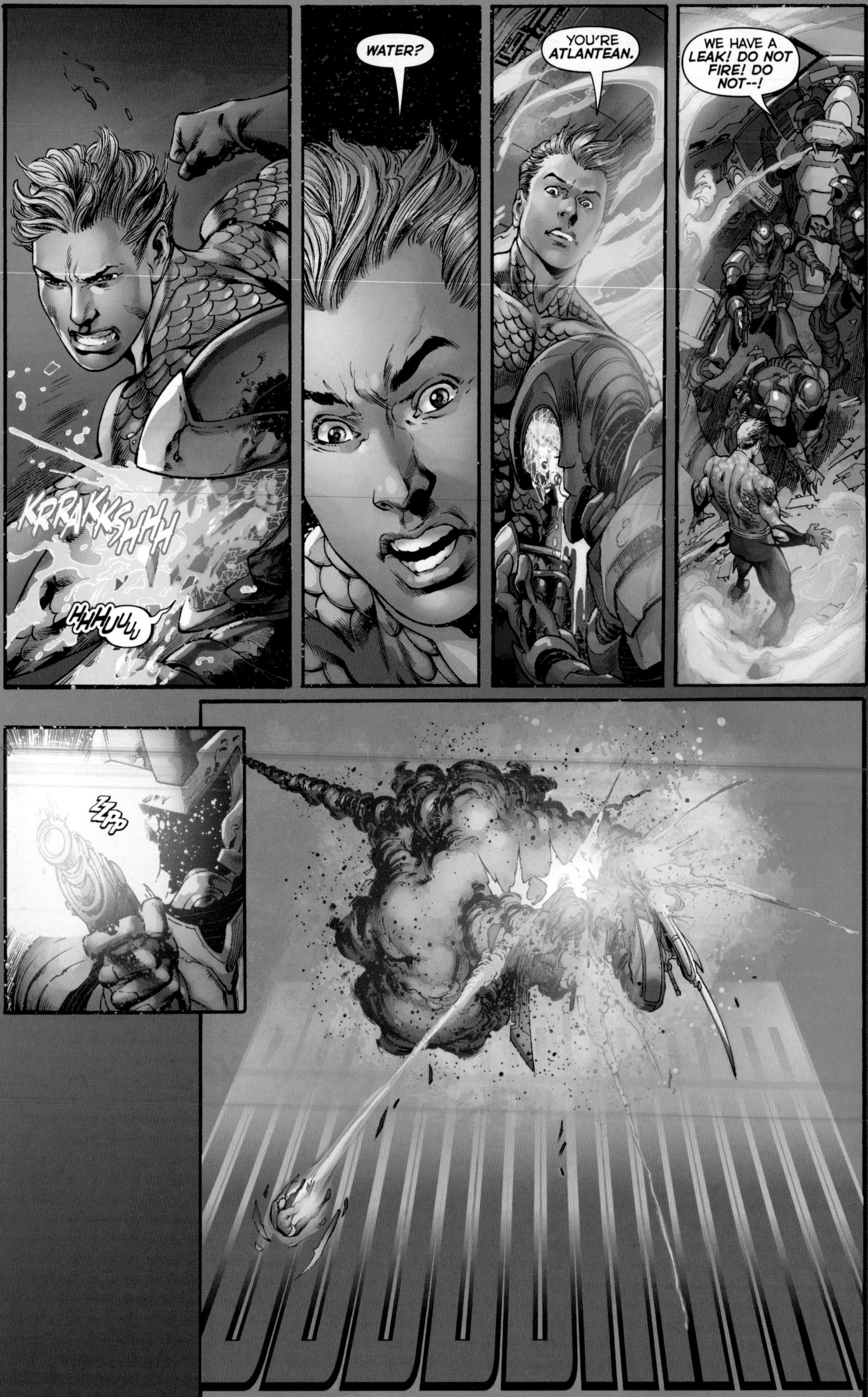
KRRAKKSHHH
HHHUUU
WATER?
YOU'RE ATLANTEAN.
WE HAVE A LEAK! DO NOT FIRE! DO NOT--!
ZZPP
DOOOMMM

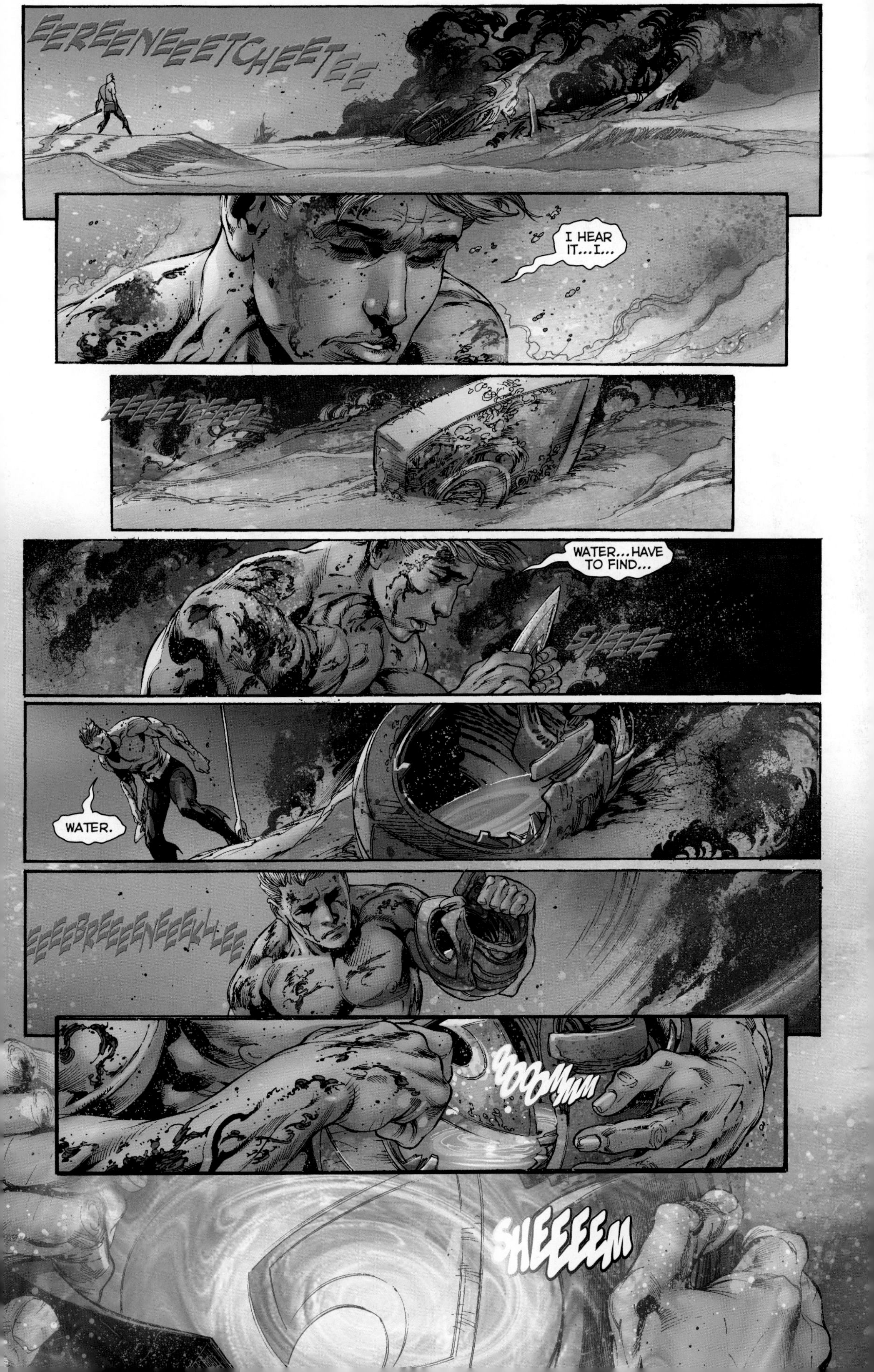
EEREEENEEETCHEETEE
I HEAR IT...I...
EEEEETEEEP
WATER...HAVE TO FIND...
SHEEEE
WATER.
EEEEBREEEENEEKLLEE
OOOOMMM
SHEEEEM

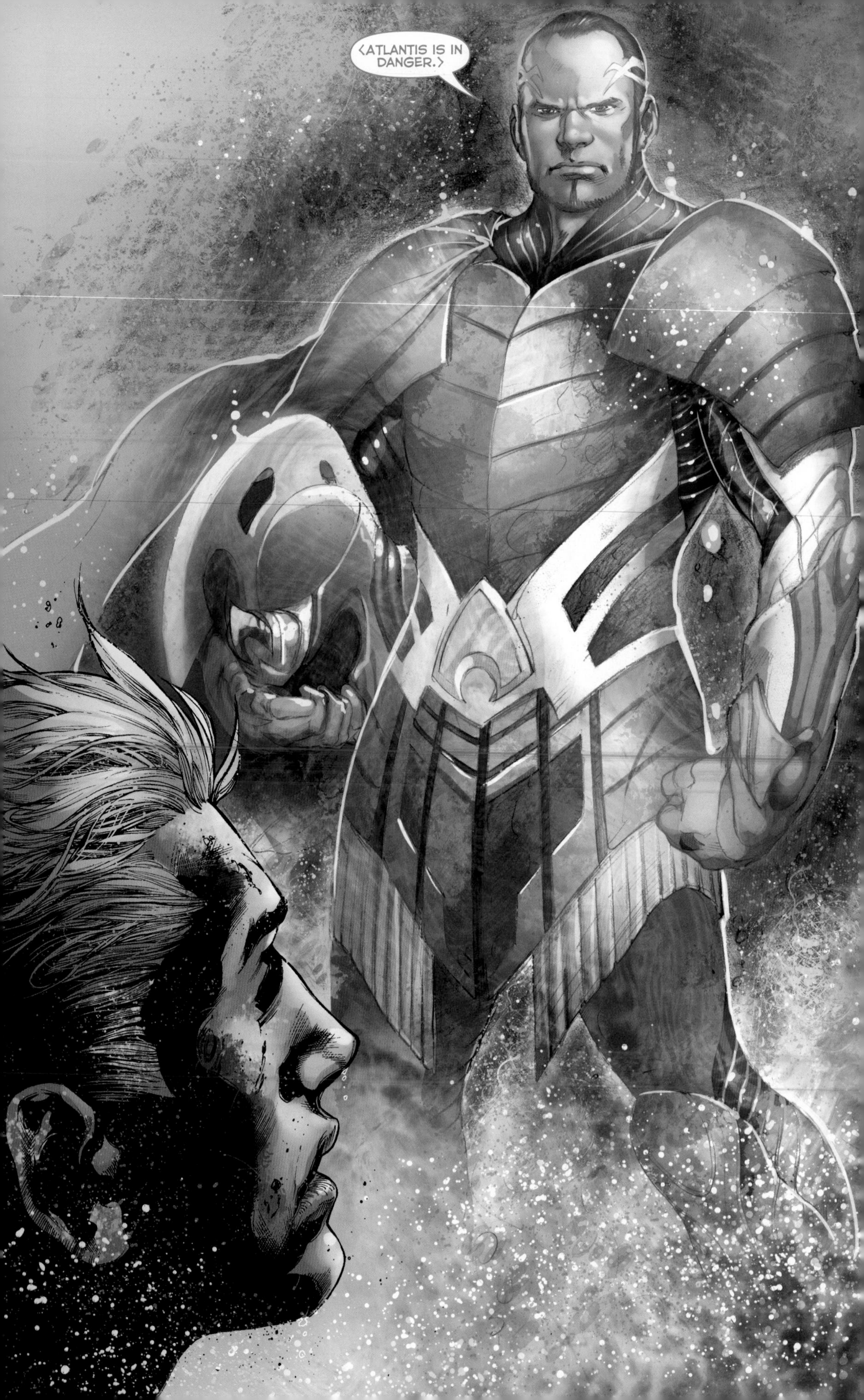
<ATLANTIS IS IN DANGER.>

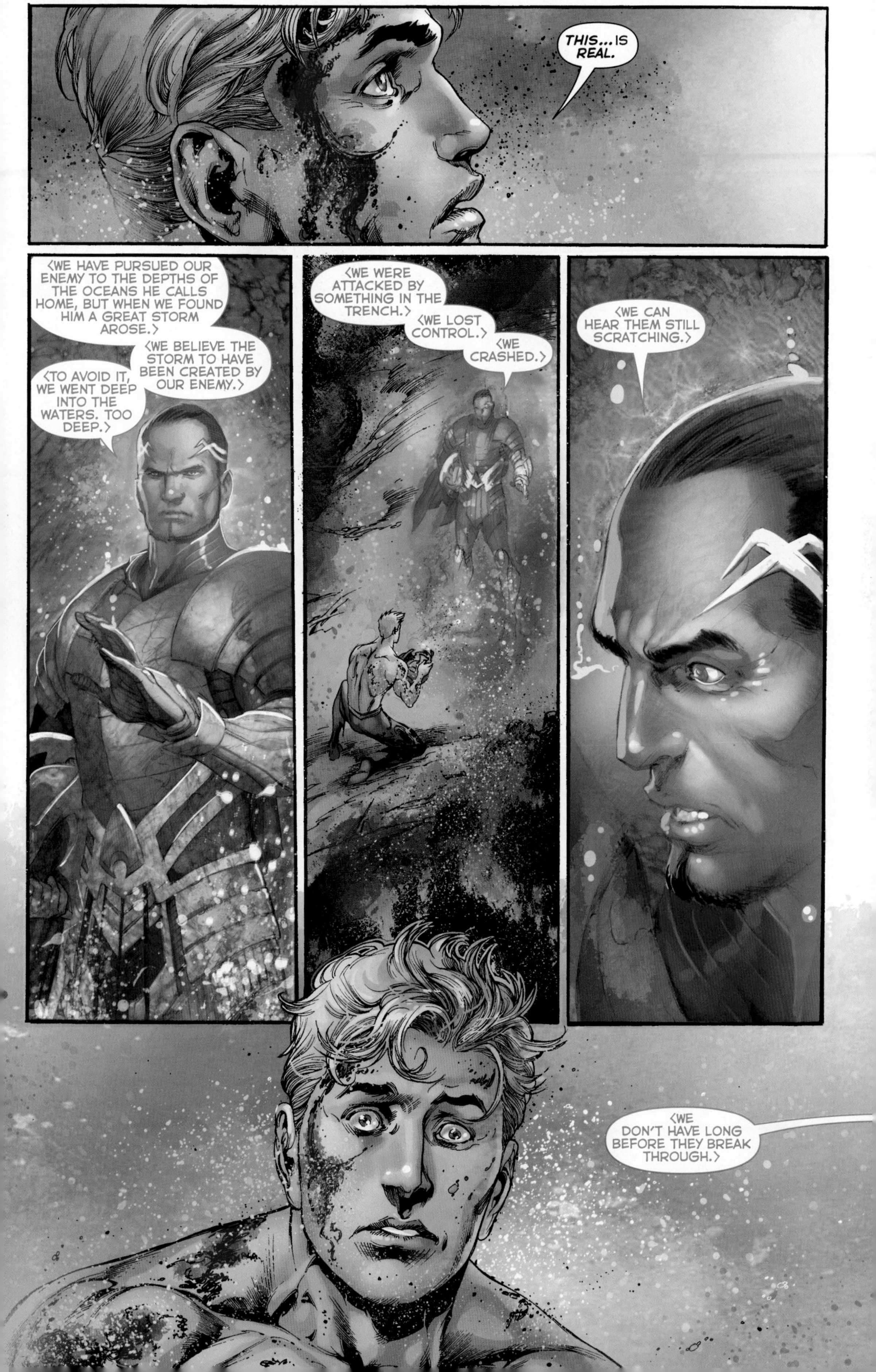
THIS... IS REAL.
<WE HAVE PURSUED OUR ENEMY TO THE DEPTHS OF THE OCEANS HE CALLS HOME, BUT WHEN WE FOUND HIM A GREAT STORM AROSE.>
<WE BELIEVE THE STORM TO HAVE BEEN CREATED BY OUR ENEMY.>
<TO AVOID IT, WE WENT DEEP INTO THE WATERS. TOO DEEP.>
<WE WERE ATTACKED BY SOMETHING IN THE TRENCH.>
<WE LOST CONTROL.>
<WE CRASHED.>
<WE CAN HEAR THEM STILL SCRATCHING.>
<WE DON'T HAVE LONG BEFORE THEY BREAK THROUGH.>

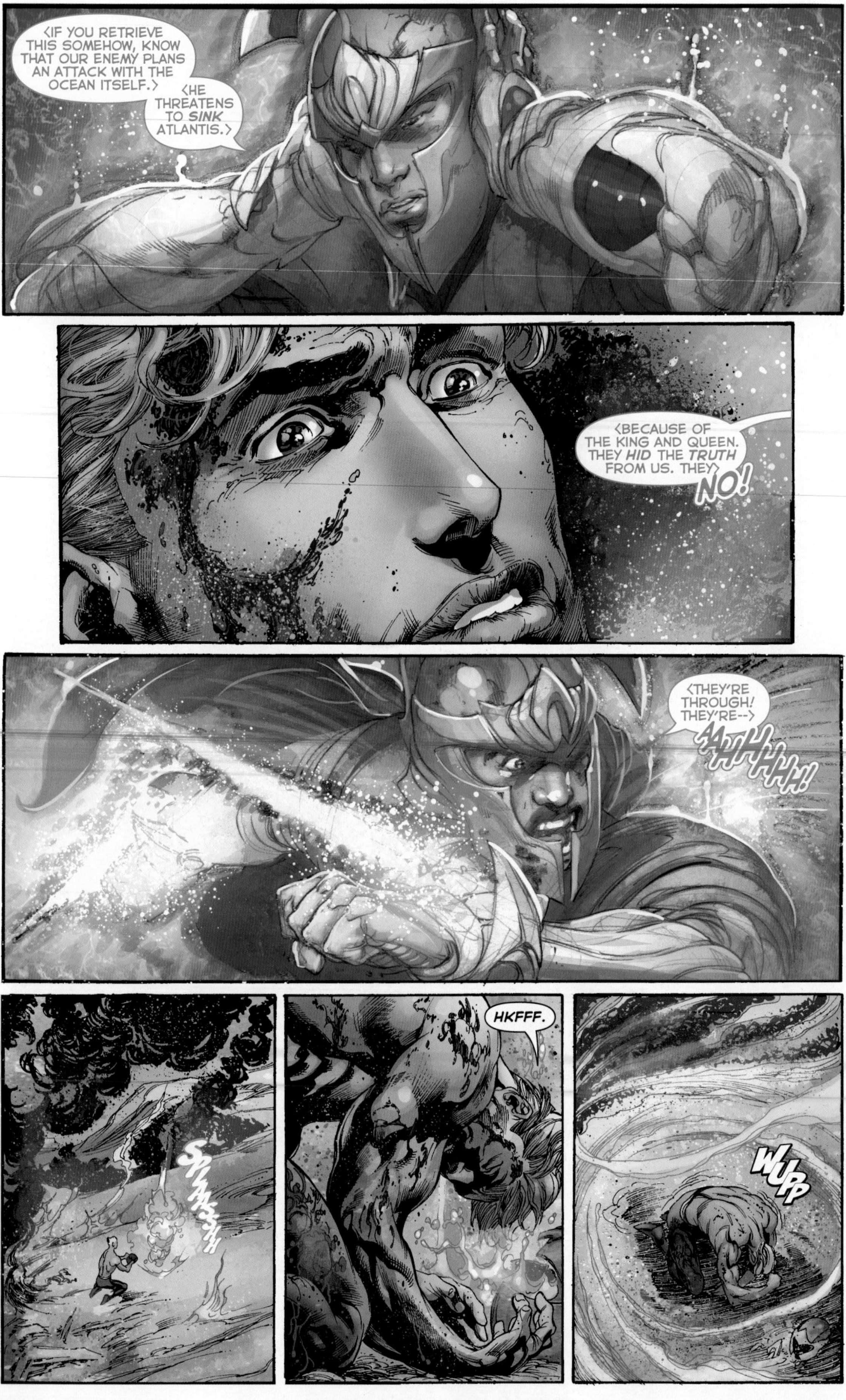

<IF YOU RETRIEVE THIS SOMEHOW, KNOW THAT OUR ENEMY PLANS AN ATTACK WITH THE OCEAN ITSELF.>
<HE THREATENS TO *SINK* ATLANTIS.>
<BECAUSE OF THE KING AND QUEEN. THEY *HID* THE *TRUTH* FROM US. THEY>
NO!
<THEY'RE THROUGH! THEY'RE-->
AAHHHHHH!
SPLASSHH
HKFFF.
WUPP

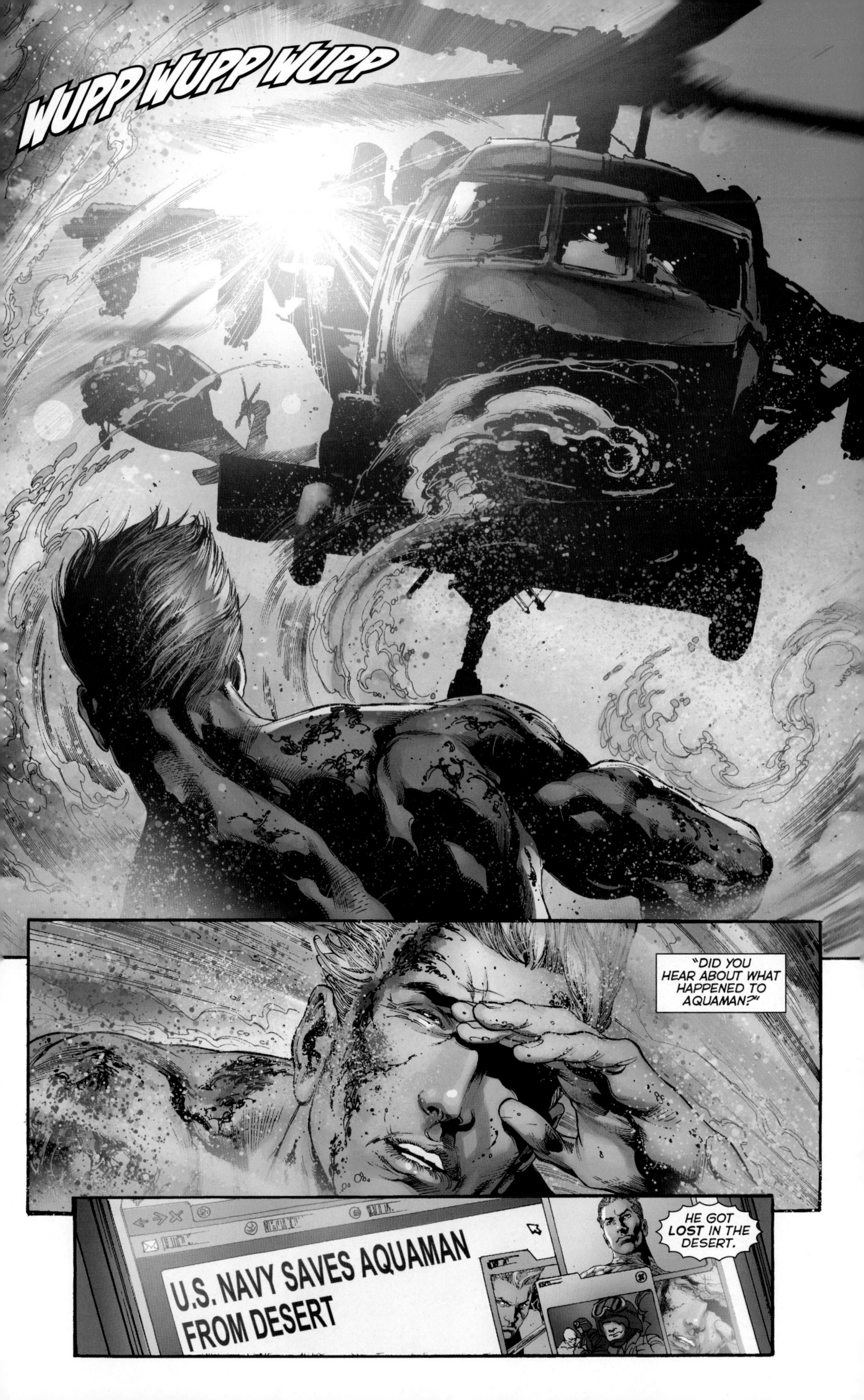
WUPP WUPP WUPP
"DID YOU HEAR ABOUT WHAT HAPPENED TO AQUAMAN?"
HE GOT LOST IN THE DESERT.
U.S. NAVY SAVES AQUAMAN FROM DESERT

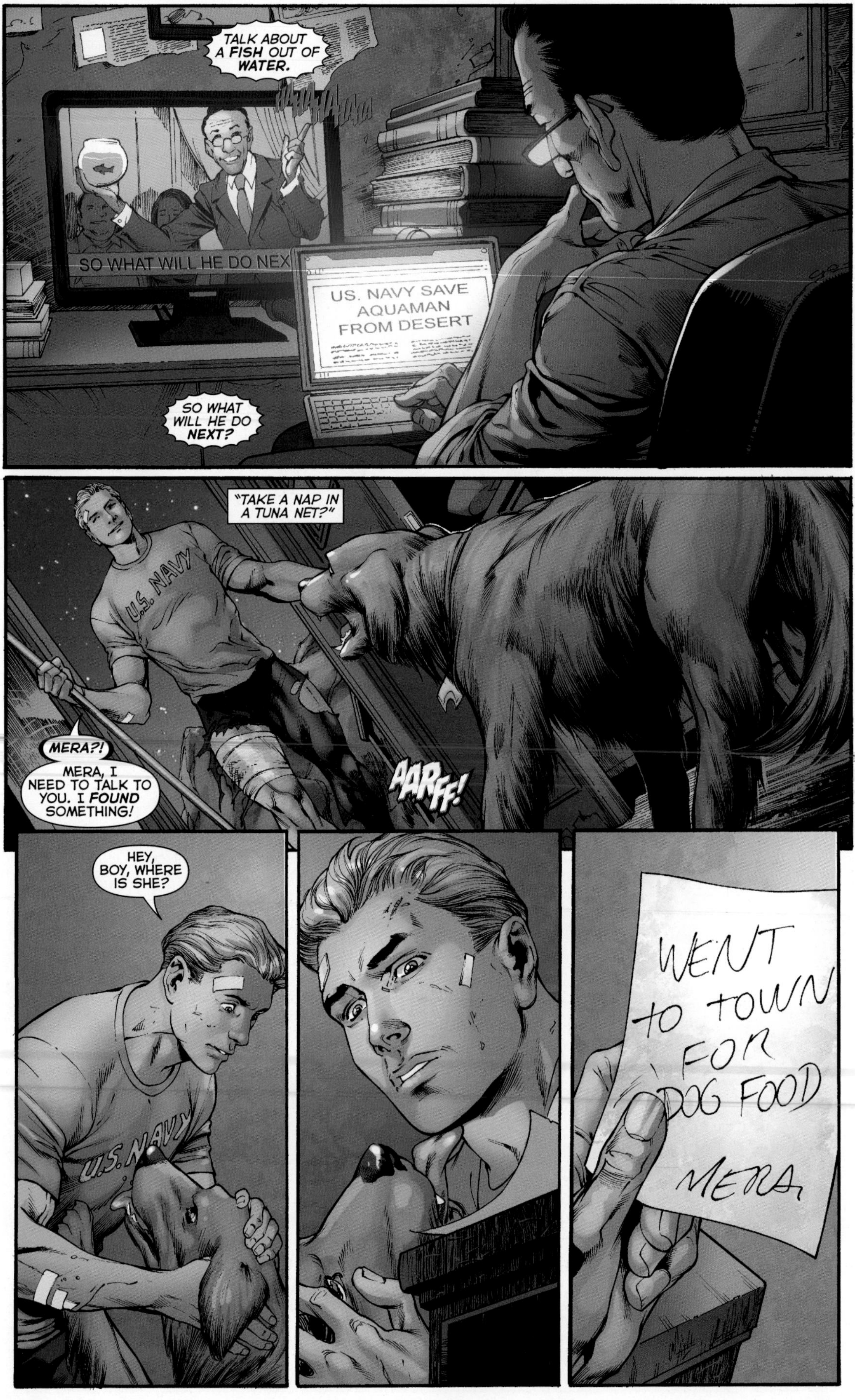
TALK ABOUT A FISH OUT OF WATER.
HAHAHAHAHA
SO WHAT WILL HE DO NEX
US. NAVY SAVE AQUAMAN FROM DESERT
SO WHAT WILL HE DO NEXT?
"TAKE A NAP IN A TUNA NET?"
U.S. NAVY
MERA?!
MERA, I NEED TO TALK TO YOU. I FOUND SOMETHING!
AARFF!
HEY, BOY, WHERE IS SHE?
U.S. NAVY
WENT TO TOWN FOR DOG FOOD
MERA

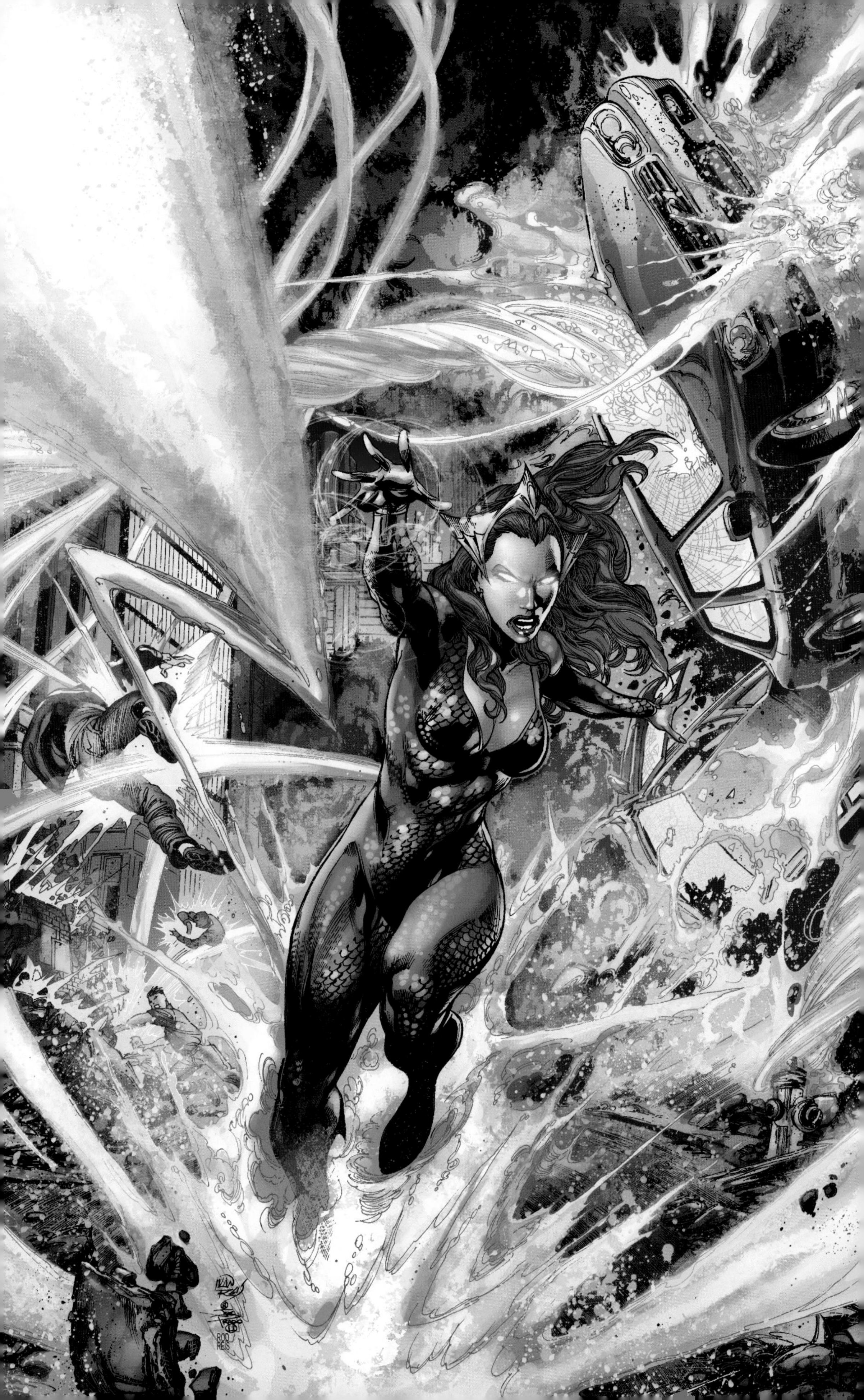

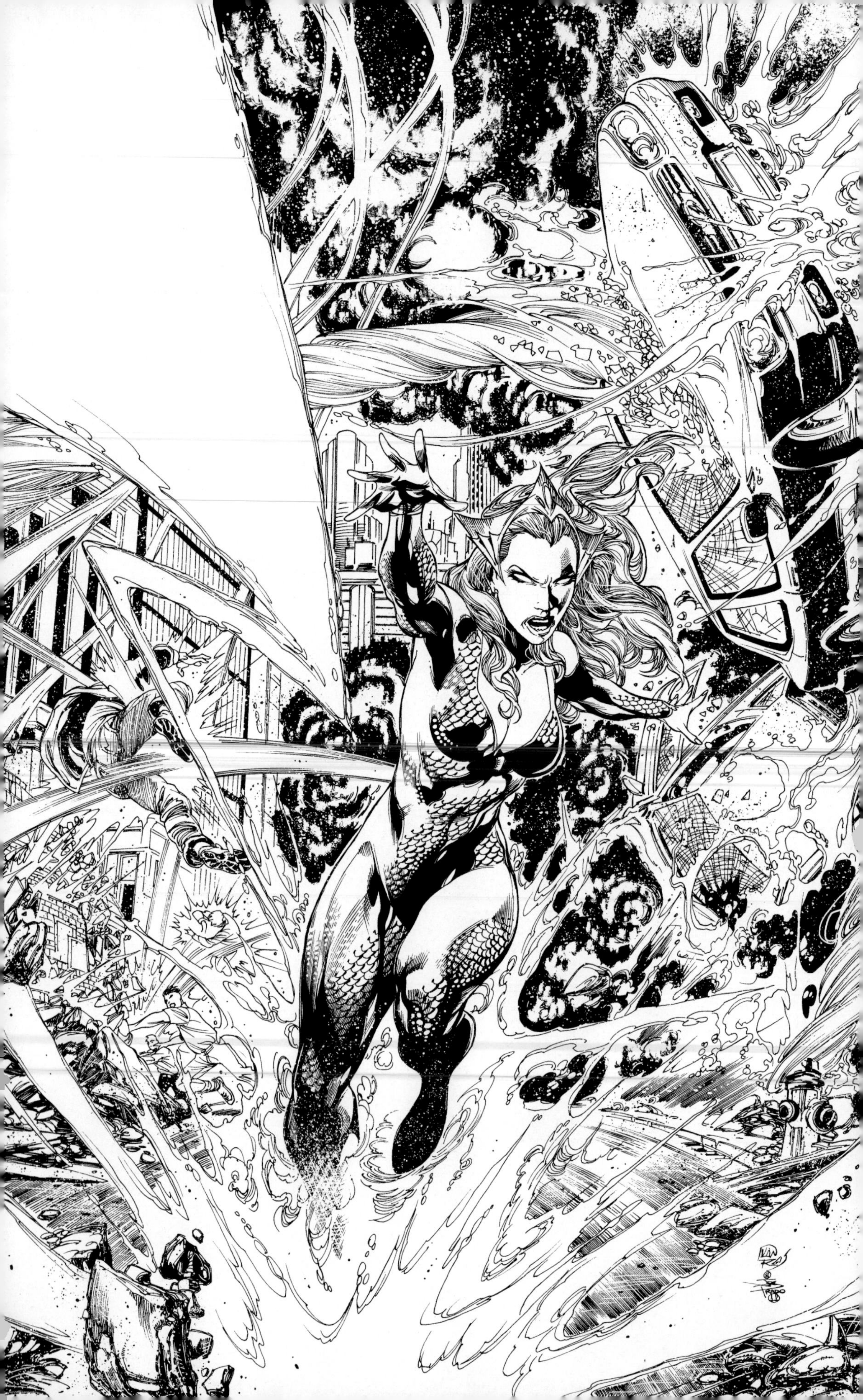

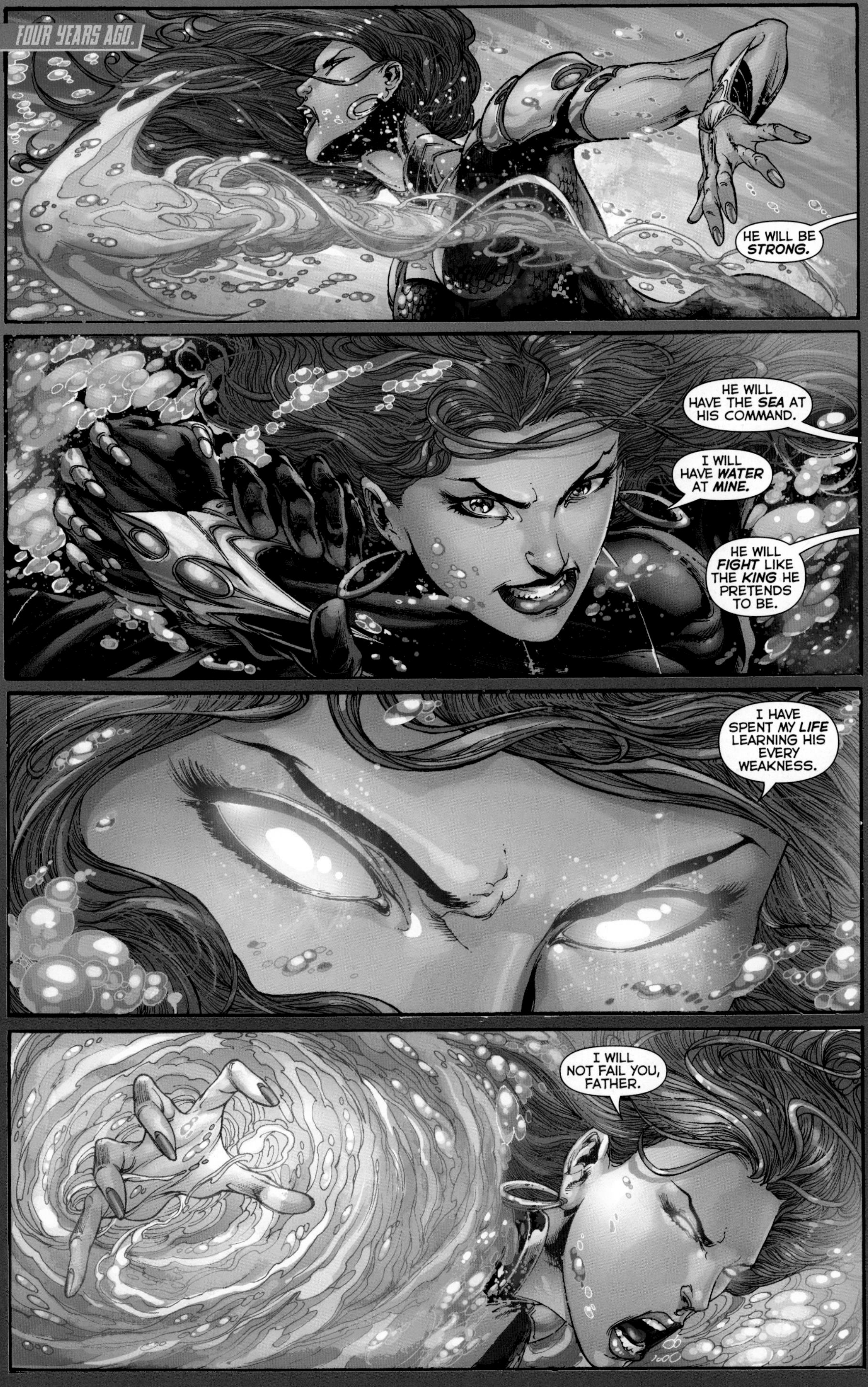

FOUR YEARS AGO.
HE WILL BE STRONG.
HE WILL HAVE THE SEA AT HIS COMMAND.
I WILL HAVE WATER AT MINE.
HE WILL FIGHT LIKE THE KING HE PRETENDS TO BE.
I HAVE SPENT MY LIFE LEARNING HIS EVERY WEAKNESS.
I WILL NOT FAIL YOU, FATHER.

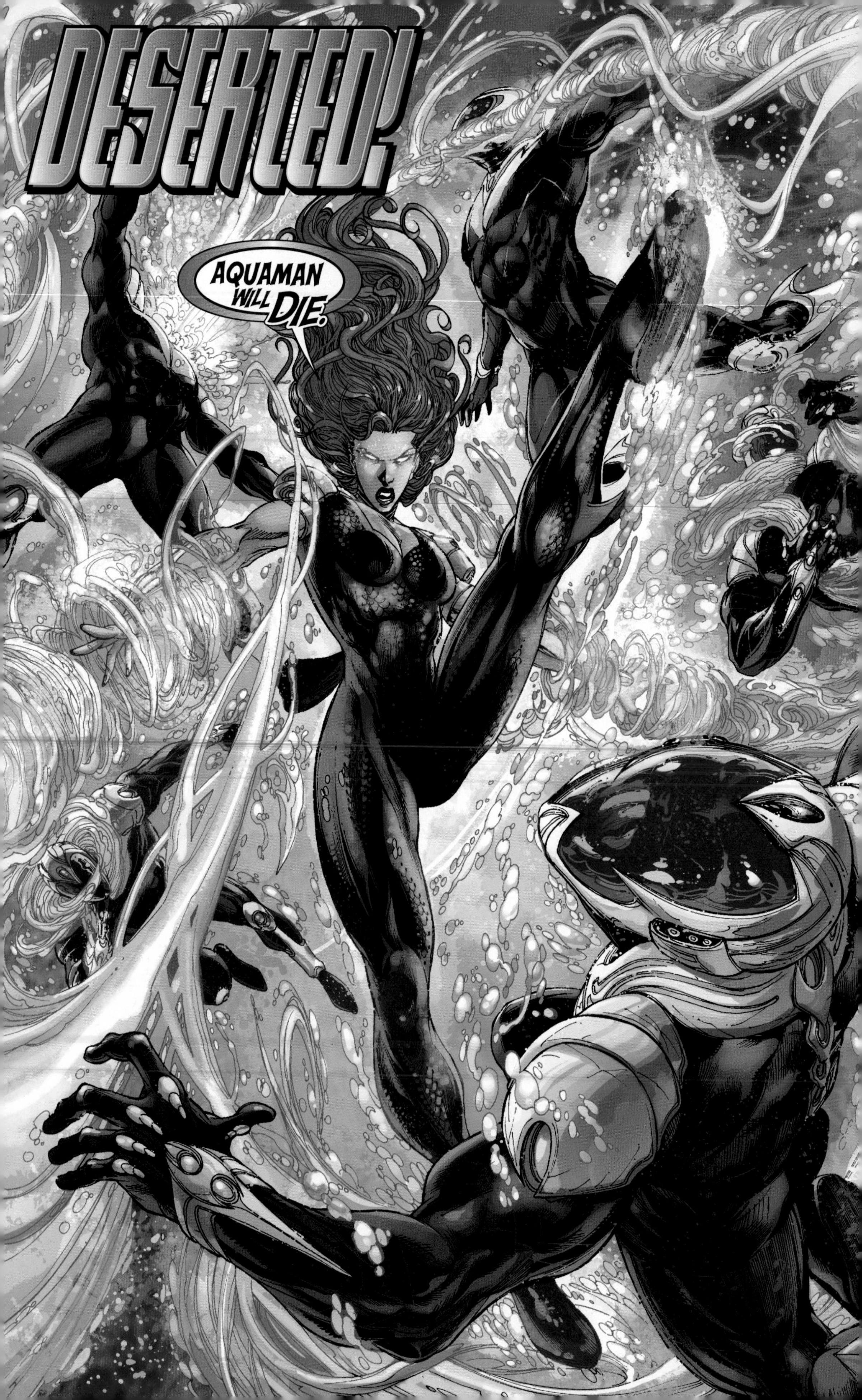
DESERTED!
AQUAMAN WILL DIE.

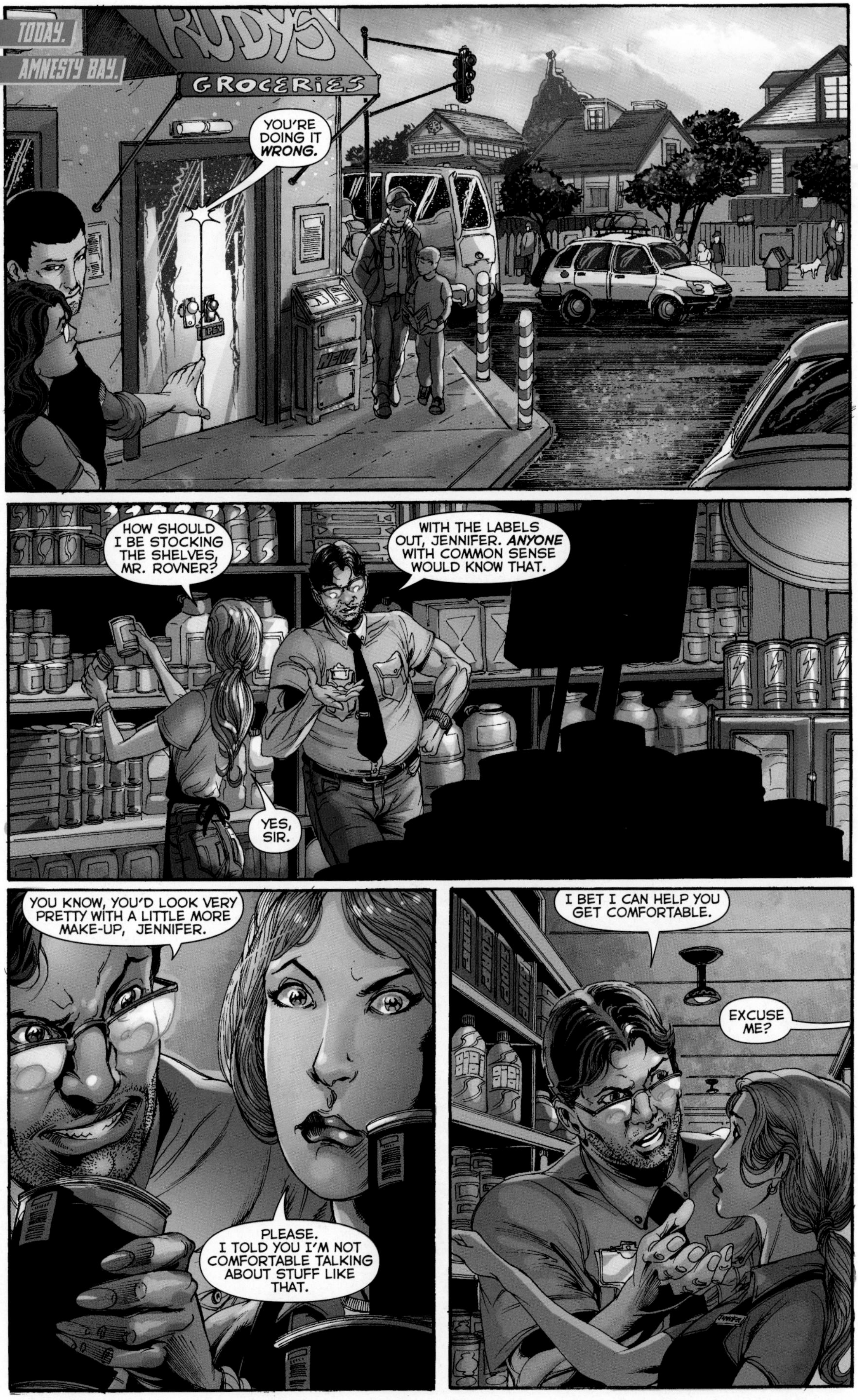
TODAY.
AMNESTY BAY.
RUDY'S
GROCERIES
YOU'RE DOING IT *WRONG.*
HOW SHOULD I BE STOCKING THE SHELVES, MR. ROVNER?
WITH THE LABELS OUT, JENNIFER. *ANYONE* WITH COMMON SENSE WOULD KNOW THAT.
YES, SIR.
YOU KNOW, YOU'D LOOK VERY PRETTY WITH A LITTLE MORE MAKE-UP, JENNIFER.
PLEASE. I TOLD YOU I'M NOT COMFORTABLE TALKING ABOUT STUFF LIKE THAT.
I BET I CAN HELP YOU GET COMFORTABLE.
EXCUSE ME?

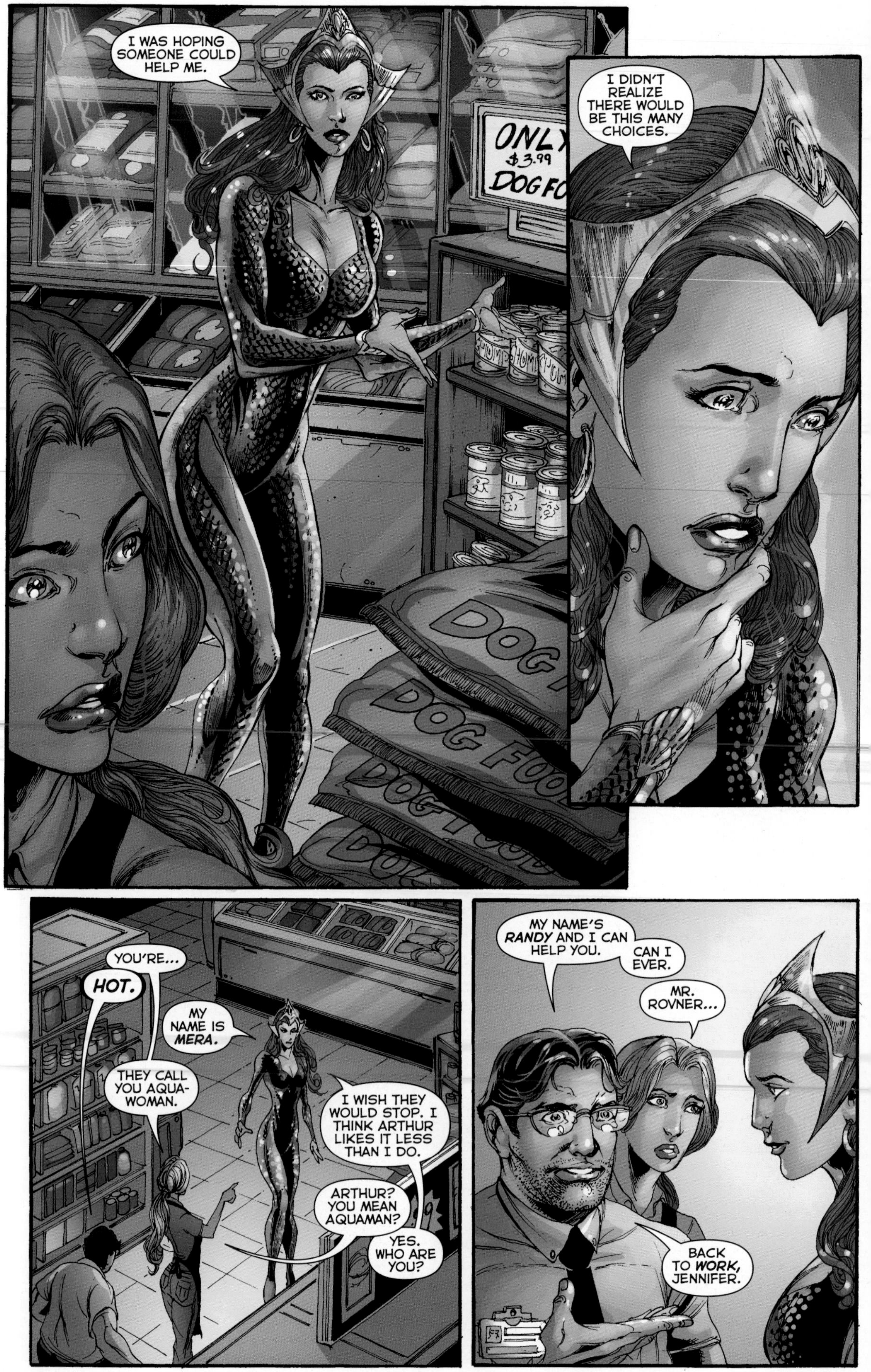
I WAS HOPING SOMEONE COULD HELP ME.
ONLY $3.99 DOG FO
I DIDN'T REALIZE THERE WOULD BE THIS MANY CHOICES.
DOG F
DOG FOO
YOU'RE... HOT.
MY NAME IS MERA.
THEY CALL YOU AQUA-WOMAN.
I WISH THEY WOULD STOP. I THINK ARTHUR LIKES IT LESS THAN I DO.
ARTHUR? YOU MEAN AQUAMAN?
YES. WHO ARE YOU?
MY NAME'S RANDY AND I CAN HELP YOU.
CAN I EVER.
MR. ROVNER...
BACK TO WORK, JENNIFER.

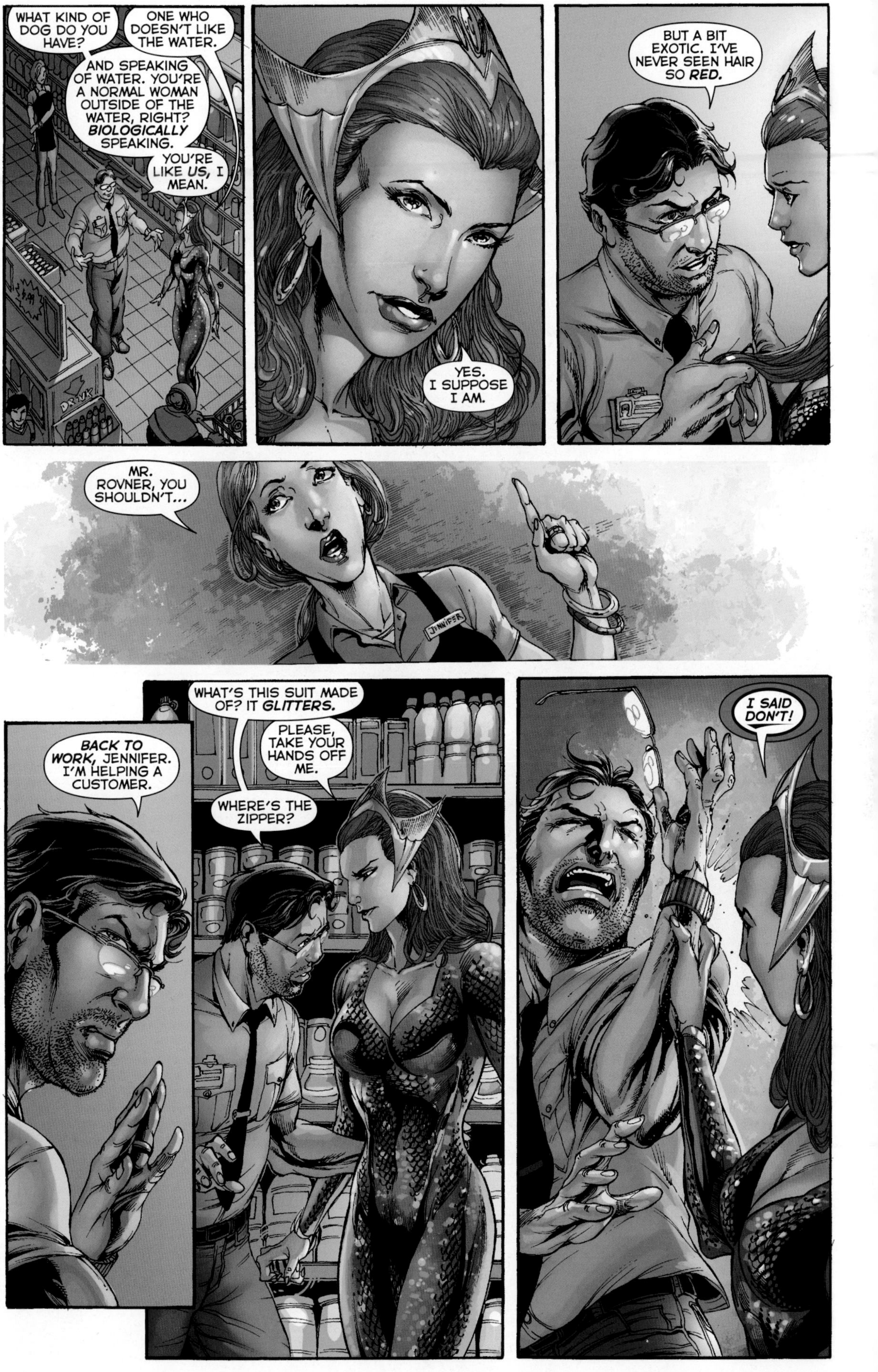
WHAT KIND OF DOG DO YOU HAVE?
ONE WHO DOESN'T LIKE THE WATER.
AND SPEAKING OF WATER. YOU'RE A NORMAL WOMAN OUTSIDE OF THE WATER, RIGHT? BIOLOGICALLY SPEAKING.
YOU'RE LIKE US, I MEAN.
YES. I SUPPOSE I AM.
BUT A BIT EXOTIC. I'VE NEVER SEEN HAIR SO RED.
MR. ROVNER, YOU SHOULDN'T...
JENNIFER
BACK TO WORK, JENNIFER. I'M HELPING A CUSTOMER.
WHAT'S THIS SUIT MADE OF? IT GLITTERS.
PLEASE, TAKE YOUR HANDS OFF ME.
WHERE'S THE ZIPPER?
I SAID DON'T!

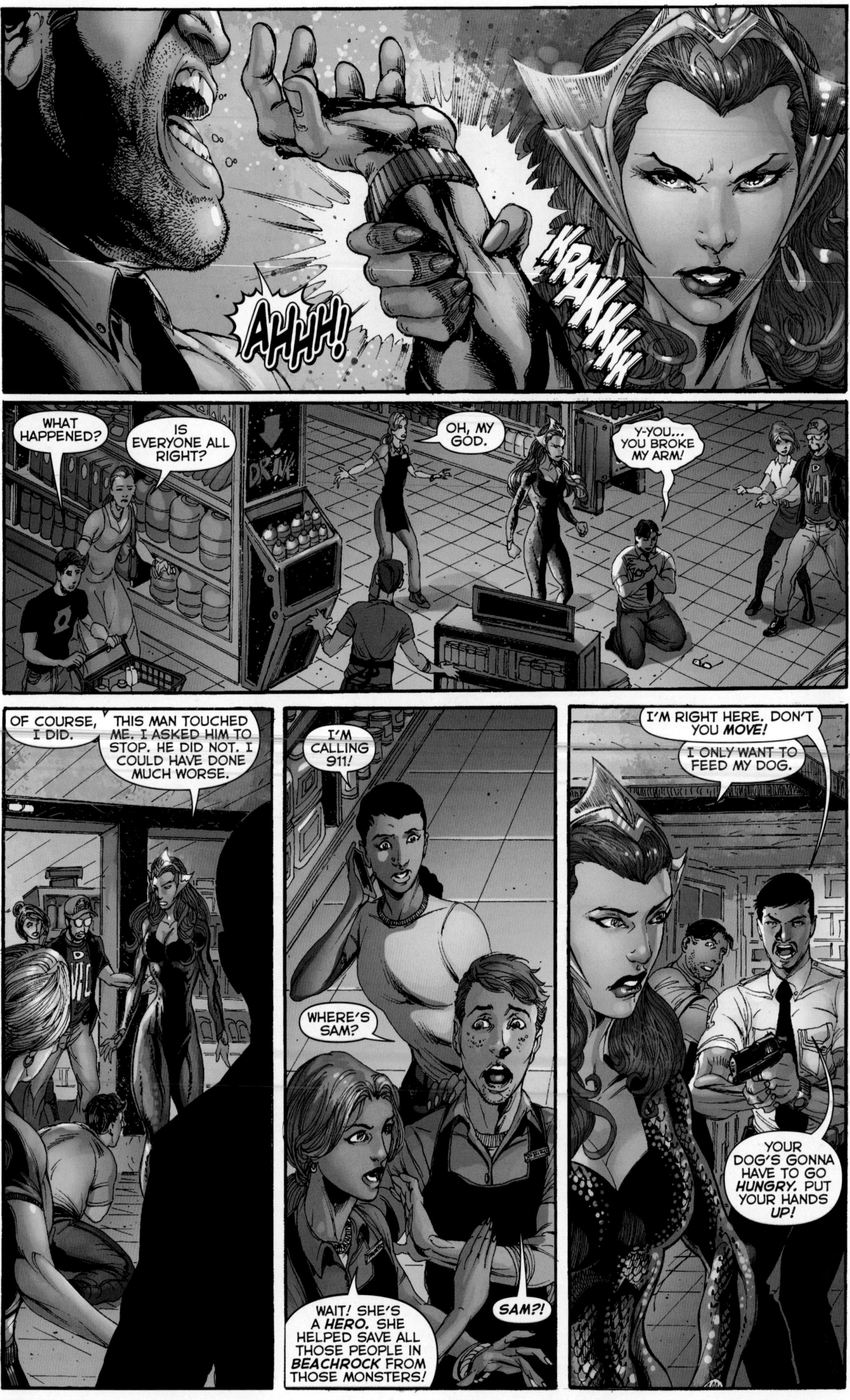

AHHH!
KRAKKKK
WHAT HAPPENED?
IS EVERYONE ALL RIGHT?
OH, MY GOD.
Y-YOU... YOU BROKE MY ARM!
OF COURSE, I DID.
THIS MAN TOUCHED ME. I ASKED HIM TO STOP. HE DID NOT. I COULD HAVE DONE MUCH WORSE.
I'M CALLING 911!
WHERE'S SAM?
WAIT! SHE'S A *HERO.* SHE HELPED SAVE ALL THOSE PEOPLE IN *BEACHROCK* FROM THOSE MONSTERS!
SAM?!
I'M RIGHT HERE. DON'T YOU *MOVE!*
I ONLY WANT TO FEED MY DOG.
YOUR DOG'S GONNA HAVE TO GO *HUNGRY.* PUT YOUR HANDS *UP!*

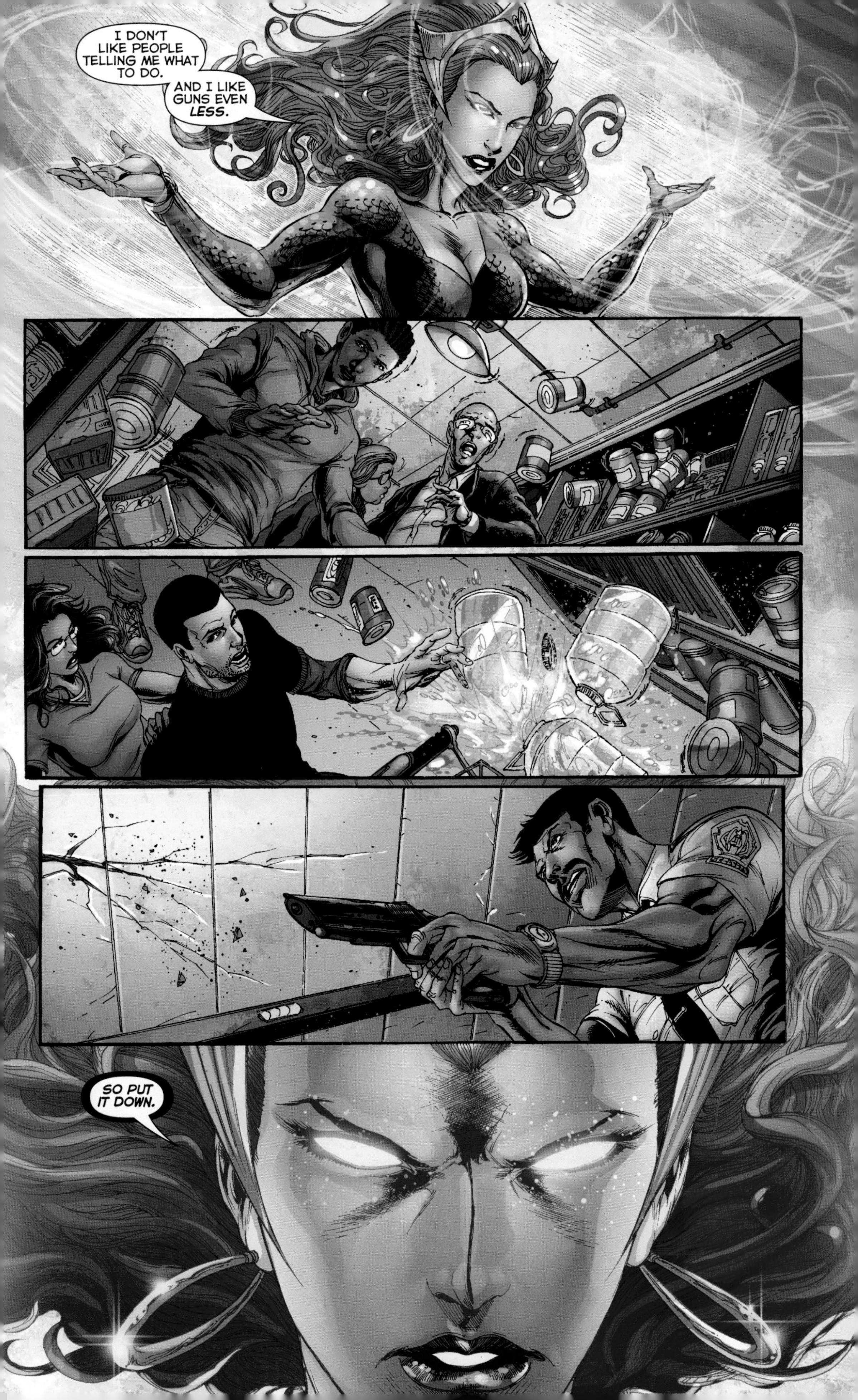

I DON'T LIKE PEOPLE TELLING ME WHAT TO DO.
AND I LIKE GUNS EVEN *LESS.*
SO PUT IT DOWN.

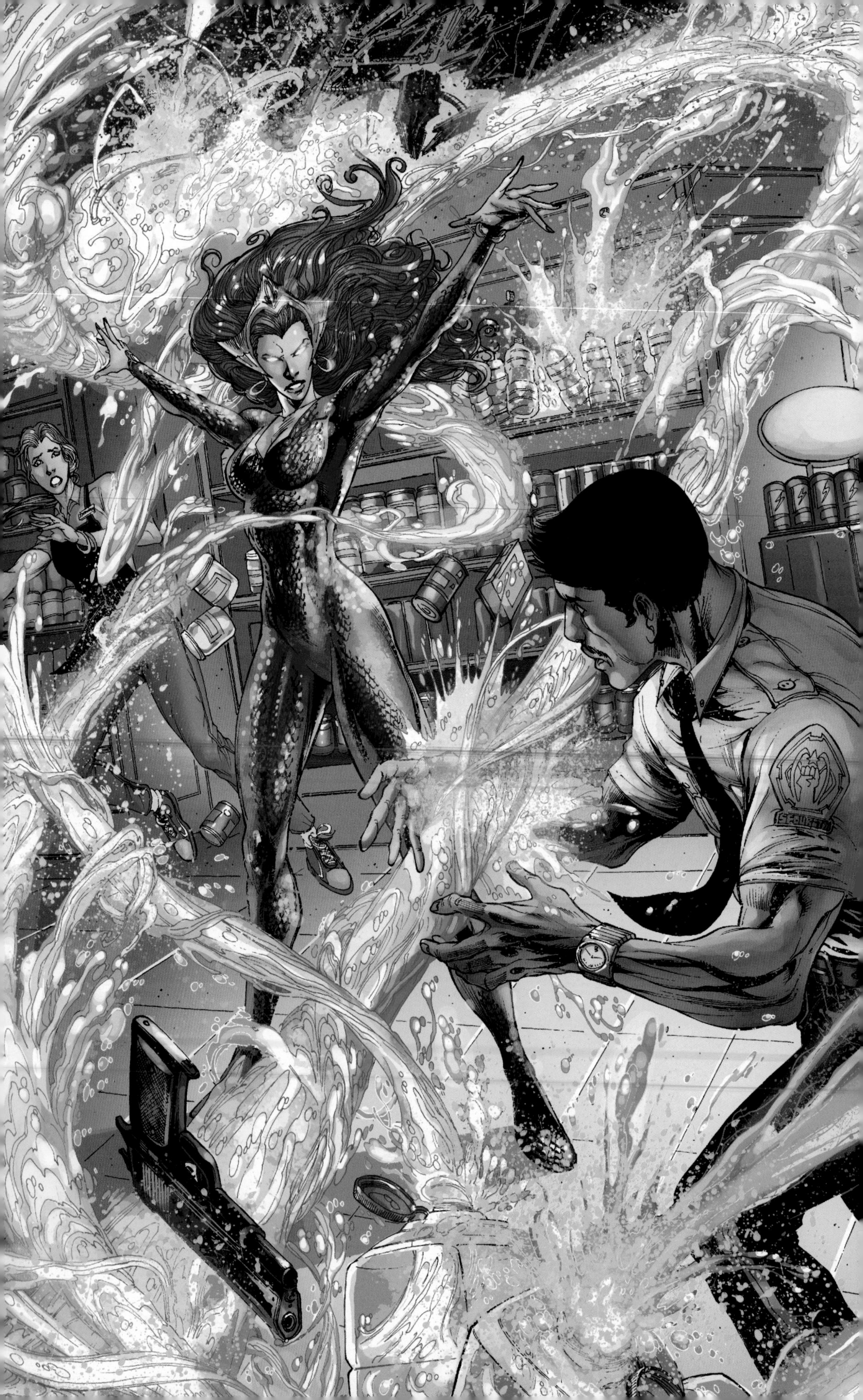

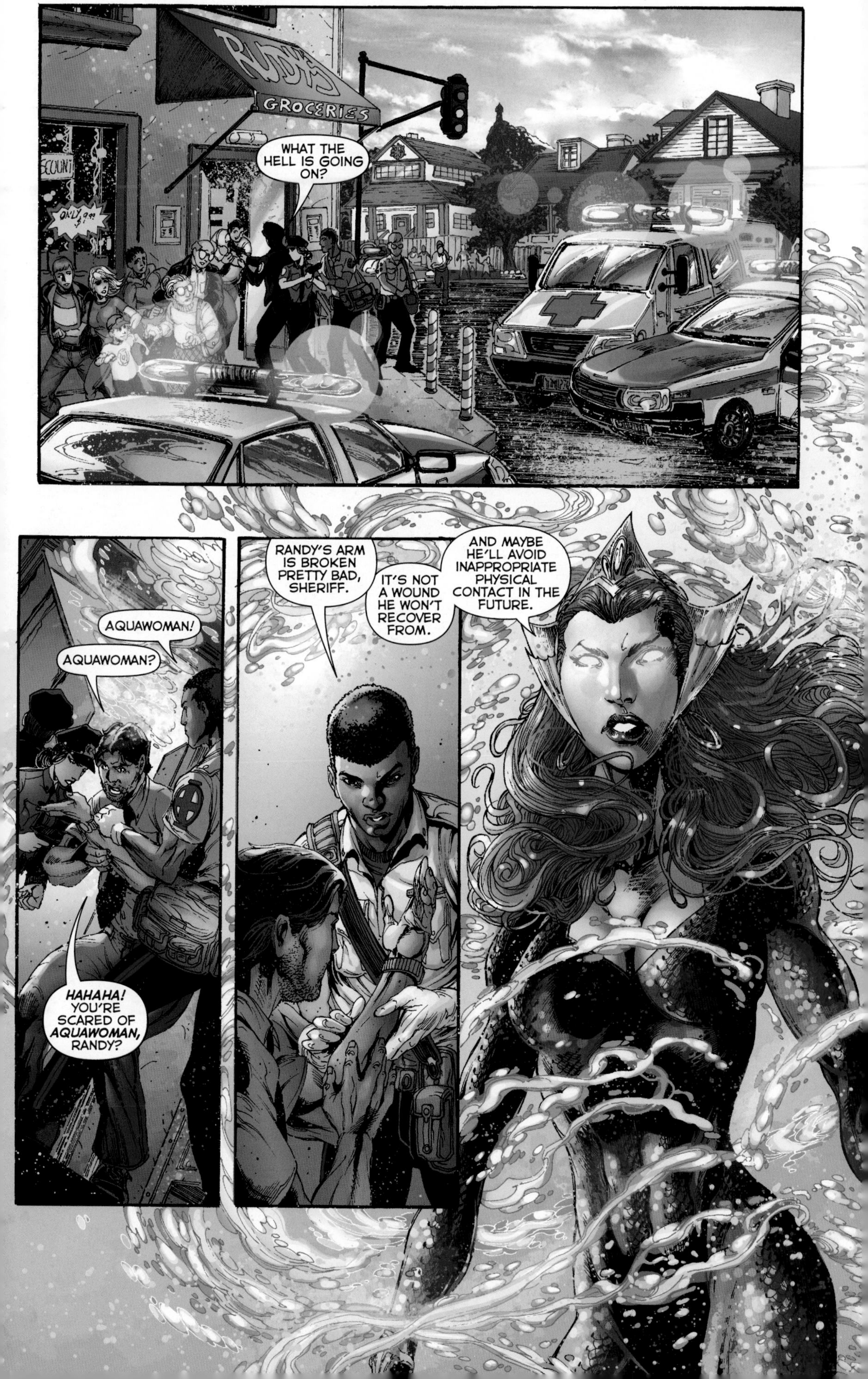
RUDY'S
GROCERIES
DISCOUNT
ONLY $9.99
WHAT THE HELL IS GOING ON?
AQUAWOMAN!
AQUAWOMAN?
HAHAHA! YOU'RE SCARED OF AQUAWOMAN, RANDY?
RANDY'S ARM IS BROKEN PRETTY BAD, SHERIFF.
IT'S NOT A WOUND HE WON'T RECOVER FROM.
AND MAYBE HE'LL AVOID INAPPROPRIATE PHYSICAL CONTACT IN THE FUTURE.

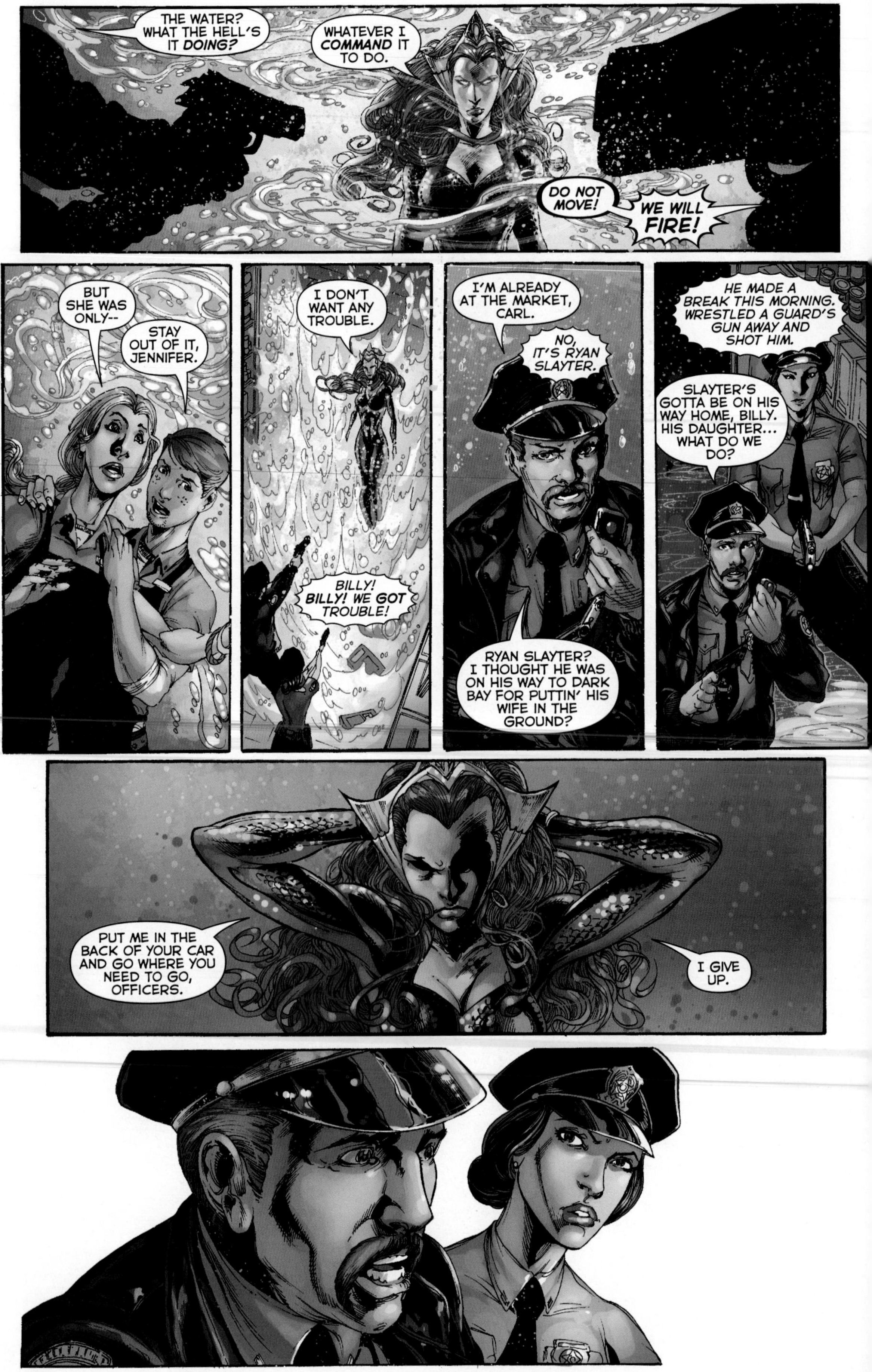
THE WATER? WHAT THE HELL'S IT *DOING?*
WHATEVER I *COMMAND* IT TO DO.
DO NOT MOVE!
WE WILL *FIRE!*
BUT SHE WAS ONLY--
STAY OUT OF IT, JENNIFER.
I DON'T WANT ANY TROUBLE.
BILLY! BILLY! WE GOT TROUBLE!
I'M ALREADY AT THE MARKET, CARL.
NO, IT'S RYAN SLAYTER.
RYAN SLAYTER? I THOUGHT HE WAS ON HIS WAY TO DARK BAY FOR PUTTIN' HIS WIFE IN THE GROUND?
HE MADE A BREAK THIS MORNING. WRESTLED A GUARD'S GUN AWAY AND SHOT HIM.
SLAYTER'S GOTTA BE ON HIS WAY HOME, BILLY. HIS DAUGHTER... WHAT DO WE DO?
PUT ME IN THE BACK OF YOUR CAR AND GO WHERE YOU NEED TO GO, OFFICERS.
I GIVE UP.

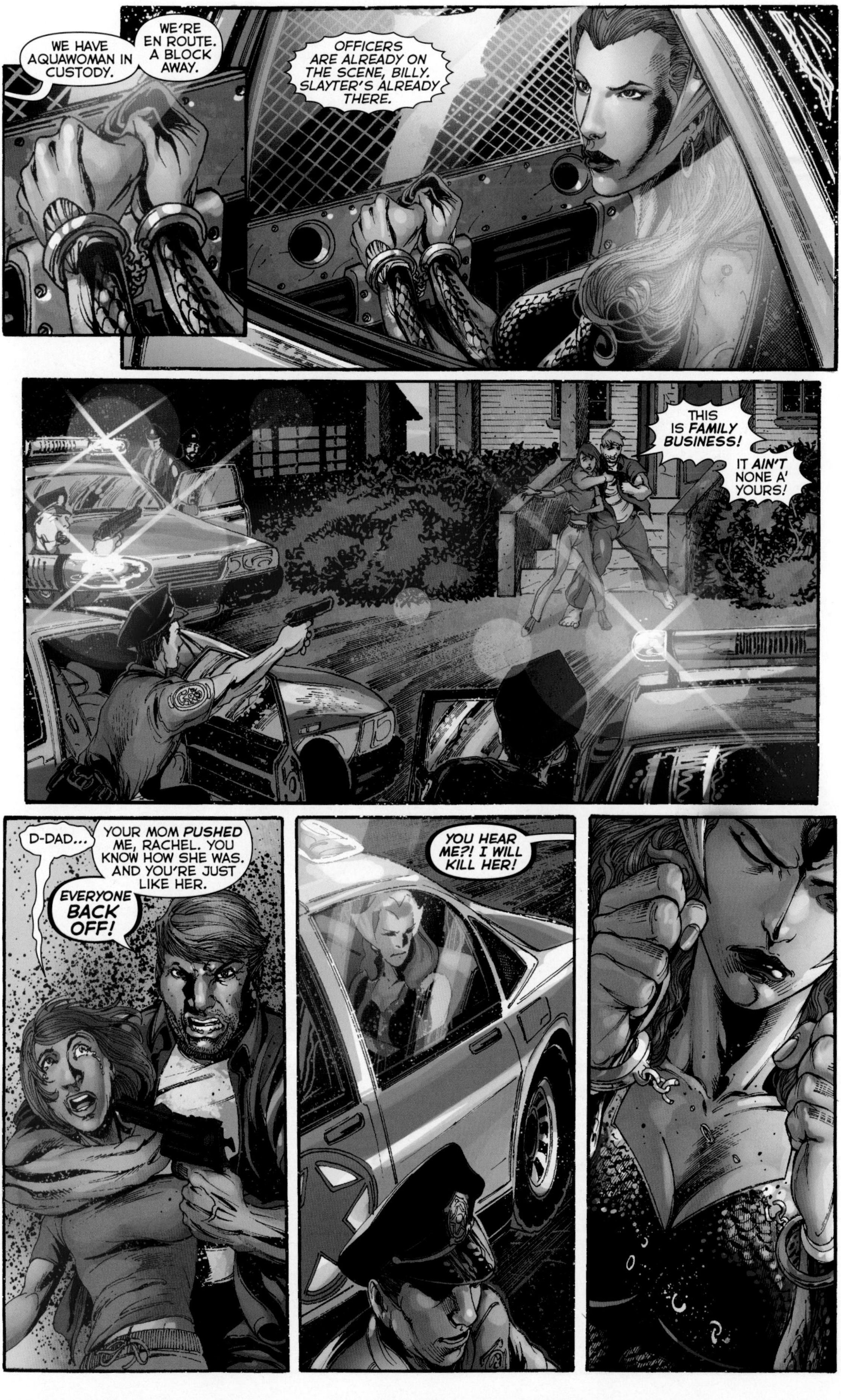
WE HAVE AQUAWOMAN IN CUSTODY.
WE'RE EN ROUTE. A BLOCK AWAY.
OFFICERS ARE ALREADY ON THE SCENE, BILLY. SLAYTER'S ALREADY THERE.
THIS IS FAMILY BUSINESS!
IT AIN'T NONE A' YOURS!
D-DAD...
YOUR MOM PUSHED ME, RACHEL. YOU KNOW HOW SHE WAS. AND YOU'RE JUST LIKE HER.
EVERYONE BACK OFF!
YOU HEAR ME?! I WILL KILL HER!

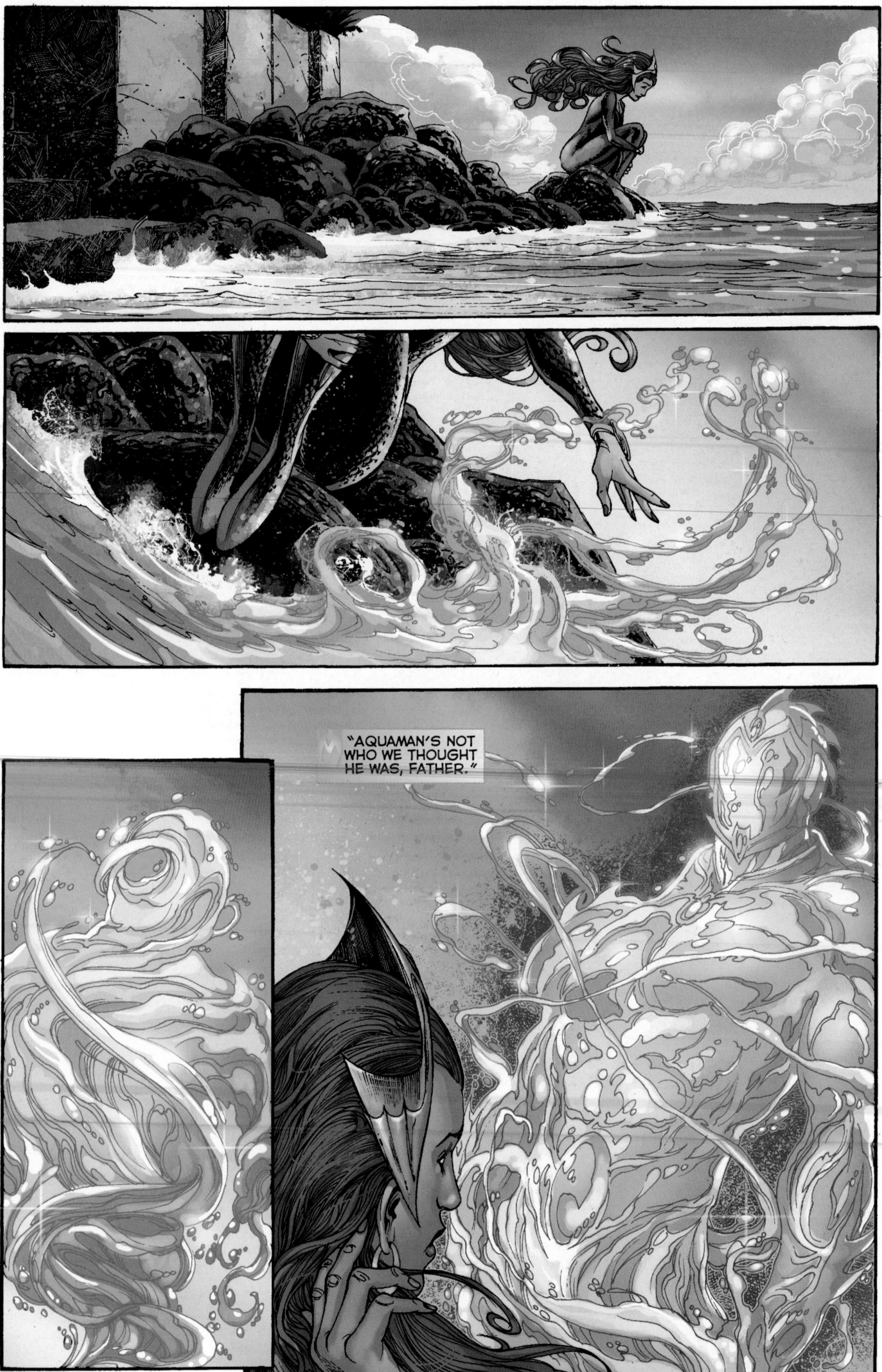
"AQUAMAN'S NOT WHO WE THOUGHT HE WAS, FATHER."

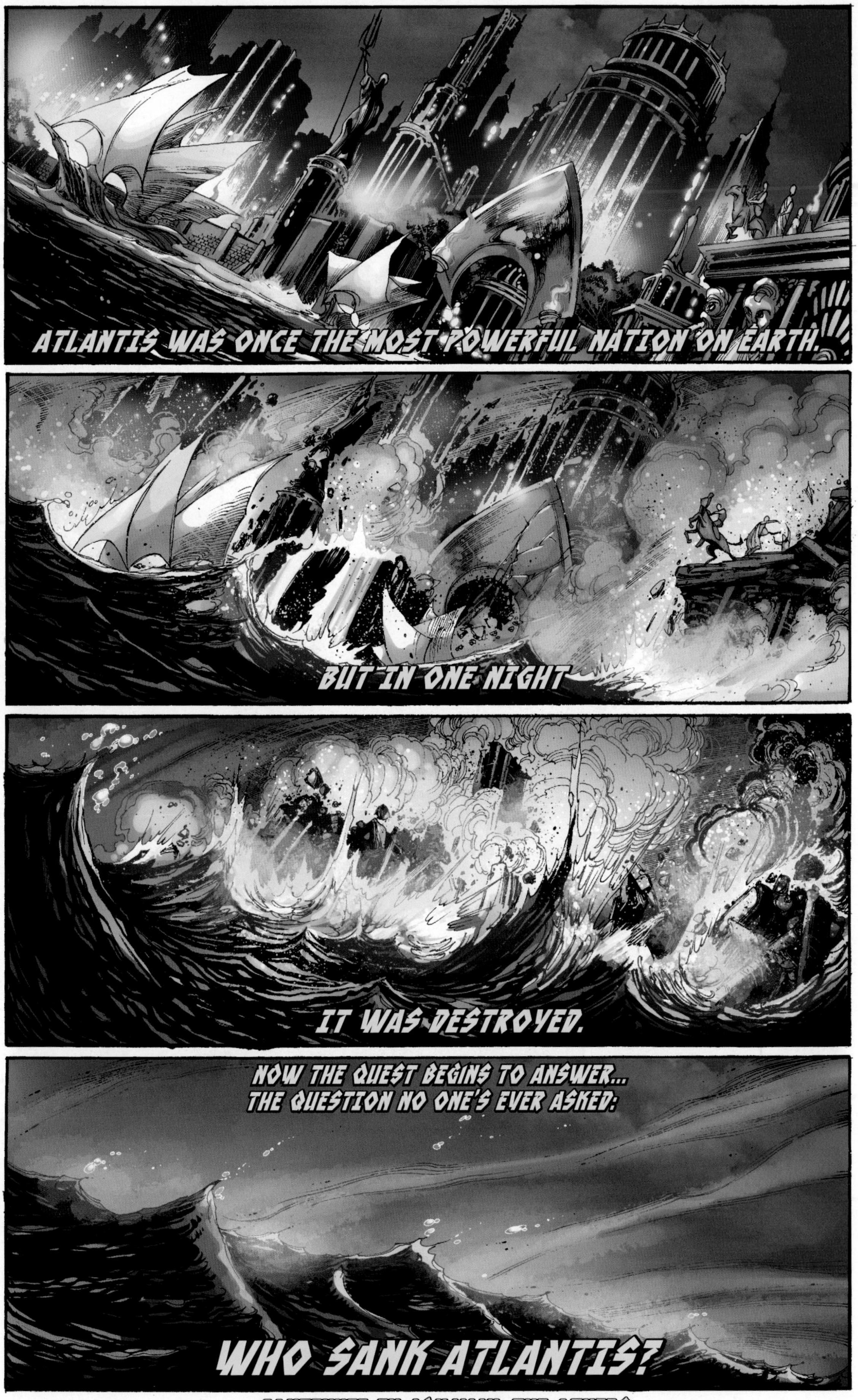
ATLANTIS WAS ONCE THE MOST POWERFUL NATION ON EARTH.
BUT IN ONE NIGHT
IT WAS DESTROYED.
NOW THE QUEST BEGINS TO ANSWER...
THE QUESTION NO ONE'S EVER ASKED:
WHO SANK ATLANTIS?

CONTINUED IN AQUAMAN: THE OTHERS

AQUAMAN

CHARACTER SKETCHES BY IVAN REIS

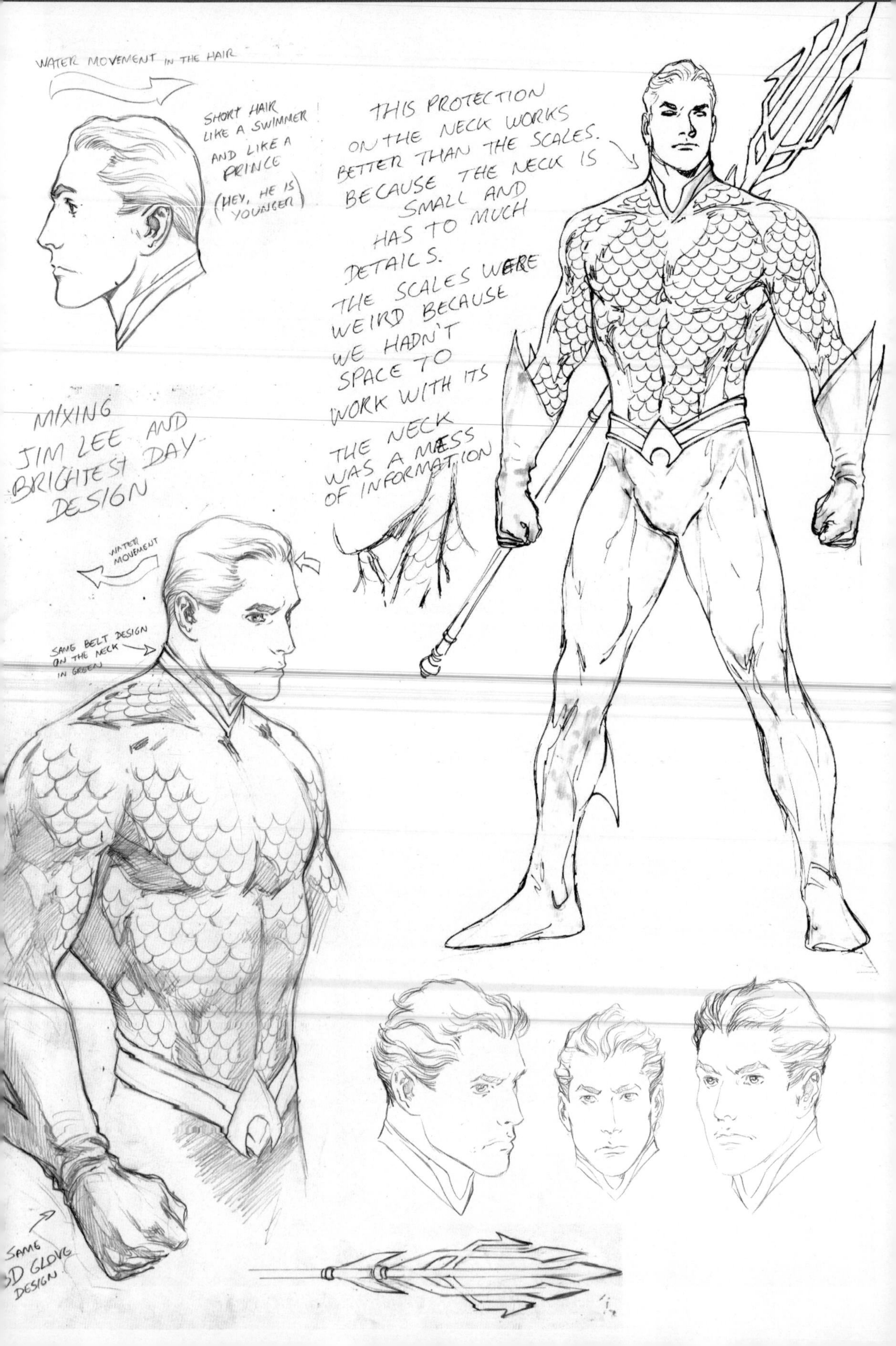
WATER MOVEMENT IN THE HAIR
SHORT HAIR LIKE A SWIMMER AND LIKE A PRINCE (HEY, HE IS YOUNGER)
THIS PROTECTION ON THE NECK WORKS BETTER THAN THE SCALES. BECAUSE THE NECK IS SMALL AND HAS TO MUCH DETAILS.
THE SCALES WERE WEIRD BECAUSE WE HADN'T SPACE TO WORK WITH ITS
THE NECK WAS A MESS OF INFORMATION
MIXING JIM LEE AND BRIGHTEST DAY DESIGN
WATER MOVEMENT
SAME BELT DESIGN ON THE NECK IN GREEN
SAME
D GLOVE
DESIGN

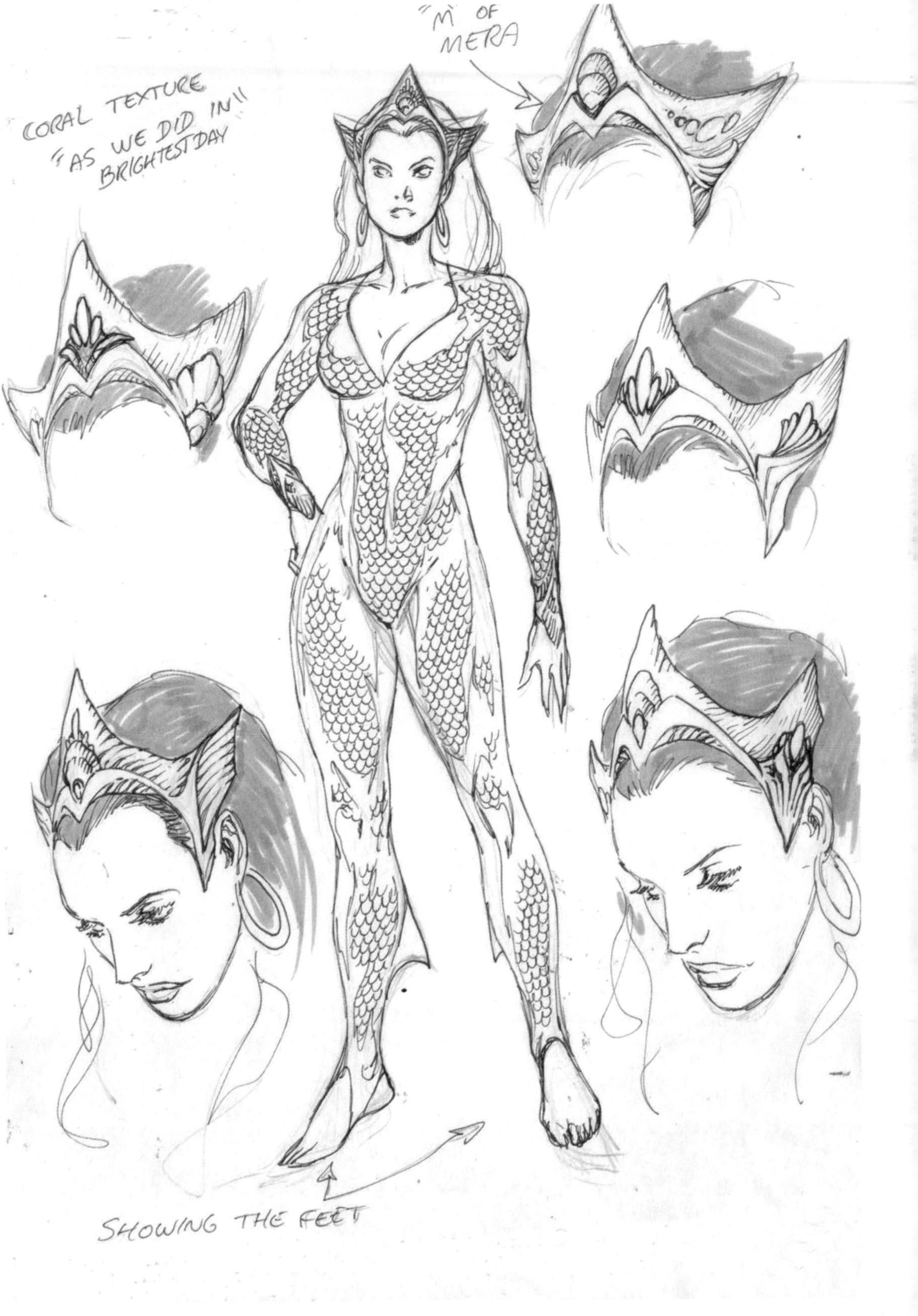
CORAL TEXTURE
"AS WE DID IN"
BRIGHTEST DAY
"M" OF
MERA
SHOWING THE FEET

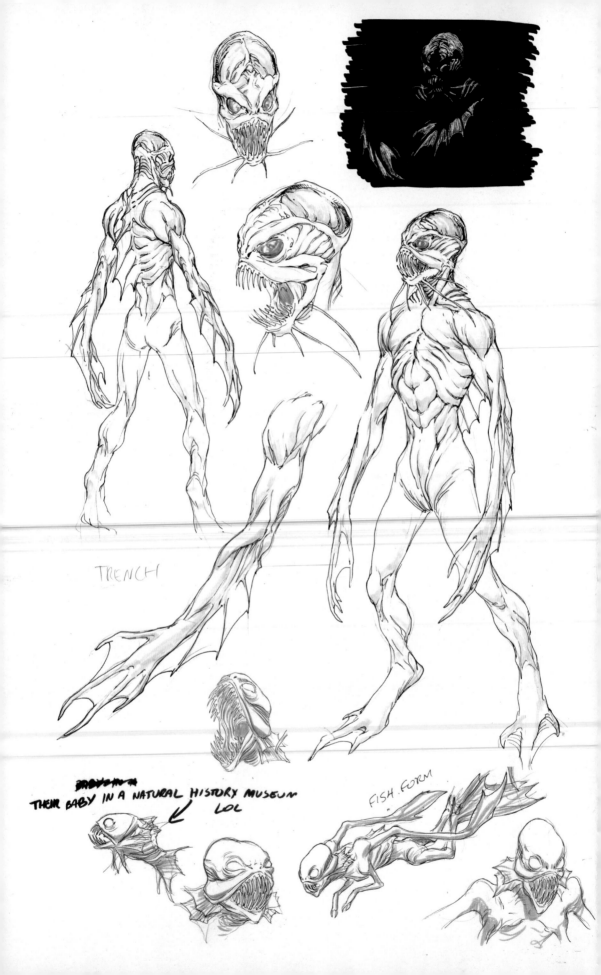

TRENCH

THEIR ~~BRODSHIT~~ BABY IN A NATURAL HISTORY MUSEUM
LOL

FISH.FORM